43299

12547

# Chekhov the Dramatist

# Chekhov the Dramatist

by

DAVID MAGARSHACK

EYRE METHUEN · LONDON

First published in paperback in Great Britian in 1980
by Eyre Methuen Ltd, 11 New Fetter Lane,
London EC4P 4EE, by arrangement with Hill and Wang,
New York

Copyright © 1980 by the Estate of the late
David Magarshack

Originally published in hardback in 1952
by John Lehmann

ISBN 0 413 46480 6 hardback
ISBN 0 413 46490 3 paperback

Printed in Great Britain by
Redwood Burn Limited
Trowbridge & Esher

# Contents

# CHRONOLOGICAL LIST OF PLAYS

# I

THE PLAYS of Chekhov, like those of any other great dramatist, follow a certain pattern of development which can be traced through all its various stages. His last four plays, moreover, conform to certain general principles which are characteristic of the type of indirect-action drama to which they belong. Chekhov himself was fully aware of that. Already on November 3rd, 1888, in a letter to Alexey Suvorin, he clearly stated that all works of art must conform to certain laws. "It is possible to collect in a heap the best that has been created by the artists in all ages," he wrote, "and, making use of the scientific method, discover the general principles which are characteristic of them all and which lie at the very basis of their value as works of art. These general principles will constitute their law. Works of art which are immortal possess a great deal in common; if one were to extract that which is common to them all from any of them, it would lose its value and its charm. This means that what is common to them all is necessary and is a *conditio sine qua non* of every work which lays claim to immortality."

Chekhov did not claim immortality for his plays. He was too modest for that. What he did claim for them, however, was something that any immortal work of art is generally supposed to possess, namely, the power so to influence people as to induce them to create a new and better life for themselves. "You tell me," Chekhov said to the writer Alexander Tikhonov in 1902, "that people cry at my plays. I've heard others say the same. But that was not why I wrote them. It is Alexeyev (Stanislavsky) who made my characters into cry-babies. All I wanted was to say honestly to people: 'Have a look at yourselves and see how bad and dreary your lives are!' The important thing is that people should realise that, for when they do, they will most certainly create another and better life for themselves. I will not live to see it, but I know that it will be quite different, quite unlike our present life. And so long as this different life does not exist, I shall go on saying to people again and again: 'Please, understand that your life is bad and dreary!'

"What is there in this to cry about?"

The misinterpretation of Chekhov's plays by the Moscow Art Theatre led to constant conflicts between their author and its two directors. These conflicts became particularly violent during the production of *The Cherry Orchard*. "The production of *The Cherry Orchard*," Olga Knipper, Chekhov's wife and one of the leading actresses of the Moscow Art Theatre, wrote, "was difficult, almost agonising, I might say. The producers and the author could not understand each other and could not come to an agreement." Chekhov himself wrote to Olga Knipper: "Nemirovich-Danchenko and Alexeyev positively see in my play something I have not written, and I am ready to bet anything you like that neither of them has ever read my play through carefully." And to a well-known Russian producer Chekhov said: "Take my *Cherry Orchard*. Is it my *Cherry Orchard*? With the exception of two or three parts nothing in it is mine. I am describing life, ordinary life, and not blank despondency. They either make me into a cry-baby or into a bore. They invent something about me out of their own heads, anything they like, something I never thought of or dreamed about. This is beginning to make me angry." And what is true of Chekhov's Russian producers is even truer of his English and American producers, though in their case the idea that the characters in Chekhov's plays represent curiously unaccountable "Russians" adequately conceals their own confusion and helplessness.

This general bewilderment would have been fatal to the

popularity of Chekhov's plays were it not that, being a playwright of genius, Chekhov paints his characters with so exquisite a brush that no caricature can strip them of their essential humanity. If neither the spectators nor those responsible for the production and performance of the plays can see the wood for the trees in them, the trees themselves are so brilliantly delineated that they are quite sufficient to ensure the comparative success of any of Chekhov's famous plays. It must not be forgotten, however, that their success is only "comparative", for so far Chekhov has failed to become a really "popular" playwright either in England or America, and it is doubtful whether one in a thousand of the regular playgoers in these countries has ever seen a play of his or, indeed, knows anything about it.

Nor has Chekhov been particularly fortunate in his critics. Disregarding the host of critics in and outside Russia whose aesthetic appreciation of Chekhov derives entirely from their own sensibilities and who seem to delight in losing themselves in a welter of half-tones and feelings too exquisite for anyone but themselves to detect, two critical appreciations of Chekhov as a playwright sum up an attitude that is still prevalent among the more thoughtful admirers of Chekhov's genius. One of them comes from Tolstoy. Peter Gnyeditch, a Russian novelist and playwright who was for some years in charge of the repertoire of the Imperial Alexandrinsky Theatre in Petersburg, recounts the following observation made by Tolstoy to Chekhov in his presence: "You know I can't stand Shakespeare, but your plays are even worse. Shakespeare after all does seize his reader by the collar and lead him to a certain goal without letting him get lost on the way. But where is one to get to with your heroes? From the sofa to the . . . and back?" And to Gnyeditch himself Tolstoy remarked that Chekhov had not "the real nerve" of a dramatist. "I am very fond of Chekhov and I value his writings highly," Gnyeditch reports Tolstoy as saying, "but I could not force myself to read his *Three Sisters* to the end—where does it all lead us to? Generally speaking, our modern writers seem to have lost the idea of what drama is. Instead of giving us a man's whole life, drama must put him in such a situation, must tie him in such a knot as to enable us to see what he is like while he is trying to untie it. Now, as you know, I have been so bold as to deny the importance of Shakespeare as a playwright. But in Shakespeare every man does something, and it is always clear why he acts thus and not otherwise. On his stage he had signposts with inscriptions: moonlight, a house. And a good thing too! For the entire attention of the spectator remains concentrated on the essential point of the drama; but now everything is the other way round."

And in an interview published in the Russian journal *Slovo* on July 28th, 1904, about a fortnight after Chekhov's death, Tolstoy summarised his objections to Chekhov's plays in these words: "To evoke a mood you want a lyrical poem. Dramatic forms serve, and ought to serve, quite different aims. In a dramatic work the author ought to deal with some problem that has yet to be solved and every character in the play ought to solve it according to the idiosyncrasies of his own character. It is like a laboratory experiment. But you won't find anything of the kind in Chekhov. He never holds the attention of the spectators sufficiently long for them to put themselves entirely in his power. For instance, he keeps the spectator's attention fixed on the fate of the unhappy Uncle Vanya and his friend Dr. Astrov, but he is sorry for them only because they are unhappy, without attempting to prove whether or not they deserve pity. He makes them say that once upon a time they were the best people in the district, but he does not show us in what way they were good. I can't help feeling that they have always been worthless creatures and that their suffering cannot therefore be worthy of our attention."

*The Seagull*, it is interesting to note, Tolstoy roundly dismissed as "nonsense." Alexey Suvorin, the well-known Russian newspaper publisher and a life-long friend of Chekhov's, records in his diary on February 11th, 1897, that Tolstoy told him that the play was "utterly worthless" and that it was written "just as Ibsen writes his plays."

"The play is chock full of all sorts of things," Tolstoy declared, "but no one really knows what they are for. And Europe shouts, 'Wonderful!' Chekhov," Tolstoy went on, "is one of our most gifted writers, but *The Seagull* is a very bad play."

"Chekhov," Suvorin remarked, "would die if he were told what you thought about his play. Please, don't say anything to him about it."

"I shall tell him what I think of it," Tolstoy said, "but I shall put it gently. I'm surprised that you think he would take it so much to heart. After all, every writer slips up sometimes."

Tolstoy, according to Suvorin, thought that Chekhov should never have introduced a writer in *The Seagull*. "There aren't many of us," he said, "and no one is really interested in us." Trigorin's monologue in Act II he considered the best thing in the play and he thought that it was most certainly autobiographical, but in his opinion Chekhov should have published it separately or in a letter. "In a play it is out of place," he declared. "In his short story *My Life*," Tolstoy concluded with what, if he only knew, would have appeared to Chekhov the most devastating criticism of his play, "Chekhov makes his hero read Ostrovsky and say, 'All this can happen in life,' but had he read *The Seagull*, he would never have said that."

Apart from his purely moral objections to Chekhov's characters Tolstoy's main criticisms of Chekhov's plays concern their structure and their apparent lack of purpose. Accustomed to the drama of direct action, Tolstoy expected the unravelling of the knot which the playwright ties round his hero to supply the key to his character, to reveal the man as a whole. He also expected a play to solve the problems society has so far failed to solve and in this way supply the answer to the question: where does it all lead to?

Curiously enough, English criticism, too, seems to regard the same apparent lack of purpose as characteristic of Chekhov's drama, though, unlike Tolstoy, most of the critics consider that as something praiseworthy. Discussing *The Seagull*, Mr. (as he then was)

Desmond MacCarthy[1] asks: "What is it all about?" and his answer is: "It is a question more than usually difficult to answer in the case of *The Seagull*. I am obliged to turn it aside," he goes on, "and say that it is a beautiful study in human nature, penetrating, detached, and compassionate. . . . It has no theme." Still, the critic admits that he often said to himself that "a work of art to have any value must somewhere carry within it the suggestion of a desirable life," which he does not apparently find in Chekhov's plays, and he therefore suggests that it is to be found "in the mind of Chekhov himself, in the infection we catch from the spirit of the whole play; in the delicate, humorous, compassionate mind which observed, understood and forgave." The same critic, in another notice of *The Seagull* eleven years later,[2] answers the same question: "What is *The Seagull* about?" as follows: "It is a study of a group of people, penetrating, detached and compassionate." As for the purpose of the play, "the point that *The Seagull* drives home," he writes, "is that the person who possesses what another thinks would make all the difference to him or her is just as dissatisfied as the one who lacks it. By means of these contrasts Chekhov shows that what each pines for makes no difference in the end."

As for *Uncle Vanya*,[3] Mr. MacCarthy finds that Chekhov's "favourite theme is disillusionment and as far as the kind of beauty he creates, beneath it might be written 'desolation is a delicate thing'." Generally, Chekhov's play, according to the same distinguished critic, reveals "an atmosphere of sighs and yawns and self-reproaches, vodka, endless tea, and endless discussion." And thirteen years later, the same critic, writing of *Uncle Vanya* again,[4] declared that "though Chekhov was far from ineffectual himself, the ineffectiveness of his generation was his inspiration. And his final conclusion about the play is: "Besides inventing the play without plot and theatrical effects, Chekhov was also the poet and apologist of ineffectualness."[5]

Discussing *The Cherry Orchard*,[6] Mr. MacCarthy states as a

[1] *The New Statesman*, November 14th, 1925.      [4] Ibid., February 13th, 1937.
[2] Ibid., May 30th, 1936.                          [5] Ibid., January 27th, 1945.
[3] Ibid., May 16th, 1914.                          [6] Ibid., October 2nd, 1926.

matter of fact ("we all know") that "the essence of Chekhov's drama" is "the rainbow effect, laughter shining through tears." And in a notice of *The Three Sisters*[1] he finds Chekhov's heroines to be "forlorn, ineffectual young women" and comes to the conclusion that "Chekhov's supreme gift was to bring the observation of character to a most delicate sense of justice," and that his method was "to develop character and situation by means of a dialogue which follows the broken rhythms of life, and by making every remark, every gesture of his characters reflect the influence of group relations of the moment."

While disagreeing entirely with Tolstoy about the value of Chekhov's plays as works of art, Mr. Desmond MacCarthy, who in this respect represents English criticism as a whole, agrees with him about the absence of a well-defined aim in them as well as about the general ineffectualness of their characters. The only trouble about this now widely held view is that Chekhov himself dissented violently from it. Before, then, deciding whether Chekhov or his critics and producers are right, it is necessary to find out what Chekhov thought the final aim and form of a dramatic work ought to be, and what his attitude to contemporary drama was. For Chekhov had very definite ideas about both, and these most certainly influenced his work for the stage.

2

CHEKHOV WAS not, as is generally supposed, a great short-story writer who took up drama seriously only during the last seven or eight years of his all too short life. He was a born dramatist whose first works of importance were three full-length plays, two written in his late teens and the third in his

---

[1] Ibid., February 5th, 1938.

early twenties. He took up short-story writing for two reasons: first, because he had to support a large family which was entirely dependent on him, and the writing of short stories was the quickest way of doing it; secondly, because the state of the Russian stage in the eighties and the nineties of the last century was such that no serious playwright could hope to have his plays performed, let alone earn a decent living in the theatre. Even Alexander Ostrovsky, whose reputation as a playwright had long been established, was not able to do so. It was indeed this hopeless position of the serious playwright in Russia towards the end of the nineteenth century that made Chekhov look on fiction as his "legal wife" and the stage as "a noisy, impudent and tiresome mistress." But the remarkable fact about a Chekhov short story is that it possesses the three indispensable elements of drama: compactness of structure (Chekhov's term for it was "architecture"), movement, that is dramatic development of plot, and action. "The reader," Chekhov wrote to the writer Ivan Leontyev on January 28th, 1888, "must never be allowed to rest; he must be kept in a state of suspense." The dialogue in Chekhov's short stories is essentially dramatic dialogue and that is what chiefly distinguishes them from the short stories of other fiction writers. Many of these short stories, particularly the early ones, have been adapted for the Russian stage, but the "adaptation" consisted mainly in lifting Chekhov's dialogue and using the descriptive passages as stage directions. Chekhov himself "adapted" five of his short stories for the stage on the same principle, that is, he merely lifted the dialogue, adding his own stage directions, and, if his story was too short, expanding it to the necessary length of a one-act play. Commenting on a play by the Norwegian playwright Bjoernstjerne Bjoernson in a letter to Suvorin on June 20th, 1896 (that is, *after* he had written *The Seagull*), Chekhov remarked that it was of no use so far as the stage was concerned because "it has no action, no living characters and no dramatic interest." This is surely the best comment ever made on the distortion the plays of Chekhov have suffered on the stage, and especially on the English and American stage, by being denied just the quality Chekhov himself valued most both as playwright and as short-story writer, namely, action.

Chekhov, then, was a born playwright and his knowledge of the stage, too, was first-hand. As a boy in his native town of Taganrog he had often appeared on the amateur and professional stage and earned general recognition as a talented actor. Replying on March 4th, 1893, to an invitation to take part in a literary evening, Chekhov pointed out that he was a bad reader and, what was even worse, suffered from stage-fright. "This is silly and ridiculous, but I can't do anything about it," he wrote. "I have never read in public in my life and never shall. A long time ago I used to act on the stage, but there I concealed myself behind my costume and make-up and that gave me courage." And writing to Suvorin on April 18th, 1895, about an amateur performance of Tolstoy's *The Fruits of Enlightenment*, planned by a number of Moscow writers in aid of some charity, in which he had agreed to take the part of the peasant, Chekhov declared: "I used to act quite well in the past, though now I fear my voice will let me down."

His purely professional attitude towards drama (as opposed to the now so common "literary" one) can further be gauged from the fact that he did not consider a play of his completed before it had been thoroughly revised by him at rehearsals. Thus he wrote on November 27th, 1889, to the poet Pleshheyev who had asked his permission to publish *The Wood Demon*, "I never consider a play ready for publication until it has been revised during rehearsals. Wait, please. It is not too late yet. When the play has been revised at the rehearsals, I shall take advantage of your kind offer without waiting for an invitation."

Chekhov's only reason for writing a play was the likelihood of its being performed on the stage. Moreover, when writing a play he usually bore in mind the actors who were most likely to appear in its leading parts and, as in the case of *Ivanov*, he never hesitated to alter a play radically if a different actor or actress took a part he had originally intended for someone else.

"I sent you two versions of my *Ivanov*," he wrote to Suvorin on January 7th, 1889. "If Ivanov had been played by a resourceful and dynamic actor, I should have altered and added a lot. I felt in the mood for it. But, alas, Ivanov is played by Davydov. That meant that I had to write shorter and duller dialogue, keeping in mind that all the subtleties and 'nuances' will be overlooked, become ordinary and tedious. Can Davydov be gentle one moment and furious another? When he plays serious parts there seems to be a kind of handmill turning round and round in his throat, dull and monotonous, which is speaking instead of him. I am sorry for poor Savina who has to play the part of my un-inspiring Sasha. I would gladly have altered it for Savina, but if Ivanov mouths his part, I can't do anything for Sasha, however much I alter her part. I am simply ashamed that Savina will have to play goodness knows what in my play. Had I known earlier that she would play Sasha and Davydov Ivanov, I should have called my play *Sasha* and made everything revolve round this part and just attached Ivanov to it. But who could have foreseen that?"

Such an attitude may appear curious to a modern playwright, but that is only because the modern playwright has become detached from the stage. To Shakespeare or (in Russia) to Alexander Ostrovsky, to playwrights, that is, whom Chekhov called "specialists of the stage," such an attitude would not have appeared at all strange, and indeed both of them wrote their plays for and around well-known members of their companies.

What was Chekhov's attitude to the theatre? What did he think of the actors of the Imperial and private stage in Moscow and Petersburg? What were his views on the problems of acting and did he think a play ought to have a well-defined aim of its own, an aim that should be intelligible to the spectator? What, finally, were his ideas on the form and structure of a play and what did he consider to be the playwright's place in the theatre?

These questions occupied Chekhov's mind continually and were of decisive importance to his whole career as a dramatist.

Chekhov left a scathing description of the state of the theatre in Moscow in an article he contributed to the Petersburg weekly

*Fragments* in 1885. What Chekhov found so appalling about the Moscow Imperial stage was the reign of mediocrity on it. "At the Bolshoy Theatre," he wrote in his article, "we have opera and ballet. Nothing new. The actors are all the old ones and their manner of singing is the old one: not according to the notes, but according to official circulars. In the ballet the ballerinas have been recently joined by Noah's aunt and Methuselah's sister-in-law." The state of affairs at the Moscow Imperial dramatic theatre, the Maly Theatre, was no better. "Again nothing new," Chekhov declared. "The same mediocre acting and the same traditional ensemble, inherited from our ancestors." As for the Moscow private theatre owned by Korsh where *Ivanov* was soon to be given its first try-out, it bore, Chekhov wrote, "a striking resemblance to a mixed salad: there is everything there except the most important thing of all—meat." There were two more private theatres in Moscow at the time, one near the Pushkin memorial, known as the Pushkin Theatre, where plays were performed for only half the season, and the theatre owned by the famous impresario Lentovsky. "Whether Lentovsky's theatre," Chekhov wrote, "will be given up to operettas, pantomimes or tragedies, or whether the celebrated clown Durov will be showing his learned pig there, is so far unknown to Lentovsky himself, who is at present preoccupied with designing vignettes for some grand, stupendous, nebulous enterprise." There were, besides, "fifty thousand amateur theatres," but Chekhov had no use for them, and even the foundation three years later of the Society of Art and Literature by Stanislavsky and the actor and playwright Fedotov was looked upon by Chekhov with unconcealed derision, the pretentiousness of the name of the society being sufficient to make Chekhov sceptical about its founders.

In a letter to Suvorin on February 14th, 1889, Chekhov roundly dismissed the Russian theatre as it existed at that time as "nothing but a sport. I don't believe in the theatre as a school without which it is impossible to exist," he declared. In *A Boring Story* which he wrote between March and September, 1889, Chekhov discussed the vexed problem of the theatre as a place of entertainment at greater length and came to the conclusion that such a theatre was a mere waste of time. "A sentimental and credulous crowd," he writes, "can be persuaded that the theatre in its present state is a 'school'. But anyone who knows what a school is really like will not be deceived by such a facile statement. I don't know what the theatre will be like in fifty or a hundred years, but under present conditions it can serve only as entertainment, and as entertainment it is too expensive to be worth while. It deprives the State of thousands of gifted young men and women who, if they did not dedicate themselves to the theatre, could have become good doctors, farmers, teachers, army officers; it deprives the public of its evening hours—the best time for intellectual work and fireside chats. Not to mention the sheer waste of money and the moral injury suffered by the public from seeing a wrongly presented case of murder, adultery or libel on the stage." This criticism of the theatre as entertainment Chekhov puts into the mouth of the hero of his story, an old professor of medicine, and Chekhov was always very careful to make his heroes speak and think "in character". But there can be no doubt that, though Chekhov himself would not have expressed these ideas in so extreme a form, they were substantially his own ideas on the theatre of his day. It was certainly Chekhov the playwright who was speaking through the mouth of his hero when he condemned the music played in the intervals between the acts of a play as "quite unnecessary" and "as adding something utterly new and irrelevant to the impression created by the play." It was only with the foundation of the Moscow Art Theatre that this "unnecessary and irrelevant" custom was abolished.

# 3

THREE NOTICES which Chekhov contributed to Moscow journals in 1881, that is to say, at the very beginning of his literary career, reveal him as a thoughtful student of the stage and a merciless critic of bad acting. Two of these deal with Sarah Bernhardt who was on tour in Russia and appeared on the Moscow stage in December of 1881. Chekhov was not an admirer of the divine Sarah. While dramatically effective, he found her too artificial. "Every sigh of Sarah Bernhardt's," he wrote, "her tears, her convulsions in the death scenes, her entire acting is nothing but a cleverly learnt lesson. Being a highly intelligent woman who knows what is and what is not dramatically effective, and who, besides, possesses most excellent taste and a knowledge of the human heart, she knows how to perform all those conjuring tricks which at one time or another take place in the human heart at the behest of fate." Chekhov's strongest objection to Sarah Bernhardt's acting was based on the fact that the great French actress always acted herself. "She transforms everyone of her heroines," Chekhov wrote, "into the same kind of unusual woman she is herself." Furthermore, Chekhov found that Sarah Bernhardt was not anxious to be natural on the stage (an interesting and highly significant criticism this). "All she cares about," he declared, "is being unusual. Her aim is to startle, astonish and stun. There is not a glimmer of talent in all her acting, but just an enormous amount of hard work." It was Sarah Bernhardt's hard work that, Chekhov thought, provided the clue to her great success on the stage. "There is not one trivial detail in her big or small parts," he wrote, "that has not passed through the purgatory of hard work." And after expressing his "most respectful admiration" for Sarah Bernhardt's "industry", Chekhov advised the Russian actors to take a lesson from her. "That the majority of our actors do very little," he wrote, "can be gathered from the fact that they all seem to stand still: not a step forward—anywhere! If only they worked as hard as Sarah Bernhardt, if only they knew as much as Sarah Bernhardt, they would go far. But, unfortunately, where the knowledge of the art of the stage is concerned, our big and small servants of the Muses lag far behind and, if an old truth is to be believed, knowledge can only be achieved by hard work.

"We watched Sarah Bernhardt," Chekhov sums up his impressions of the French actress, "and we were thrown into raptures by her great industry. There were moments in her acting which almost moved us to tears. If our tears did not flow it was only because the whole charm of her acting was spoilt by its artificiality. But for that confounded artificiality, those deliberate conjuring tricks and over-emphasis, we should most certainly have burst into tears, and indeed the whole theatre would have shaken with thunderous applause. Oh, genius! Cuvier said that genius was always at loggerheads with mere agility, and Sarah Bernhardt is certainly very agile."

There was one important quality of acting, however, that Chekhov did appreciate in Sarah Bernhardt: it was her ability to *listen*. That ability, though, was shared by the rest of her French company. They were all excellent listeners, and that was why, Chekhov thought, they never felt out of place on the stage. It was different with the Russian actors. "This is how we do it:" Chekhov wrote, "when Mr. Mashkeyev is saying his lines on the stage, Mr. Wilde, who is listening to him, has his eyes fixed on some far-away point and keeps coughing impatiently, and as you watch him, you cannot help feeling that what he is thinking of at the moment is: 'That has nothing to do with me, old man'!"

What Chekhov admired, therefore, and what he demanded from his actors, was natural acting, the sort of acting for which the great Russian actor Shchepkin became famous and which Stanislavsky later on made into the cornerstone of his own system of acting. He realised, as Stanislavsky did many years later, that such acting required a great deal of hard work as well as observation of life. "Our actors," Chekhov complained in a letter to Suvorin on November 25th, 1889, "never observe ordinary people. They know nothing of landowners, business men, priests, or Civil Servants. On the other hand, they are quite capable of representing billiard markers, rich men's mistresses, drunken card-sharpers, and generally those individuals whom they happen to observe incidentally during their pub-crawls and drinking-bouts. The real trouble is that they are so frightfully ignorant."

Chekhov's dissatisfaction with the state of the Russian stage of his time is expressed even more forcibly in a notice on a performance of *Hamlet* at the Pushkin Theatre which he wrote on January 11th, 1882. It is the only dramatic criticism of a Shakespearean performance Chekhov ever wrote, and for that reason alone it deserves to be quoted at length. Chekhov begins his notice with a parable of a sage who could not be dragged away from his books but whom one of his disciples discovered one night in "a far from respectable place" with a pretty French girl on his knees, sipping champagne.

"What are you doing, Herr Professor?" his disciple exclaimed in dismay, turning pale with surprise.

"A foolish thing, my son," the sage replied, pouring out a glass of wine for his disciple. "I am doing a very foolish thing."

"But why?" the disciple asked.

"To let in a little fresh air, my son," the sage replied, lifting his glass. "To wine and women!"

The disciple drank, turning even paler with surprise.

"My son," went on the sage, stroking the hair of the pretty French girl, "clouds have gathered in my head, the atmosphere has grown heavy, and lots and lots of things have accumulated. All that has to be aired and purified and put in its proper place. It is to do that that I am committing this piece of folly. Folly is a regrettable thing, but very often it does freshen things up. Yesterday I felt like rotting grass, but tomorrow morning, *O bone discipule*, I shall be as fresh as a daisy. Three cheers for an act of folly committed once a year! *Viva stultitia!*"

"If folly," Chekhov continues, "sometimes acts in so refreshing a manner, how much more must it be true of its opposite extreme." And he goes on to explain that nothing needed refreshing so much as the Russian stage. "Its atmosphere," he writes, "is leaden and oppressive. It is covered inches-thick in dust and enveloped in fog and tedium. You go to the theatre simply because you have nowhere else to go. You look at the stage, yawn, and swear under your breath."

But, Chekhov contends, it is impossible to put new life into the stage by an act of folly because the footboards are all too used to acts of folly, as it is. It must be brought to life by the opposite extreme, and, he adds, "this extreme is Shakespeare. I have often heard people ask whether or not it is worth while performing *Hamlet* at the Pushkin Theatre," Chekhov writes. "It is an idle question. Shakespeare must be played everywhere for the sake of letting in fresh air, if not for the sake of instruction or some other more or less lofty purpose."

*Hamlet*, Chekhov was glad to report, was accorded a delighted welcome by the audience of the Pushkin Theatre which seemed to enjoy itself hugely. Chekhov goes on to criticise the performance, and again in these criticisms a clue can be discovered to his own ideas of acting.

"Mr. Ivanov-Kozelsky,"[1] he writes, "is not strong enough to play Hamlet. He understands Hamlet in his own way. Now, for an actor to understand a character in his own way is not a fault, provided the actor does not let his author down. Mr. Ivanov-Kozelsky whined through the whole of the first act. Hamlet never whined. No man's tears are cheap, and certainly not Hamlet's. On the stage," Chekhov declares, as though in anticipation of the fate that would befall his own characters, "tears must not be shed without reason. Mr. Ivanov-Kozelsky," he goes on, "was frightened of the ghost, so greatly frightened indeed was he that I felt sorry for him. He made a hash of Hamlet's speech to his father. Hamlet was an irresolute man, but he was no coward, all the more so since he had already been prepared for the meeting

[1] A famous Russian actor.

with the ghost. The scene in which Hamlet invites his friends to swear on the hilt of his sword was not successful: Ivanov-Kozelsky did not speak but hissed like a gander chased by boys. His conversation with Rosencrantz and Guildenstern lacked dignity. He gave himself airs in their presence. It is not enough," Chekhov goes on, again as though in anticipation of the way in which his own characters would be mangled and distorted on the stage, "it is not enough to feel and to be able to convey one's feelings correctly on the stage; it is not enough to be an artist; an actor must also possess a great fund of knowledge. An actor who undertakes to play Hamlet must be an educated man. The scene between Hamlet and his mother was excellently played. So was the scene in the churchyard. There was a great deal of charm in Ivanov-Kozelsky's acting, but all this charm was due to his ability to feel, and to that alone. He underlined every word, watched his every movement, counted his steps. This is the fault of every beginner. Hamlet's death in horrible convulsions and a fearful voice should have been replaced by a natural one."

As for the other actors, Chekhov found that "Claudius was not bad," and, he added significantly, "he knew how to kneel." On the other hand, "the queen, the ghost, Horatio and the rest were bad. Still, the First Player was good enough and though I am told that Ophelia had a better voice than Miss Baranova, she did not play so badly."

After criticising the small stage, the bad scenery and costumes, and the unnecessary cuts, Chekhov concludes his notice by praising "the genius of the man who first suggested a performance of *Hamlet* on the stage of the Pushkin Theatre. Far better," he declares, "a badly acted Shakespeare than some dreary trash."

This being Chekhov's opinion of the Russian stage and the Russian actors, what did he think of the Russian audiences? There were moments when the Russian audiences made him lose heart. "Why and for whom do I write?" he exclaims in a letter to Suvorin on December 23rd, 1888. "For the public? But I do not see it and I believe in it less than in house demons: it is uneducated, badly brought up, and its better elements are unfair and ill-disposed to us. I can't make up my mind whether this public does or does not need me." But he drew the line at blaming the Russian audiences for the bad state of the theatres. "The public," he wrote to Suvorin in November of the same year, "is everywhere the same: intelligent and foolish, generous and ruthless, all depending on its mood. It always was a herd in need of good shepherds and dogs and it always went where the shepherds and dogs made it. You profess to be outraged that it should laugh at silly jokes and applaud high-sounding phrases; but it is the same audience that packs the theatre to see *Othello* and that weeps when listening to Tatyana reading her love letter in *Eugene Onegin*. However foolish it may be, it is in general more intelligent, more sincere and more good natured than Korsh or any actors and playwrights, while Korsh and the actors imagine that they are the more intelligent ones. A mutual misunderstanding."

4

A SCATHING description of the type of playwright who was all too common in his day, was given by Chekhov in 1886 in a small sketch under the title of *Dramatist*. The playwright, "a dim personality with lustreless eyes and a catarrhal physiognomy," is shown paying a visit to his doctor. His complaints include breathlessness, belching, heartburn, depression and a bad taste in the mouth.

"What do you do for a living?" asked the doctor.

"I am a playwright," the individual replied not without pride.

The doctor, filled with respect for his patient, smiled deferentially. Since such an occupation implied great nervous strain, he asked his patient to describe his mode of life. The playwright told him that he usually got up at twelve, and at once smoked a cigarette and drank two or three glasses of vodka. After breakfast he again had some beer or wine, the choice depending "on his finances". Then he usually went to a pub and after the pub he had a game of billiards. At six o'clock he went to a restaurant to have his dinner, but his appetite was so bad that to stimulate it he was forced to have six or seven glasses of vodka. Then at the theatre he felt so nervous that he again had to consume large quantities of drink. From the theatre he went to some night-club where he usually stayed till the morning.

"And when do you write your plays?" asked the doctor.

"My plays?" the playwright shrugged. "Well, that depends..."

Asked by the doctor to describe "the process of his work," the playwright gave this illuminating, though not by any means exaggerated, account of the way "popular plays" were usually written in those days: "First of all, I get hold of some French or German piece either by accident or through some friends (I haven't got the time to keep an eye on all the new foreign plays that are published myself). If the play is any good I take it to my sister or hire a student for five roubles. They translate it for me and I, you see, adapt it for the Russian stage: I substitute Russian names for the names of the characters and so on. That's all. But don't run away with the idea that this is easy. It isn't at all easy!" the "dim individual" declared, rolling up his eyes and heaving a sigh.

The Russian stage in the eighties and nineties of the last century was indeed flooded with such "adaptations" of, mostly, French plays, and one of Chekhov's own brilliant one-act comedies actually owed its origin to one such adaptation of a French play.

Two years later Chekhov gave the following description of an original Russian play by E. P. Karpov, who was later to become the producer of the Petersburg Alexandrinsky Theatre and who was chiefly responsible for the failure of *The Seagull*:

"The other day I saw *Crocodile Tears*, a rubbishy five-act play by a certain Karpov, author of *On the Meadow*, *The Agricultural Board*, *The Free Bird*, etc." he wrote to Suvorin on November 11th, 1888. "The whole play, even if one overlooks its wooden naïvety, is an utter lie and travesty of life. A dishonest headman of a village gets a young landowner, a permanent member of the local agricultural board, into his power and wants him to marry his daughter, who is in love with a clerk who writes poetry. Before the marriage a young, honest land-surveyor opens the eyes of the landowner, who exposes his would-be father-in-law's crimes, the crocodile, i.e., the headman of the village, weeps, and one of the heroines exclaims: "And so virtue is triumphant and vice is punished!' which brings the play to an end.

"Horrible! After the play Karpov stopped me and said: 'In this play I have shown up the liberal milksops and that is why it was not liked and was abused. But I don't care a damn!'

"If ever I say or write anything of the kind, I hope that you will hate me and have nothing to do with me any more."

And in a letter to Leontyev on the same day Chekhov wrote:

"You want to have an argument with me about the theatre. By all means, but you will never convince me that I am wrong about my dislike of these scaffolds where they execute playwrights. Our contemporary theatre is a world of confusion, stupidity and idle talk. The other day Karpov boasted to me that he had shown up 'the silly liberals' in his third-rate *Crocodile Tears* and that that was why his play was disliked and abused. After that my hatred of the theatre grew more violent and I grew even more fond of those fanatics who are trying to make something decent and wholesome out of it."

It was in another letter to Leontyev that Chekhov summed up his attitude to his contemporary playwrights in these words: "Our gifted writers have a great deal of phosphorus, but no iron. We are, I am afraid, no eagles, but just pretty birds who know how to sing sweetly."

It is an amazing fact that the accusation of lacking "iron", which Chekhov brought against the writers of his own day, should even in his lifetime have been brought against him by those who were so influenced by this general absence of a clearly perceived aim in their own writings that they naturally assumed that Chekhov, too, was like them. And yet there was no more outspoken a critic of this contemporary trend in literature than Chekhov. Writing to Suvorin on October 27th, 1888, Chekhov declared: "I dislike everything that is being written today. It makes me feel bored. Everything in my own head, however, interests, moves and excites me—and from this I conclude that nobody is doing what ought to be done, and that I alone know the secret of how to do it." Chekhov was quick enough to modify this seemingly arrogant statement from a young man of twenty-eight by adding that he supposed every writer thought the same, but in his case it happened to be true. Among his contemporaries, that is to say, among the young popular writers of the eighties and nineties, he was the only one to demand from the creative artist "a conscious attitude towards his work", though at first he insisted that it was not the business of a writer to provide a solution of social problems. "In *Anna Karenina* and *Eugene Onegin*," he wrote to Suvorin in the same letter, "not a single problem is solved, but they satisfy you completely because the problems in them are formulated correctly. It is the duty of the judge to put the questions to the jury correctly, and it is for the members of the jury to make up their minds, each according to his own taste." In another letter to Suvorin earlier in the same year Chekhov is even more specific. "The creative artist," he writes, "must not set himself up as a judge of his characters or of their opinions, but must be an impartial witness. If I happen to hear a rather confused discussion about pessimism which does not solve anything, I have to report this conversation in the form in which I heard it, and it is for the members of the jury, i.e. for my readers, to express an opinion about it. My business consists in being talented, that is, in being able to distinguish the important depositions from the unimportant ones and in being able to throw light on my characters and to speak their language. . . . It is time that writers, and particularly those of them who are artists, should admit that it is impossible to make anything out in this world, as indeed Socrates and Voltaire so admitted. The mob thinks that it knows and understands everything, and the more stupid and ignorant it is, the wider does the scope of its knowledge and understanding seem to stretch. But if an artist in whom the mob believes is bold enough to declare that he does not understand anything of what he sees around him, then that alone will be a big step forward."

The vexed problem of the ultimate aim of art is of particular importance so far as Chekhov the playwright is concerned. Chekhov's insistence on the absolute objectivity of the writer led him at first to assume a standpoint which is barely distinguishable from that of the art-for-art's sake school. Indeed, it led him to write the only purely naturalistic play he ever wrote—*On the Highway*, a play that was forbidden by the censor on the ground that it was "sordid". The failure to differentiate between Chekhov's plays of direct-action and his later plays of indirect-action is to a certain extent due to the failure to realise that Chekhov's attitude towards the ultimate aim of art underwent a complete change during the seven years that separate his last play of the direct-action type from his first play of the indirect-action type. It is not only the purely structural form of the plays that underwent a change but also their inner content. If during his first period as a playwright Chekhov seemed to assume that artistic objectivity was incompatible with the presence of a "message" in a work of art, it was due mainly to his own struggles to achieve personal freedom and eradicate all traces of slavishness which his upbringing by a bigoted and despotic father had left on his mind. "My holy of holies," he wrote to the poet Pleshcheyev on October 4th, 1888, "is the human body and brain, talent, inspiration, love and personal freedom—freedom from force and lies, whatever form the last two may take. That is the programme I should like to have followed if I were a great artist. . . . I am not a liberal, or a conservative, or an evolutionist, or a monk or an indifferentist," he declares in the same letter. "I should like to be a free artist and—that is all. . . . I hate lies and violence of any kind. Phariseeism, stupidity and licence are to be found not only in middle-class homes and police stations; I see them in science, in literature, and among our young people. I consider a label or a trade-mark of any kind to be a prejudice." In a letter to Suvorin on

January 2nd, 1889, he replied to the assertion of the Russian novelist Dmitry Grigorovich who wrote to him that "talent and freshness will overcome everything". It was much truer to say, Chekhov declared, that "talent and freshness may spoil a great deal. For in addition to the profusion of material and talent, something no less important is required. First of all, a mature mind and, secondly, *a feeling of personal freedom*, which I did not possess before."

But even during the period when Chekhov drove his conception of the creative artist's objectivity to the extreme of denying that a work of art must possess what is commonly known as "a message", he deeply resented any accusation of being merely a naturalistic writer. In reply to the criticism of his short story *Slime* (an early story published in September, 1886) by Maria Kisselev, an old friend of his, who accused him of being too much preoccupied with "dunghills" and urged him to concentrate on finding "the pearl in the dunghill", Chekhov made a detailed statement on his attitude to literature and the aims that should animate a serious writer in clothing contemporary life in an artistic form, a statement that is of the greatest possible significance to his early work for the theatre.

"I do not know who is right," Chekhov wrote on January 14th, 1887, "Homer, Shakespeare, Lope de Vega or, in general, the ancients who were not afraid of rummaging in 'dunghills' but were much more steadfast than we are so far as morals are concerned, or our contemporary writers who are prudes on paper but cold cynics in spirit and in life. I do not know whose taste is worse: the taste of the ancient Greeks who were not ashamed of glorifying love as it really is, or the taste of the readers of Emile Gaboriau, Eugenia Marlitt or Peter Boborykin?" At the age of twenty-seven Chekhov did not feel himself competent to give an answer to this question, just as he felt incompetent to give the right answer to the question of nonresistance to evil or the freedom of conscience. His correspondent's references to Turgenev and Tolstoy, who, she claimed, avoided the "dunghill" Chekhov brushed aside as irrelevant. "Their fastidiousness," he

wrote, "proves nothing; after all, the generation of writers before
them considered even descriptions of peasants and low-grade
civil servants as beneath their dignity. And, besides," he goes
on, "one period of literature, however rich in content, does not
give us the right to draw any conclusions in favour of one literary
movement or another. References to the corrupting influence of
a certain literary movement do not solve the problem, either.
Everything in the world is relative and approximate. There are
people whom even children's books will corrupt and who seem
to derive delight from reading the piquant passages in the Psalms
and Solomon's Proverbs. But there are also people who remain
unaffected by 'dirt'; indeed, the more familiar they become with
it, the cleaner they are. Publicists, lawyers, and doctors, who are
familiar with all the secrets of life are, as a rule, much more moral
than bishops. And, finally," Chekhov maintained, "no literature
can possibly outdo life by its cynicism: you can't make a man
drunk on a glass of liquor if he has already drunk a whole barrel."

As for his correspondent's claim that it was the duty of literature
to dig for "the pearl" in "the dunghill", that, Chekhov contended,
meant disowning literature itself, for literature, he wrote, "is a
creative art just because it shows us life as it is. Its purpose," he
went on, "is absolute and honest truth, and to narrow down its
functions to such a specialised field as the extraction of 'pearls'
is as fatal as, for instance, compelling Levitan to paint a tree
without showing its dirty bark and yellow leaves." Chekhov
was ready to admit that the "pearl" was an excellent thing in
itself, "but a writer," he insisted, "is not a confectioner, a cos-
metician or an entertainer. He is a man who has to fulfil certain
duties; he is a man who has entered into a contract with his
conscience and his sense of duty, and however much he may hate
it, he must overcome his fastidiousness and soil his imagination
with the dirt of life . . . To a chemist," Chekhov went on, "the
notion of dirt does not exist. A writer must be as objective as a
chemist. He must renounce every subjective attitude to life and
realise that dunghills play a very honourable part in a landscape
and that vicious passions are as much a part of life as virtuous ones."

On the other hand, Chekhov admitted that writers must observe the rules of decency, but, he added, "it is only that that we are entitled to demand from the realists."

Chekhov concluded his letter by deploring any outside interference with literature. "The fate of literature would be lamentable indeed," he declared, "if it were left to the mercy of personal prejudice. That is first of all. Secondly, no police exists that could possibly consider itself competent in literary matters. I admit that self-restraint is necessary, for charlatans, too, find their way into literature, but, however much you tried, you could never invent a better police for literature than the critic and the author's own conscience. People have been inventing all sorts of things since the creation of the world, but they have not invented anything better than that."

This letter was written shortly before Chekhov wrote *Ivanov*, his last direct-action play, and the views expressed in it are therefore important in assessing the literary merits of his plays of that period. He had acknowledged himself to be a realist pure and simple and had taken for his watchword the phrase "life as it is". But it would be a grave mistake to think that Chekhov never budged from this position. Indeed, the seven years that separate *The Wood Demon* (1889), the play in which he had unsuccessfully attempted to find a different approach to drama, from *The Seagull* (1896), the first play in which he was supremely successful in his new medium of indirect action plays, were years of great heart-searchings for Chekhov, years in which his formula "life as it is" underwent a profound change. His endless recasting of *Ivanov* and his final dissatisfaction with the play, to which he began to refer in his letters as *Bolvanov* (*bolvan* meaning "blockhead" in Russian), shows that even at that early date Chekhov was beginning to be conscious of the dilemma inherent in the strict adherence to the principle of complete objectivity. In his letter to Suvorin of October 27th, 1888, he summed up the problem in these words: "If one were to deny the problem and the intention in creative art, then one would have to admit that the artist worked without premeditation under the influence of some mental aberration, and if, therefore, some writer were to boast to me that he had written a story without any previously thought out design but just by inspiration, I should call him a madman." But he still insisted that while it was right to demand from an artist a conscious attitude towards his work, it was only "the correct formulation of the problem" and not its solution that was compulsory for him. Two years later, however, in reply to Suvorin's criticism of his short story *Thieves*, he admitted that "no doubt it would be pleasant to combine a sermon with art," but, he pointed out, he found such a combination personally impossible for technical reasons. "For to depict horse-thieves in seven hundred lines," he wrote on April 1st to Suvorin, "I have to think and talk all the time in their tone and feel as they do, otherwise, if I were to add subjectivity, my characters would become blurred and the story would not be as compact as all short stories ought to be. When writing I rely entirely on the reader to add the missing subjective elements in the story."

But Chekhov soon discovered that it was impossible to rely on the reader to draw the right moral from his stories. Indeed, one of the "fat", i.e. "highbrow", monthlies in Moscow, *Russian Thought*, to which he was to become a regular contributor later on, had so misunderstood the whole purpose of his writings that it bluntly accused him of being "an unprincipled writer". That was the last straw. On April 10th, 1890, Chekhov wrote a furious letter to Vukol Lavrov, the editor of the monthly, in which he repudiated the accusation of lack of principle as a libel which made any future business relations between them and the usual civilities of acquaintanceship impossible. This letter is important in that it reveals the inner conflict that was going on in Chekhov's mind at that particular time. Indeed, his defence against Lavrov's criticism is rather lame, and the fury of his letter must be chiefly ascribed to his own realisation of its lameness. "I have never been an unprincipled writer," he declared, "or, which is the same thing, a scoundrel. It is true that my whole literary career is an uninterrupted sequence of mistakes, sometimes gross mistakes, but that is explained by the limitation of my gifts and not at all by my being a good or a bad man. I have never blackmailed anyone, I have never written anything of a libellous nature, I have never informed on anyone, flattered anyone, or lied to anyone, or insulted anyone—in short, I have never written a single line of which I need be ashamed. If I were to assume that by 'unprincipled' you have in mind the melancholy fact that I, an educated man, who have often appeared in print, have done nothing for those I love, and that my activity has vanished without a trace, without, for instance, being of the slightest use to our agricultural boards, our new courts of justice, the freedom of the press, and so on, then *Russian Thought* ought in justice to consider me as its colleague and not accuse me, for it never did more than I—and that not because of any fault of mine."

Chekhov went on to defend himself against an accusation which obviously hurt him to the quick by claiming that even if he were to be judged as a writer pure and simple, he did not deserve to be publicly stigmatised as unprincipled, and he advanced the curious plea that he was really a doctor and not a writer at all, and that even as a writer he had so far got on excellently with all his literary friends. Finally, he pointed out that in the conditions of the strict censorship that prevailed at the time, it showed a peculiar lack of tact on Lavrov's part to bring such an accusation against writers.

5

CHEKHOV'S REFERENCE to the stringent censorship was the only valid argument he used to rebut Lavrov's criticism. In his great plays he had to resort to all sorts of evasions in order to circumvent that particularly obnoxious obstacle. But his letter undoubtedly reveals a great uneasiness of mind and is indeed an indirect admission that there was some justice in

Lavrov's accusation. His fury with *Russian Thought* was short-lived. He was, above all, honest with himself. On November 25th, 1892, in a letter to Suvorin he re-defined his position as a writer by finally relinquishing his standpoint of strict objectivity and placing the "aim" of a work of art, i.e. its moral purpose, at the head of all its other distinguishing marks.

Chekhov began his letter by casting a critical eye over the successful writers and artists of his time. His main objection to them was that they lacked "alcohol" to make their readers "drunk and enthralled". Had any of these writers ever given the world "one drop of alcohol?" Were not "Korolenko, Nadson and all our modern writers just lemonade? Have the paintings of Repin and Shishkin," he asked Suvorin, "ever turned your head?" And he went on to characterise these writers in the phrase he later put into Trigorin's mouth: "Charming, talented. You are delighted," he wrote, "but at the same time you can't forget that you want to smoke." Comparing the achievements made in his day by science and technology, Chekhov could not help concluding that the writers of his time found life "flabby, sour and dull" and that they themselves, too, were "sour and dull. All this," he concluded, "is not caused by our stupidity or lack of talent or, as Victor Burenin[1] thinks, by our self-conceit, but by an illness which is for an artist worse than syphilis or sexual impotence." These writers lacked "something", something very essential, something that made all the difference between mere entertainment and real art. What was that "something"? Chekhov went back to the classics in search of it. "Remember," he wrote, "that the writers whom we consider immortal or even just good, the writers who have the power of keeping us enthralled, all possess one highly important characteristic in common: they get somewhere and they call upon us to go with them, and we feel not only with our reason but with the whole of our being that they have some aim, like the ghost of Hamlet's father, who did not come back for nothing and did not trouble Hamlet's imagination for nothing. Some of them, according to how great they

[1] A member of the staff of Suvorin's paper, *Novoye Vremya*.

are, have aims that concern their own times more closely, such as the abolition of serfdom, the liberation of their country, politics, beauty, or simply vodka, others have more remote aims, such as God, life beyond the grave, human happiness, and so on. The best of them are realists and depict life as it is, but because every line they write is permeated, as with a juice, by a consciousness of an aim, you feel in addition to life as it is, also life as it should be, and it is that that delights you. But what about us? We depict life as it is, but we refuse to go a step further. We have neither near nor remote aims and our souls are as flat and bare as a billiard table. We have no politics, we do not believe in revolution, we deny the existence of God, we are not afraid of ghosts, and so far as I am concerned, I am not afraid of death or blindness, either. But he who wants nothing, hopes for nothing and fears nothing cannot be an artist." In another letter belonging to the same period, he wrote that the writers of his time were "like maniacs who are writing books and plays for their own pleasure. One's own pleasure is of course an excellent thing while one is writing," he declared, "but afterwards?"

So the great realisation had come at last, and though for the time being Chekhov pretended that he, too, was suffering from the same illness, it was merely his modesty speaking. Already in his short story *Ward No. 6*, which he wrote shortly before his letter to Suvorin, he had shown "a consciousness of an aim" that entitled him to a place among the foremost creative artists in fiction, but that consciousness was already discernible in many of his earlier stories in spite of his adherence to the principle of strict objectivity. For objectivity is as much the hallmark of a great artist as the consciousness of a high moral purpose, and, as Chekhov points out, it is the combination of the two that is characteristic of all great art, or, in other words, of realism as opposed to mere naturalism.

Having reached that conclusion, Chekhov later not only refused to include *On the Highway* in the collected edition of his works, but entirely suppressed it. And the main reason for his bitter conflict with the directors of the Moscow Art Theatre was their failure to see the high moral purpose of his plays, a failure that is still characteristic of most of his producers in England and America. What differentiates Chekhov's early from his four last plays is not only a difference of technique. It is the much more important question of the final aim of the plays, the moral purpose that is absent from his early plays and forms so essential a part of his later ones. For it is these later plays that, in Chekhov's own words, "are permeated by a consciousness of an aim", and are meant to make the spectator see not only "life as it is", but also "life as it should be".

The greatest mistake English and American producers of Chekhov's plays have been making is to accept the view that Chekhov's drama is essentially a drama of frustration. This is only true of his two plays of direct action; of his last four plays the opposite is true: it is a drama of courage and hope. It was Stanislavsky who was mainly responsible for treating Chekhov's plays as plays of frustration and it was he who imposed this view on the rest of the world. But the bitter conflict between Chekhov and Stanislavsky is well known, and the most obvious mistake some producers make is in either overlooking this conflict altogether or drawing the wrong conclusion from it. They all ignore the final aim of the four great plays. Indeed, they usually go so far as to deny that such an aim exists and purposely play down or entirely ignore those parts of the plays which deal with this aim. Hence the spurious "Chekhovian" atmosphere which is laid on so thickly in every production of a Chekhov play. Ironically enough, it is they who, instead of expressing Chekhov's ideas, express the ideas of the Russian woman critic Sazonova, which appalled Chekhov when he read her strictures of his letter to Suvorin of November 25th, 1892. Suvorin himself was so astonished to read Chekhov's views on the ultimate aims of a work of art, which were so much at variance with Chekhov's former views, that he sent his letter to Sazonova for her comment and then sent those comments on to Chekhov, whose reply to Suvorin is both illuminating and decisive.

"That the last generation of writers and artists had no aim in their work," Chekhov wrote to Suvorin on December 3rd, 1892, "is quite a legitimate, consistent and interesting phenomenon, and the fact that Sazonova was aghast at my letter does not mean that I was insincere or acted against my conscience. It is you yourself who have read insincerity into it, for otherwise you would not have sent her my letter. In my letters to you I am often unjust and naïve, but I never write anything I do not believe in. But if you want insincerity, there are tons of it in Sazonova's letter. 'The greatest miracle is man himself, and we shall never grow tired of studying him.' Or 'The aim of life is life itself'. Or 'I believe in life, in its bright moments, for the sake of which one not only *can* but also *must* live; I believe in man, in the good sides of his nature,' and so on. Do you really think this is sincere, or does it indeed mean anything? This is not an outlook on life, but sheer nonsense. She underlines 'can' and 'must' because she is afraid of speaking about what is and what must be taken into account. Let her first of all tell us what is, and then I shall be glad to listen to what can and must be done. She believes in 'life', which means that she does not believe in anything if she is intelligent or that she simply believes in the peasant's God and crosses herself in the dark as if she were a silly old woman.

"Under the influence of her letter," Chekhov goes on, "you write to me about 'life for life's sake'. Thank you very much. Why, her letter which is supposed to be so full of the joy of life is more like a graveyard than mine. I wrote that we had no aims and you rightly drew the conclusion that I considered them necessary and that I would gladly go in search of them, while Sazonova writes that it is wrong to tempt man with all sorts of benefits which he will never get—'you must be thankful for your present mercies', and in her opinion our misfortune consists solely in our looking for some more remote and higher aims. If this is not just female logic, then it is the philosophy of despair. He who is sincerely convinced that higher aims are as unnecessary to man as they are to a cow and that 'our whole misfortune' lies in having those aims, has nothing left but to eat, drink and sleep, and when he gets sick of all that, to take a good run and smash his head on the sharp edge of a trunk. I am not abusing Sazonova. All I mean is that she does not appear to be a very cheerful person."

# 6

MENTION HAS already been made of Chekhov's views on the paramount importance of action in a play. What are the other general conditions that Chekhov regarded as necessary to an aspiring playwright? First of all comes a thorough, first-hand knowledge of the stage. "Beginning with the next season," Chekhov wrote to a fellow-dramatist in March 1889, "I shall start visiting the theatre regularly and educating myself scenically." To his eldest brother Alexander, who had sent him a general outline of a play he was proposing to write, Chekhov wrote: "Don't forget to visit the theatre a few times and make a thorough study of the stage. You'll then be able to compare and that is important." Another rule that Chekhov was never tired of enjoining on his fellow-dramatists was the need for originality. "Try to be original in your play," he advised his brother, "and, as far as possible, intelligent, but do not be afraid to appear silly. Complete freedom of expression is necessary, but remember that only he is free to express his views who is not afraid to write stupid things. Incidentally, love declarations, infidelities by husbands and wives, and tears shed by widows, orphans and other people have been described long ago." In a further letter to his brother he gives another list of characters that a playwright should avoid: "Retired captains with red noses, drunken press reporters, starving writers, consumptive and hard working wives, honest young men without a blot on their characters, lofty-minded young ladies, and dear old nannies." Eleven years later, in a letter to Suvorin, he adds this illuminating note on the need for originality in a playwright's characters: "An educated nobleman who wants to become a priest—this is rather old-fashioned and does not arouse curiosity. You should have taken a young scientist, or a secret Jesuit who dreams of the union of the churches, or anyone else who would have cut a much more imposing figure than a nobleman who is about to take holy orders." Discussing another character in Suvorin's play, Chekhov remarks: "The father seems to have no weakness of any sort. He does not drink, he does not smoke, he does not play cards, and he is not ill. You ought to attach some kind of quality to him and give the actor something to hang on to." And he adds this rather significant note on the importance of sex in plays: "Whether the father does or does not know about his daughter's false step is not very important. Sex, no doubt, plays a great role in the world, but not everything depends on it, not by any means; and it is not everywhere that it is of decisive importance."

A play, in Chekhov's view, must above all be compact. "The more compact and the tighter a play is," he writes to a fellow dramatist, "the brighter and more expressive it is." He warns the same dramatist against becoming a professional playwright, that is to say, a playwright to whom the mere tricks of the stage are more important than the subject matter of his plays. A playwright, he insists, must above all be a poet and an artist. He must conquer the stage and not let the stage conquer him. All the same, so keen was Chekhov's perception of the requirements of the stage that in a letter to another fellow dramatist he coined the aphorism: "You must never put a loaded rifle on the stage if no one is going to fire it."

In addition to compactness and expressiveness, Chekhov laid great stress on "plasticity of phrase". He warned his brother against preciosity of language. He objected to the dialogue of one of Suvorin's plays because the language of its characters was "like a white silk dress which is all the time reflecting the sun and on which it hurts you to look. The words 'vulgarity' and 'vulgar'," he adds, "are old-fashioned now." Writing to Gorky in January 1899, Chekhov warned him against lack of gracefulness and restraint in his first play, defining "gracefulness" in these words: "When a man spends the least possible number of movements on some definite action, then that is gracefulness."

Another principle of writing plays Chekhov stuck to all through his career as a playwright concerned the elimination of what he called "the personal element". Writing to his eldest brother in May, 1889, he declared: "Your play will be no good at all if all the characters are like you. Who cares about your life or mine or about your ideas or mine?" A further principle, which is very characteristic of Chekhov's later plays especially, is that "an author must always be humane to the tips of his fingers". But admirable as this last principle is, it has undoubtedly been responsible for a great deal of "sensitive" criticisms of Chekhov's plays which tend to obscure their more important points.

There is another piece of advice Chekhov gives to his brother which is characteristic of the external form of a Chekhov play and which might as well be noted here. Every full-length play of Chekhov's has four acts and the importance of each act in its relation to the play as a whole was defined by Chekhov as early as May 8th, 1889, in a letter to Alexander: "The first act," he wrote, "can go on as long as an hour, but the others must not last longer than thirty minutes. The climax of the play must occur in the third act, but it must not be too big a climax to kill the fourth act."

It was Chekhov's custom first to produce a rough draft of a play and then go on improving it. With *Ivanov* and *The Wood Demon (Uncle Vanya)* this procedure was much more drastic, the two plays in their final form undergoing vital alterations. This process of re-shaping a play Chekhov considered required much greater ability from the playwright than the initial process of writing the play. In a letter to the poet Pleshcheyev on January 15th, 1889, written soon after the completion of the final draft of *Ivanov*, he referred to this particular aspect of the playwright's craft in connexion with the "tragic laugh" that was one of the characteristics of his friend and fellow dramatist Ivan Leontyev (Shcheglov). "No," he writes, "I do not envy Jean Shcheglov. I understand now why he laughs so tragically. To write a good play for the theatre one must possess a special kind of talent (one can be an excellent novelist and at the same time write bunglingly incompetent plays); but to write a bad play and then attempt to make a good one out of it, to resort to all sorts of tricks, to delete, re-write, insert soliloquies, resurrect the dead, bury the living— to do all that one must possess a much greater talent. That is as difficult as making a silk purse out of a sow's ear. Here you will not only laugh tragically, but neigh like a horse."

One more important aspect of Chekhov's attitude to the stage still remains to be elucidated, namely his views on the playwright's place in the theatre. It was undoubtedly Chekhov's great good fortune that among the greatest admirers of his genius was Nemirovich-Danchenko, one of the founders of the Moscow Art Theatre, who prevailed on Stanislavsky almost by main force to put on *The Seagull* during the Moscow Art Theatre's first season, thus being responsible for Chekhov's close association with one of the most progressive theatres in Russia. But this association with Stanislavsky and Nemirovich-Danchenko was also one of Chekhov's greatest misfortunes inasmuch as both producers were, at the outset of their stage careers at any rate, what is commonly known as producer-autocrats who brooked no interference either from their actors or from their authors and who quite honestly held the view (all too common among producers) that they had a right to interpret a play any way they liked. Ordinarily this would have brought about an early break between Chekhov and the Moscow Art Theatre, for Chekhov would never have agreed to his elimination from the production of his plays and the complete disregard of his own interpretation of them. As early as 1887, he insisted on the playwright's right to have a deciding voice in anything that concerned the production of his plays. Writing to Nicolai Leykin, editor of the humorous weekly *Fragments* to which he had been contributing regularly during the early years of his authorship, Chekhov made it quite plain that he would never resign his position in the theatre to the producer. Leykin had written to him: "An author who habitually interferes with the production is a nuisance to the actors, his instructions being mostly silly." To which Chekhov replied: "The author is the owner of the play and not the actors. Everywhere the casting is left to the author, provided he is not absent. Besides, till now *all* my instructions were helpful and the actors did as I told them. If the author is to be completely eliminated from the production of his plays," he concluded, prophetically as it turned out, "then goodness knows what will happen. Remember how Gogol used to fly into a temper when his play was being produced! Wasn't he right?"

Holding such views, how did it happen that Chekhov let Stanislavsky and Nemirovich-Danchenko ride roughshod over his own conception of his plays? The answer to this question is simple: at the time his plays were being performed at the Moscow Art Theatre Chekhov was already a stricken man who could take no direct part in their production. He was condemned to live in the Crimea and the few rehearsals he managed to attend in Moscow were insufficient for him to correct the cardinal misunderstanding of his ideas by the two producers. (He did, however, take an active part in the rehearsals of *The Three Sisters* before the revival of the play in the autumn of 1901.) That was the reason for his frequent outbursts of anger during the rehearsals and his refusal to advise the actors how to play their parts. His stock reply to the actors, "You'll find it all in the text," was just an evasion forced on him by his complete helplessness to make his producers see the positive ideas he had taken so much pains to present in an artistic form. In face of such utter blindness on the part of his producers and their inability to raise themselves above the prevailing ideas of their time, Chekhov was powerless: he was too ill to do anything. The irony of it was that this cardinal misinterpretation of his plays seems to have agreed with the mood of that particular period in Russian history so that in spite of it the plays were (after a time) successful. There is, of course, the further fact that with so great a playwright as Chekhov the failure to grasp the ruling ideas of his plays, the inability to understand their structure, and even the plain distortion of their characters, leaves so much that is original and artistically true that the spectator has plenty left he can thoroughly enjoy. That, however, does not justify the view that Chekhov's outbursts of angry protests against the misinterpretation of his plays were merely the unaccountable tantrums of genius. Chekhov, as is plainly evident from his letters, does not belong to the type of writer who is devoid of critical ability. He was, in fact, a very profound literary critic as well as a man who possessed the invaluable capacity for self-criticism. It took him about seven years to work out his new formula of the play of indirect action, and there can be no doubt that he arrived at his new form of dramatic expression only after a careful and painstaking analysis of the technique of playwriting, including a thorough study of Greek drama,[1] a fact of some consequence to the understanding of the structure of his last four plays.

[1] Among the large number of well-thumbed books Chekhov sent to the public library of his native town of Taganrog were the best available translations of the complete plays of the Greek dramatists.

# PART II

---

## Plays of Direct Action

# 7

## Vaudevilles:

*Kalkhas* or *The Swan Song, The Bear, The Proposal, A Tragedian in Spite of Himself, The Wedding, The Anniversary, On the Harmfulness of Tobacco*

CHEKHOV'S DRAMATIC work can be divided into two main periods. The plays belonging to one period differ from the plays belonging to the other, both in their structure and their final aim. There is an interval of about seven years between them during which Chekhov evolved the original type of drama which has made him famous. The first period includes four full-length plays, of which two have been preserved, and eleven one-act plays, eight of which are light comedies. All of them are characteristically direct-action plays, that is, plays in which the main dramatic action takes place on the stage in full view of the audience. The four plays of the second period, on the other hand, are indirect-action plays, that is, plays in which the main dramatic action takes place off stage and in which the action that does take place on the stage is mainly "inner action".

*The Wood Demon* does not strictly speaking belong to either of these categories and represents Chekhov's first attempt to write an indirect-action play or, as he first called it, a "lyrical" play.

Chekhov's one-act comedies are perhaps the most perfect examples of direct-action plays, since their characters only exist on the stage and the spectator is not expected to imagine them as having any existence beyond it.

By the time Chekhov tried his hand at writing "vaudevilles", they had been firmly established on the Russian stage for almost a century. They were first imported from France and even in Chekhov's day most of them were adaptations of French stage hits. Originally, they were musical farces written in verse, but with time the verse gave place to prose, and occasionally a more serious note of social criticism crept into them. They remained, however, entirely plays of situation and their characters bore no resemblance to living people. Chekhov, as his friends testify, loved to see "gay" plays. He was a true humorist and incongruity, even of a most mechanical kind, fascinated him. It is not surprising therefore that he should have taken to writing gay one-act comedies based on situations of an out-spokenly farcical nature. But in his hands these "vaudevilles" underwent a radical change, for his characters were all living people. That was the main reason why they were so successful financially. "Chekhov," Nemirovich-Danchenko writes, "often advised me to write vaudevilles because they were sure to bring me in a good income. The charm of these 'jokes' of his is due not only to their comic situations but also to the fact that their characters are living people and not stage vaudeville figures and that their dialogue is full of humour and characteristic dramatic surprises."

"To write a good vaudeville," Chekhov used to say, "is far from easy. It requires a special kind of mood, a mood full of high spirits." And in a letter to Suvorin, written shortly after the great success of *The Bear* on the Moscow and Petersburg stages, Chekhov declared: "When I have written myself out, I shall write nothing but vaudevilles and live on them. I feel as if I could write a hundred a year. Subjects for vaudevilles simply gush out of me like oil from a Baku well." And five years later, on January 2nd, 1894, he wrote to Suvorin: "Sergeyenko[1] is writing a tragedy based on the life of Socrates. These obstinate peasants are always after something big because they are not capable of creating something small; they bubble over with the most extravagant pretensions because they completely lack literary taste. It is much easier to write a play about Socrates than about a young girl or a cook. Which merely shows that I do not consider the writing of vaudevilles a frivolous occupation. Nor do you consider it as such, much as you may pretend that it is nothing but a lot of frivolous

[1] Peter Sergeyenko, novelist and dramatist, was an old friend of Chekhov's who conducted the negotiations for the sale of Chekhov's complete works with the publisher Marx.

nonsense. If a vaudeville is nonsense, then a five-act play by such a man as Burenin is nonsense."

Shortly after writing his first "vaudeville", *Kalkhas* or *The Swan Song*, Chekhov proposed to his friend Lazarev-Gruzinsky, who at the time was also a contributor to humorous journals, that they should collaborate in writing a skit on the acting of *Hamlet* on the Russian stage under the title of *Hamlet, Prince of Denmark*. He himself wrote the beginning of it and sent it on to Lazarev-Gruzinsky to finish. In his two letters to Lazarev-Gruzinsky, written on the 15th and the 24th of November, 1887, Chekhov gives a detailed description of his technique of "vaudeville" writing, a great deal of which is equally applicable to his other plays. "This letter is a strictly business one," Chekhov begins his first letter. "The point is that when I gave the actors a brief outline of the plot of *Hamlet, Prince of Denmark*, they were so excited about it that they expressed a wish to put it on not later than January, that is to say, as soon as possible. Strike while the iron is hot. Have you written anything? Are you getting what is wanted? Have you mastered the subject and the stage requirements? . . . The requirements are: 1) complete confusion; 2) each character must possess individual features and idiosyncrasies and must speak in a language of his own; 3) no long speeches; 4) uninterrupted movement; 5) the parts must be written for Gradov, Svetlov, Schmidthof, Kisselevsky, Solovtsov, Vyazovsky, Valentinov, Kosheva, Krasovskaya, and Borozdina;[1] 6) it must be full of criticisms on the prevailing conditions of the stage, for without criticism our vaudeville won't be any use."

And having received Lazarev-Gruzinsky's version of the play, Chekhov wrote back a long letter in which he further explained the technical principles of playwriting which he held at the time. "Your version of *Hamlet*," he wrote, "consists entirely of dialogues which have no organic connexion. Such dialogues are unthinkable. The number of characters must grow with each new scene according to the following progression:

[1] All actors and actresses of Korsh's Theatre.

.
. .
. . .
. . . .
. . . . .
.....................................

"By heaping up the episodes and characters and creating a connexion between them, you will make sure that during the entire action the stage will be crowded and noisy.

"You forget that the Tigrovs and Co.[1] feel the eyes of the audience on them all the time. Which means that the cross-examination of your Ophelia by Hamlet is unthinkable. All you want here is just one flash of anger and a lot of noise. Hamlet is indignant, but at the same time he does his best to conceal his unhappiness.

"The representative of the press can only speak from the orchestra. How the devil would he get on the stage? He makes a short and impressive speech. Think of Belyankin.[2]

"In the second act we must insert a scene from *Hamlet*.

"The end of the first act is very stilted. It is impossible to end an act like that. In the interests of the second act you must end the first act with a reconciliation of the parties.

"Incidentally, Tigrov's part is for Gradov.

"To judge by your draft, you won't be sufficiently brief. Don't forget that half of the time will be taken up by the actors rushing about the stage."

So here we have a general outline of Chekhov's methods as a dramatist. The play must be compact; the dialogues must possess an inner connexion; the number of characters in each scene must grow according to a well-defined progression; the characters must conform to the well-known idiosyncrasies of certain actors; the curtains must be carefully planned so as to contribute to the organic unity of the play; and the playwright must always allow

---

[1] The characters in the proposed play.
[2] A well-known cartoonist and contributor to humorous journals.

for the time it takes the actor to perform a certain stage action or in other words, he must possess a sense of stage timing.

*Hamlet, The Prince of Denmark* was never finished and no unfinished versions of it are extant. Chekhov was never successful in his collaboration with other writers. He also proposed to another friend of his, the playwright Leontyev, to write a "vaudeville" with him under the title of *The Power of Hypnotism*, but nothing came of it, either. Finally, he began writing *The Wood Demon* in collaboration with Suvorin, but that partnership, too, was soon dissolved. The truth is that collaboration between a genius like Chekhov and any of his second-rate fellow-writers was, to use Chekhov's own expression, "unthinkable", for the simple reason that they could never understand what he was driving at. The irony of it is that these second-raters actually thought themselves better playwrights than Chekhov and were never slow in telling him how he should write his plays. The blindness of the second-rater in face of genius is one of the most astonishing facts in literary history.

Chekhov's first "vaudeville" *Kalkhas*, was written in December, 1887. (It was actually his second one-act comedy, since his first one—*Diamond Cuts Diamond*—was written while he was still at school in Taganrog, but it has not been preserved.) Like five of his other one-act plays, it is an adaptation of one of his short stories. The story *Kalkhas* was first published in November 1886 in *The Petersburg Gazette*. The play follows the story very closely, Chekhov simply lifting the dialogue and incorporating it in his play and adding the few excerpts from Pushkin's *Boris Godunov*, *King Lear*, *Hamlet*, *Othello*, Pushkin's poem *Poltava*, and the final four lines from Griboyedov's comedy *The Misfortune of Being Clever*. The first indication of the completion of the comedy is contained in a letter Chekhov wrote to Maria Kisselev on January 14th, 1887: "I have written a play on four small pages of note-paper. It will take between fifteen and twenty minutes to act. The smallest drama in the world. The famous Davydov, who is now playing at Korsh's Theatre, will act in it. It is going to be published in *The Season* and that means that everyone will read it. On the whole, it is much better to write little things than big ones: few pretensions and a good chance of success—what more do I want? I wrote my drama in one hour and five minutes. I started another, but didn't finish it because I couldn't spare the time." At the end of December he wrote to Davydov, who was to play the part of the old actor, that he was sending him two copies of the play. On February 19th, 1888, just over three months after the successful première of *Ivanov*, the play was performed for the first time at Korsh's Theatre. On November 15th he wrote to Alexey Kisselev, the owner of the country estate of Babkino, where Chekhov used to spend his summers, and the husband of Maria Kisselev: "My silly little one-act play will be performed on Friday." In October, 1888, he decided to alter its title to *Swan Song*. "I have changed the title of *Kalkhas* to *Swan Song*," he wrote to Alexander Lensky, the leading actor of the MalyTheatre, who was anxious to act in it. "It's a long, bitter-sweet title, but I could not think of another one, however hard I tried." And in a letter to the poet Pleshcheyev earlier the same month he wrote: "The play has little merit and I do not think it is important in any way, but Lensky is anxious to act in it. Will you please have it read by the Dramatic and Literary Committee of the Imperial Theatres and pass it as fit for performances on the Imperial stage." Pleshcheyev was a member of the powerful Dramatic and Literary Committee whose approval was necessary before any play could be performed on the Imperial stage. The play was passed by the Committee on October 25th. Chekhov revised the text of the play several times, the last time in 1897 when he altered the age of the actor from 58 to 68, and the phrase "I have acted on the stage for 35 years" to "45 years".

*Swan Song* (*Kalkhas*), described by Chekhov as "a study in one act", is what it claims to be, a dramatic study of the Russian actor and the conditions of the Russian stage towards the end of the nineteenth century. At that time the actors enjoyed no social standing of any kind and even the best of them were in the end ruined by drink. Stanislavsky was the first to fight against the prevalence of drunkenness among the actors and to raise the social status of the actor generally. He had a hard struggle to achieve his reforms of the stage, but in the end he triumphed, with the result that the Svetlovidovs had a much better chance of being good and useful actors in their old age.

Chekhov's second "vaudeville", *The Bear*, was an original play which instantly became a great success and assured him a steady income for many years. The history of this brilliant comedy is a curious one. It derives directly from the French "vaudeville" *Les Jirons de Cadillac* by the French dramatist Pierre Berton, a Russian adaptation of which under the title of *Conquerors Are Above Criticism* Chekhov saw at Korsh's theatre. The French play deals with the taming of a coarse but good-natured sea-dog by a beautiful society woman. Two actors of Korsh's company, Rybchinskaya and Solovtsov, the latter a good friend of Chekhov's, were particularly successful in the parts of the society woman and the sailor. Solovtsov's big physique and thunderous voice made him an ideal sailor of the type demanded by the play, and Chekhov liked him so much in that part that he decided to write a part of a "Russian bear" for him. He wrote the play in February, 1888. "Having nothing to do," he told Leontyev in a letter on February 22nd, "I sat down and wrote a vaudeville under the title of *The Bear*." And in a letter to another correspondent on the same day, he wrote: "Having nothing to do, I wrote a silly little French vaudeville under the title of *The Bear*."

The play was performed at Korsh's Theatre with Rybchinskaya and Solovtsov in the main parts on October 28th. ("I usually write my plays in winter for the next autumn season," Chekhov declared in a letter to Lazarev-Gruzinsky on November 23rd, 1889. "Otherwise I find it impossible to compete.") It was a resounding success. "Solovtsov," Chekhov wrote to Leontyev on November 2nd, 1888, "played phenomenally. Rybchinskaya was sweet and not bad. The theatre roared with laughter; the dialogue was constantly interrupted by applause. During the first and second performance both the actors and the author had to take calls. All the newspapermen, lauded it to the skies, except

Vassilyev[1]." And yet Chekhov added this significant note: "But my dear chap, Solovtsov and Rybchinskaya are not playing artistically. They act without any nuances, harp on one and the same note, are timid, etc. Their acting is clumsy." And in a letter to Suvorin on November 7th, he again complained: "Rybchinskaya and Solovtsov are not playing artistically. My sister and I would have acted much better." And again three days later in a letter to Pleshcheyev: "My *Bear* is very successful in Moscow, though the bear and the she-bear are acting rather badly." On 23rd December he wrote to Suvorin: "The second edition of my *Bear* is just being published and you say that I am not a good playwright." And to another correspondent on January 16th, 1889: "My *Bear* should really be called the *Milchcow*. It has brought me more money than any of my short stories. Oh, the public!" Writing to Pleshcheyev on January 15th, he complained, not for the first time, of being in financial straits. "But for my *Bear* and Suvorin, who gave me a hundred roubles for some of my stories for his popular library, I should have had nothing to live on. May the Lord bless them both!" In March of that year *The Bear* earned him 500 roubles in royalties from the Alexandrinsky Theatre. "A gipsy," he wrote to Suvorin, "would not have got as much from a live bear as I got from a dead one." And two years later, in April, 1891, he wrote to his sister from Naples that his only hope of paying back the debt he had incurred to defray the costs of his journey abroad rested with "the fools of amateurs who will play my *Bear*". (This reference to the amateurs is characteristic of Chekhov, who, like Ostrovsky, could not bear to see his plays mangled by incompetent actors.) In August of the following year he wrote to Suvorin from his small estate of Melikhovo: "I am waiting for them to thresh and sell the rye, and till then I shall live on my *Bear* and on mushrooms." The play continued to be a constant source of income to Chekhov. It was, by the way, the only play of Chekhov's that Tolstoy seemed to like. In a letter to Chekhov on December 16th, 1900, his wife, Olga Knipper, told him that Tolstoy had seen *The Bear* performed

[1] The dramatic critic of the *Moscow News*.

in Moscow and liked it very much. "He roared with laughter," she wrote.

*The Proposal*, Chekhov's second original "vaudeville", was written in November, 1888, about six months after *The Bear*. Chekhov wrote it "specially for the provincial stage", as he told Leontyev in his letter of November 7th, but it became an instantaneous success in Moscow and Petersburg, too. Indeed, it was put on at a special performance before the Czar in Czarskoye Selo, the Czar's summer residence, in September, 1889. "I am told," Chekhov wrote to Leontyev on September 29th, "that at the performance in Czarskoye Selo Svobodin[1] was inimitable in *The Proposal*; he and Varlamov[1] got something out of a bad little play which made even the Czar pay me a compliment. I am expecting the order of Stanislaus and an appointment as a member of the State Council." On January 20th, 1890, the play was performed at the Maly Theatre in Moscow on the benefit night of Prince Sumbatov-Yuzhin, one of the theatre's leading actors. In a letter to Sumbatov-Yuzhin on December 14th of the same year, Chekhov wrote that he had re-read his play and found that "after *Macbeth*, when the audience is still under the influence of Shakespeare, it risks appearing as a hideous anti-climax. And who indeed could be expected to enjoy seeing this insignificant and petty rabble after the beautiful Shakespearean villains". But Chekhov need not have worried. He had invested "the insignificant rabble" with so many human attributes that the success of the comedy was a foregone conclusion. It was published for the first time in December, 1888, under Chekhov's initials A.P. (Anton Pavlovich).

This comedy is interesting for a feature which throws light on Chekhov's use of technical terms in his plays. He was fond of picking up all sorts of odd second-hand books and browsing through them. One of these, *The Diary of an Insignificant Man*, by Yegot Driansky, a little-known novelist and playwright of the sixties, abounded in hunting terms. It was from it that Chekhov "lifted" the many hunting terms in *The Proposal*. Another literary

[1] Two famous Petersburg actors.

curiosity he picked up second-hand was a dictionary of English naval terms used in the Russian navy. These gave him the idea for his short story *A Wedding with a General*, which he wrote in 1884, incorporating it five years later in his one-act comedy *The Wedding*. When writing *The Cherry Orchard*, he resorted to a somewhat similar expedient for the billiard terms used by Gayev in the play. He asked Alexander Vishnevsky, a schoolmate of his and an actor of the Moscow Art Theatre, to listen to people playing billiards and note down as many of the terms as he could, intending to put them in where necessary afterwards. "I don't play billiards," he wrote, "or rather I did play once but have forgotten it all now."

Chekhov wrote two more "vaudevilles" in 1889: *A Tragedian in spite of Himself* and *The Wedding*, both of them adaptations of his short stories. He finished the first on May 3rd, having promised the famous Petersburg actor Varlamov to write a comedy for him. In a letter to Leontyev on May 6th, he referred to it as "a stale joke" made out of "an old, motheaten story." The story in question was *One of Many*, written in 1887 and describing the sad lot of a much married man who has to leave his summer cottage in the country for his office in town every day and who is burdened with all sorts of commissions by his wife and friends. The play is practically a faithful transcription of the dialogue in the story, except that here and there Chekhov made some alterations to preserve the decencies of the stage. He was always deeply conscious of the fact that what might pass without criticism in a short story might be an unpardonable breach of good manners and good taste in the theatre. Thus, the episode of the child's coffin is left out of the play, and Chekhov also left out Tolkachov's description of the greatest horror that awaited him each night after his wife had finished practising her duets with her "tenor friends". In the play Tolkachov ends his story of the tortures inflicted upon him at night by his wife by an account of the method he has invented for drowning the noise of singing in the drawing-room by tapping his temple above the ear. "And so," he goes on, "after a sleepless night I get up at six o'clock and rush off to the station to catch my train." In *One of Many* his account is more circumstantial. "The moment they have gone," Tolkachov says, "a new punishment is inflicted upon me. My dear wife comes in and demands that I should carry out my marital duties. She has worked herself up into such a state of ecstasy while practising with her tenors in the moonlight that now I am expected to work it off for her. Believe me, my dear fellow, I am so terrified that when she comes into our bedroom at night I am thrown into a sweat and scared out of my wits."

The play, though not as successful as *The Bear* or *The Proposal*, was revived again and again during Chekhov's lifetime. At each revival Chekhov was very anxious that the part of Tolkachov should be played by the right kind of actor. "If Bibikov agrees to play the part of Tolkachov," he wrote to a theatrical manager on September 21st, 1889, "I shall be glad to shorten the long monologue, which, I fear, is rather tiring for a performer." Again, writing to Suvorin in October, 1897, he refused to let Suvorin put on the play at his theatre in Petersburg because the actor Chekhov considered as capable of performing Tolkachov's part had left the company. When, a month later, Suvorin proposed that the part should be played by another actor, Chekhov pointed out that the actor in question was too young and lacked the "solidity" of a middle-aged married man and that it would therefore be better to put the performance off till next year.

*The Wedding*, which Chekhov wrote in October, 1889, provides a good example of his method of gathering material for a play. It is based on a humorous sketch, *The Marriage Season*, illustrated by Chekhov's brother Nicholai and published in November, 1881, that is, at the very beginning of Chekhov's literary career, and two short stories, *A Marriage of Convenience* and *A Wedding with a General*, published in November and December of 1884 respectively. *The Marriage Season* has two short references which Chekhov incorporated in his play. The bridegroom in the sketch was "a retired telegraphist" who married for money, while the bride, who was "beautiful and innocent", married for love. In the first short story as well as in the play this telegraphist is introduced as an invited guest whose discourse on electricity precipitates a quarrel between him and the bridegroom. In the sketch, too, Chekhov included among the different items of expenditure one of 27 roubles and 22 copecks to "the pastrycook and the General". In two articles which Chekhov contributed to the Petersburg humorous weekly *Fragments* in 1884, he refers to the custom which was at the time prevalent among Moscow lower middle classes "to hire a General . . . without whom no shopkeeper's wedding is complete." In his short story *A Marriage of Convenience* Chekhov used only the telegraphist incident, which he later included almost without alterations in the play. The "General" motif Chekhov expanded into the short story *A Wedding with a General*, and having in the meantime been fascinated by the naval terms in the old dictionary he had picked up, he transformed the General into a Vice-Admiral. The second part of the play is based on this second short story, but to heighten the comic effect he reduced the rank of the distinguished guest from that of a Vice-Admiral to that of a mere Lieutenant-Commander, corresponding, as the retired naval officer himself explains, only to the rank of lieutenant-colonel in the army, while transferring the naval officer's dialogue with hardly any alterations from the short story to the play. Chekhov, however, introduced two new characters into his play, a flirtatious midwife and a Greek pastrycook, the latter being a further link with his first sketch *The Marriage Season*. The play as a whole is a much more ambitious attempt at light comedy, having a cast of over ten characters as compared with the two or three characters of his previous "vaudevilles". The play also becomes a link with Chekhov's personal life. The flat above the one in which the Chekhov family lived in 1885 in Moscow was hired out for weddings and Chekhov had an excellent opportunity of being an unseen witness of such occasions with their interminable toasts preceded by a flourish from the band, the dances at which the best man acted as the master of ceremonies, and so on. Indeed, it seems that Chekhov and his brothers and friends often amused themselves by improvising a wedding party while a real one was taking place in the flat above and dancing to the music of the band. In *The Wedding*, therefore, Chekhov used the material taken directly out of his own private life as well as that gleaned from his personal observation of life and from his own short stories. Practically the same method was used by him in *The Seagull* and to a larger or smaller extent in his other famous plays.

Two years after completing *The Wedding*, Chekhov wrote what was in effect his last one-act comedy, *The Anniversary*. He finished it in December 1891, and revised it thoroughly in 1902, altering the names of two of the leading characters as well as the dialogue and the stage directions, and cutting out a whole scene after the departure of the deputation of the members of the bank's directorate. This "vaudeville", which Chekhov again subtitled "a joke in one act", is also based on one of his short stories, *A Helpless Creature*, published in February 1887. But this story, the dialogue of which was again incorporated with few alterations into the play, forms only one incident of the comedy: the arrival of the old lady, the wife of a retired low-grade civil servant, who seems to think that the bank ought to pay her the wages her husband was unsuccessful in claiming from his department. The comedy as a whole, however, in spite of its broad comic elements, is a great deal more serious in intention than any other of Chekhov's one-act curtain-raisers, representing as it does a biting exposure of the private banks in Russia.

Chekhov wrote two more one-act comedies or "vaudevilles". One of them, a monologue entitled *On the Harmfulness of Tobacco*, first written in 1886, he kept revising again and again, and there can be little doubt that he used it chiefly as an experiment for the type of dialogue he was devising for his indirect-action plays. Its monologue form was just the thing he wanted for his experiments in an entirely new dramatic medium. The other play, *The Night before the Trial*, an adaptation of a story of the same title written about 1895, he left unfinished. He was at the time already developing his technique of indirect-action plays and he most probably no longer felt like writing a play of direct action.

# 8

# *Platonov*

URING HIS first period as a playwright, Chekhov wrote, in addition to the nine one-act comedies, four full-length plays, a one-act "dramatic study", and a one-act parody, *Tatyana Repina*, being Chekhov's version of the last act of Suvorin's play of the same title. His first three plays Chekhov wrote at the age of 18 while still at school in Taganrog. All that has been preserved of them are their titles, which his eldest brother Alexander mentions in a letter he sent to Chekhov on October 14th, 1878. They are: *Without Fathers*, a drama, *Laugh It Off If You Can*, a comedy, and *Diamond Cuts Diamond*, a one-act comedy. Alexander found that Chekhov possessed dramatic talent and technique worthy of greater scope, but he condemned his plays as immature. *Without Fathers* he thought "an inexcusable, though innocent, lie." The one-act comedy, Alexander, who had already entered on the thorny path of authorship in Moscow, wrote, "is written in an excellent style and its dialogue is typical of each character, but its subject-matter is rather trite. This last work of yours I read to my colleagues, giving it out to be my own play, and they all agreed that its style was excellent and that it showed ability, but they thought that it lacked observation and experience of life. In time, *qui sait*, you may become a capable writer."

Curiously enough, *Without Fathers* was for a long time confused by Russian critics with Chekhov's third full-length play, probably written in 1881, which was discovered in manuscript after his death, and which for the purposes of identification may as well be referred to by the name of its chief character, Platonov.[1] Its date is uncertain, but it is more than a coincidence that a pun in

[1] The MS. of the play consists of one hundred and thirty-four closely written pages. The title page is missing and the lower half of the last clean page has been torn off.

Chekhov's sketch *The Marriage Season* (the description of the female sex as "female polonaise", the word for sex in Russian being *pol*) should also occur in his third full-length play. As *The Marriage Season* was written in 1881, it is a fair inference that the play, too, was written in that year. This seems to be confirmed by the reference Chekhov's younger brother Michael makes to this play in his introduction to the second volume of Chekhov's letters. "While a student," he writes, "Chekhov wrote a long play, and hoping to have it performed at the Maly Theatre, took it to the famous actress Yermolova. It was a very unwieldy play, with a railway train, horse-thieves and the lynching of a gipsy." It is evident from this reference that Michael had only a hazy recollection of the play, for Osip, the only horse-thief in it, is not a gipsy. Chekhov himself was so disappointed with the rejection of the play that on his return from this visit to Yermolova he tore up his clean copy of it. The copy that has been preserved is his rough draft and for that reason alone perhaps it is unfair to judge it as a sample of Chekhov's early work for the theatre. It is certainly exceedingly long and "unwieldy". His repeated insistence on compactness as one of the most important requirements of a well-written play is most probably a result of his realisation that the length of *Platonov* (it runs to over 164 printed pages, that is, it is almost as long as his three last plays put together) was its most glaring fault. According to a modern Russian critic, the whole interest of the play lies in that "it enables one to follow up the genesis of certain themes and characters which were fully developed afterwards. The figure of its hero, Platonov, shown as a 'weak-willed character of contemporary life' will soon grow into the more universal character of Ivanov, the theme of the decay of the landed aristocracy will become the central theme of *The*

---

The four acts of the play are intact, but the text has been corrected many times in black and blue pencil as well as in ink. The MS. is not dated, but an examination of the handwriting shows that it must have been written in the early eighties.

A somewhat untidy version of the play, under the wrong title, *Without Fathers*, was first published in 1923. A second fully revised edition of it appeared in 1949. A garbled English version under the title *That Worthless Fellow Platonov* was published in London in 1930. It omits the long Act I entirely and starts the play with Act II, Sc. 1. The fact of this omission is not mentioned.

*Cherry Orchard*, and so on. But intrinsically the play lacks artistic merit, being rather weak from the point of view of architectonics and built up on external melodramatic effects: two attempts on Platonov's life, the attempted suicide of one of the heroines who tries to throw herself under a train, the final murder of the hero, etc. Chekhov is here entirely under the influence of the prevailing theatrical clichés and of the "problem' drama of the popular Russian dramatists of his time."[1]

This judgment is a little too sweeping. What is so significant about *Platonov* is that it represents Chekhov's first attempt to paint a large canvas of the social forces that were moulding Russian life in the last two decades of the nineteenth century. In spite of its obvious shortcomings, it not only contains a gallery of well realised, if at times "theatrical", portaits taken from the different strata of Russian society, but also shows the clash between the self-destructive economic forces his characters represent, and affords, in a symbolic form, a glimpse of the inevitable outcome of this struggle. (The only other similar "prophecy" contained in Chekhov's plays is Tusenbach's declaration on the future of Russia in Act I of *The Three Sisters*: "The time has come and something huge is about to overwhelm us—a mighty hurricane is on the way, and soon, very soon, it will sweep away from our society laziness, complacency, prejudice against work and effete boredom. I shall work, and in another twenty-five or thirty years everyone will work—everyone!")
It is, surely, a remarkable fact that at the age of twenty-one when he was only just becoming known as a writer of humorous trifles, Chekhov should have undertaken a major dramatic work in which he appraised the whole social fabric of his times and passed his judgment upon it.

The play, then, is a microcosm of Russia in the eighties of the last century. Its characters include the young widow of a General, Anna Voynitsev, and her improvident idealist of a step-son, Sergey, whose estate, like the Ranevsky estate in *The Cherry Orchard*, is to be sold at a public auction, as well as other typical

[1] S. Danilov. *An Outline of the History of the Russian Theatre*. Moscow, 1948.

representatives of the landowning class, Glagolyev, Petrin and
Shcherbuk, and Platonov himself, a former rich landowner who
has squandered his patrimony and is now a village teacher, a
representative of the army, Colonel Triletsky, and the colonel's
son, Dr. Triletsky, representing the liberal professions. This is
how the young Chekhov introduces the colonel in Act I.

ANNA. The colonel is such a darling! I shall be going shooting
    quail with him on St. Peter's Day.
COLONEL TRILETSKY. Ho, ho! Quail? Why, my dear lady, we
    shall organise a campaign against snipe. A Polar expedition
    to the Devil's Dyke.
ANNA. We'll try out your new English shotgun.
COLONEL TRILETSKY. So we shall, so we shall, divine Diana.
    (*Kisses Anna's hand.*) Remember last year, dear lady? Ha, ha!
    I like high-spirited women like you, ma'am. Damme, if I
    don't. Can't stand timid creatures. Women's emancipation!
    Why, bless my soul, here you have the best example of it
    before you. Go near her and you get a whiff of gunpowder.
    She simply reeks of Hannibals and Hamilcars! A field-
    marshal, a regular fieldmarshal! Give her a pair of epaulettes
    and she'll conquer the world. We'll go shooting, ma'am.
    We'll show 'em what military blood is worth, my dear
    lady, divine Diana, Alexandra of Macedon!
PLATONOV (his son in law). I can see you've had a couple, colonel.
COLONEL TRILETSKY. Why, of course, my boy.
PLATONOV. So that's why you're in such good form.
COLONEL TRILETSKY. You see, my boy, I arrived at eight o'clock
    this morning. They were all asleep. I walked in here and
    raised a hell of a row. Then her ladyship came in and—burst
    out laughing. Well, so we opened a bottle of Madeira.
    Diana had three glasses and I had the rest of the bottle.

Then there are the business men, Vengerovich and Bugrov,
who between them will buy up the Voynitsev estate. This is how
they are introduced:

DR. TRILETSKY. What a marvellous article I've just published in
    the *Russian Courier*, gentlemen! Have you read it? Have you
    read it, Mr. Vengerovich?

VENGEROVICH. I have.

DR. TRILETSKY. Don't you agree it is a splendid article? I've written you up as a real man-eating tiger, haven't I? Enough to make all Europe gasp with horror.

PETRIN (*roars with laughter*). So that's who it is! So that's who this V. is! And who, pray is B.?

BUGROV (*laughs*). That's me. (*Wipes his forehead.*) Who cares?

VENGEROVICH. Not bad, not bad at all. If I knew how to write, I should certainly write for the papers. To begin with, you get paid for it, and, secondly, we seem for some reason inclined to regard people who write as intelligent. Anyway, doctor, you didn't write that article at all. Mr. Glagolyev wrote it.

GLAGOLYEV. That's funny. It's true I wrote it, but how the devil did you find out?

VENGEROVICH. Oh, one can find out everything if one wants to badly enough. You sent it off by registered post and—well— the clerk at the post office has an excellent memory. That's all. There's nothing mysterious about it.

And as a contrast to the two representatives of the new acquisitive class Chekhov presents Osip, a thief, who, too, is a beast of prey like them, but who makes no bones about it.

PLATONOV. I have the honour, ladies and gentlemen, to present a most interesting specimen to you. One of the most interesting wild animals of our present day zoo. (*Turns Osip round.*) Known to all and sundry as Osip the horse thief, parasite, murderer and burglar. He was born in Voynitsevka, committed all his murders and robberies in Voynitsevka and is always to be found in and around Voynitsevka. (*Laughter.*)

OSIP (*laughs*). You are a caution, sir.

DR. TRILETSKY (*examining Osip closely*). What's your trade, my good man?

OSIP. Theft, sir.

DR. TRILETSKY. I see. Quite a pleasant occupation. What a cynic you are, though.

OSIP. What's a cynic, sir?

DR. TRILETSKY. Cynic is a Greek word which translated into your language means a pig who does not care if the whole world knows that he is a pig.

What Osip and Vengerovich possess in common is their contempt for the people on whom they batten. Asked why he had not been sent to Siberia, Osip explains that "according to the law, sir, you can only be sent to Siberia if they're able to prove something against you or if they catch you redhanded. Now I admit," he goes on, "that everyone knows that I'm a thief and a robber, but not everyone can prove it. You see, sir, the common people have no guts nowadays. They're stupid. And so, of course, they are afraid of proving anything against me. They could have sent me to Siberia, but they don't know the law. They're terrified of everything. They're always trying to do things behind your back, in a crowd. They're an ignorant, beggarly, scurvy lot, sir. It serves them right if they get hurt." And he goes on to assure Platonov that he is not the only one who thinks that way. "Nowadays," he declares, "everyone thinks like that. Take Mr. Vengerovich, for instance."

PLATONOV. Yes, but he, too, is above the law. Everyone knows, but not everyone can prove it.

VENGEROVICH. I'd be glad if you'd leave me out of it.

PLATONOV. It's no use talking about him. He's been made in your image, but he's much cleverer than you. It isn't quite safe to tell him what he is in his presence, but one can tell you. You're birds of a feather, but, my dear fellow, he owns sixty pubs—sixty pubs, and you haven't even got sixty copecks.

VENGEROVICH. Sixty-three pubs.

PLATONOV. He'll have seventy-three next year. He contributes to public charities, he gives dinners, he is a respected member of society, everybody bows and scrapes before him, and you—you're a fine fellow, to be sure, but you don't know how to live. You don't know how to live, you bad man!

Against this background of the decay of the old order, the insatiable greed of the new and the seemingly inert mass of millions of the exploited and expropriated, Chekhov places his drama of human passion and frustration. Its hero Platonov expresses in his person the uncertainty of that period. Glagolyev, the representative of the old order who is the only one to have preserved his fortune (his son, Chekhov makes it quite clear, will squander it for him), a man whom everyone looks on as an incurable romantic, gives this characterisation of Platonov: "He is an admirable representative," he tells Anna in Act I, "of our modern uncertainty. He is the hero of the best, but, unfortunately, still unwritten, modern novel. By uncertainty," he explains, "I mean the present condition of our society: the Russian novelist feels this uncertainty. He finds himself in a quandary. He feels lost. He doesn't know what to seize on. He doesn't understand. His novels are abominably bad, everything in them is forced and cheap, and no wonder. Everything is so uncertain and un-intelligible. Everything is so terribly confused. Everything is in such a hopeless muddle. And Platonov, in my opinion, expresses this uncertainty admirably."

Platonov himself is quite aware of his own weakness and ineptitude. "Fate," he tells Sonia, Sergey Voynitsev's young wife, with whom he was in love as a student, "has played a trick on me which I could never have foreseen at the time when you looked upon me as a second Byron and I saw myself as a future Cabinet Minister and Christopher Columbus." But he has a great sense of justice, he is intelligent and he is admired for his honesty and sincerity, though, as Osip tells his wife Sasha, he has one great fault: he has not enough charity. To him the world is "a world of fools, stupid, hopeless fools." Human folly, laziness and ineptitude make him angry. He is never tired of preaching to people and insulting people, though, being a gentleman, he usually apologises afterwards. But he himself is incapable of doing anything. "I can see iniquity all round me," he tells Sonia in Act II, Sc. 7. "I can see it defiling the earth, swallowing up my brothers in Christ and my countrymen, but I just sit about without doing anything: I sit, look, and keep still. I'm twenty-seven, but when I'm thirty I shall be just the same as I am now—I anticipate no change—and as the years go by, I can just see myself growing fat, dull and indifferent to everything except the lusts of the flesh, and then—death! A life completely ruined! My hair stands on end when I think of this kind of death!" And in Act II, Sc. 2, he cries in despair: "Nothing will come of us, the lichens of the earth! We are lost! We are utterly worthless!"

Unable to lift himself out of this slough, Platonov, this amalgam of Byron, Hamlet and, above all, Chatsky, the hero of Griboyedov's famous comedy *The Misfortune of Being Clever*, the personified social conscience of the Russian intellectual of the first half of the nineteenth century, falls back upon the old palliatives to which members of his class have resorted in all ages—wine and women. But—and this is where Chekhov's genius as a dramatist reveals itself—the four women with whom he gets involved to his undoing are carefully drawn individual characters as well as personified moral types. There is, to begin with, the young widow Anna, who, as in a morality play, stands for lust. "There is nothing worse," she tells Platonov in Act III, "than an educated woman who has nothing to do. What use am I? What do I live for? (*Pause.*) I can't help being immoral. I am an immoral woman, Platonov. (*Laughs.*) And I love you too, perhaps because I'm an immoral woman. And I'm quite sure to make a mess of my life. Women like me always do. I should have been a headmistress or a professor. If I'd been a diplomat I'd have set the whole world by the ears. An educated woman without anything to do, and that means that I'm not wanted. Horses, cows and dogs are wanted, but I am not—I am redundant." While her husband was alive she let Osip make love to her and, though she soon got rid of him, he remained her slave ever after. When the play opens, she has already made up her mind to capture Platonov. "What's the matter with her ladyship today?" Dr. Triletsky asks Platonov in Act II, Sc. 2. "She laughs, moans, tries to kiss everybody. Just as if she were in love." And Platonov with that insight into people which raises him above everybody else in the play, promptly replies: "Who should she fall in love with? With herself? Don't you believe in her laughter. It is impossible to believe in the laughter of an intelligent woman who never cries: she only laughs when she wants to cry. And, as a matter of fact, she does not even want to cry—she wants to shoot herself. You can see it in her eyes."

Lust born of despair is the most dangerous kind of lust as Anna presently proves to Platonov. She starts her attack gently enough, but Platonov is not slow to guess her intentions, and his answer is short and to the point: "I shall be brief. All I want to tell you is —whatever for? Honestly, it isn't worth it, Anna." He goes on to point out to her that if they were to become lovers, they would soon get tired of one another, and that it would be absurd to endanger their friendship which was a thousand times dearer to him than the kind of love she had in mind. Anna dismisses Platonov's plea as nonsense and decides to take by force what she could not get by argument. Platonov, when she arrives at his cottage at night, is at first loath to believe that she should want him so much. "You've come," he tells her, "to conquer, to take a fortress. But I am not a fortress. I am weak—weak! Don't you understand?" But Anna will not be put off. "It's a very simple matter, really," she tells him. "A woman who loves you and whom you love has come to you. The weather is lovely. What could be simpler?" And when Platonov declares that he will not allow himself to become her plaything, the truth again bursts out of her: "I want to forget myself. You don't know, you don't understand how awful life is and how much I want to live!" And flinging herself on his neck, she cries: "I shan't let you go. I don't care what happens, but you will be mine, mine!"

But what Anna did not count on was that another woman would undertake the impossible task of saving Platonov. That woman is Sonia, the wife of Anna's stepson. Platonov and Sonia had been in love with one another five years before the action of the play starts when Platonov was still a student. They meet again after her marriage. She remembers him as a young man of great promise and is surprised to learn that he is only a village teacher. She is an idealist, and her disappointment on learning that Platonov has not even finished his course at the university is so great that she remarks rather enigmatically: "This should not prevent you from being a man, should it?"

PLATONOV. I beg your pardon? I don't understand.

SONIA. I'm sorry I didn't express myself clearly enough. What I
    mean is that this should not prevent you from being a man—
    working hard for—well—for freedom, the emancipation of
    women–I mean it shouldn't prevent you from working for an
    ideal.

This unexpected meeting has its inevitable result. Platonov
cannot forget that he once kissed Sonia's beautiful hair and he
feels that he is too young to be satisfied with memories alone.
Sonia, in the second act, realises that her marriage is a mistake
and that her husband's pretensions to be "a man of the future" is
merely a pose. He finished the philological faculty, but he does
not dream of getting a job, not even as a teacher. On his return
home he falls back into his old habits of drinking and raising
loans from the two men who will in the end sell his estate and
ruin him. She discovers to her horror that for days now she has
not even been thinking of him, that she pays no attention to what
he says, that he is becoming a burden to her. "What am I to do?"
she asks herself in her soliloquy in Act II, Sc. 5. "It's awful! So
soon after our marriage and already—and it's all Platonov's fault!
I haven't the strength to resist him. He pursues me all day long,
he is constantly looking for me, he does not leave me alone with
those meaningful eyes of his. I can't trust myself. If he should
take one step, anything might happen!" And when Platonov
does corner her, she tells him frankly that she has been avoiding
him on purpose. She couldn't stand his constant reminders that
they had once been in love with one another. "A student," she
tells him, "loved a young girl, a young girl loved a student. It's
an old story and too ordinary for you or me to take it seriously."
She asks him to stop following her about. He accuses her of being
a coward and of imagining that he is still in love with her. They
quarrel and part. Sonia decides that the only thing for her to do in
the circumstances is to go abroad with her husband, but it does
not take Platonov long to persuade her to stay. She does more:
during the garden party given in her honour, she goes for a sail
on the river with Platonov. She comes back looking pale and
with her hair dishevelled.

SONIA (*alone*). I can't! This is too much—it's more than I can bear! It's either ruin or happiness for me! It's so close here! Yes, he'll either ruin me or else he is the messenger of a new life. A new life! My mind's made up!

A new life! The theme is to occur again in *The Cherry Orchard*, and it is not the only one Chekhov took from this play for his last one. Indeed, there can be no doubt that when writing *The Cherry Orchard* Chekhov went back to the manuscript of his early play for a great many more themes. At the end of Act II, Platonov receives a letter from Sonia (which bears rather a marked resemblance to Nina's message to Trigorin). "I am taking the first step. Come, let us take it together. Come and take me. I am yours. I shall be waiting for you in the summer house near the four pillars. My husband is drunk. He's gone hunting with young Glagolyev. I am all yours." And again the hope of a new life overwhelms him. "Does Sonia really love me?" he wonders. "Why, that means real happiness! It is my happiness! It's a new life, with new people and new scenery. I'm going. I'm going to the summer house near the four pillars. I'm going. You were and you will be mine!" But after Sonia has become his mistress, he is again overwhelmed with doubts. Sonia tells him that she has told her husband everything, and in her passionate appeal to him to go away with her, Chekhov for the first time introduces the theme of work, which was to become one of the main themes of his last three plays. When Platonov agrees to leave with her, she promises to put him on his feet, to make a man of him, to make him happy. "I shall make you work," she says. "We shall eat our own bread, we shall work hard. I shall work." And she leaves him with the words: "Tomorrow you will be a different man, a new man! We shall breathe fresh air and new blood will course through our veins. (*Laughs.*) Away, decrepit man! Here, take my hand! Shake!"

But there was his wife, Sasha, and their little boy. When Sergey Voynitsev asks him in Act I if he is happy with Sasha, Platonov replies: "I'm a family man, my dear chap. Take my family away from me and I'm utterly lost. I wouldn't sell my

Sasha for a million. We get on marvellously together. She's a fool and I'm a failure." When, in Act II, Sc. 2, Platonov asks Sasha if she loves him, she looks at him in surprise. "What a silly question," she says. "How is it possible for me not to love you?" She may be a fool, but she is loyal. While he: "I take no bribes, I don't steal, I don't beat my wife, I think as a decent man should, and yet I'm a cad. A ridiculous cad! An unusual cad!" After he runs off to Sonia, Osip, who has witnessed the scene between him and Anna, thinks that he has gone off to Anna, and he tells Sasha at the end of Act II about it. Sasha tries to commit suicide by throwing herself on the railway lines in the path of an approaching train. At the last moment, however, she remembers her little son and shouts to Osip to save her. Osip, who has sworn to kill Platonov because he thinks he is his rival, is just in time.

OSIP (*picks her up and carries her into the cottage*). I shall kill him, don't you worry!

The third act opens with the scene between Sonia and Platonov. Several weeks have elapsed after the melodramatic ending of the second act. Sasha has left Platonov and is living with her father. After Sonia has gone, Platonov begins to pack, but he is interrupted by the arrival of a bailiff who brings him a summons. The summons is from the fourth woman in the play, a young girl of twenty, Mary Grekova, a scientist, whom Dr. Triletsky favours with his attentions. "I drive down to her place," Dr. Triletsky tells Anna at the beginning of Act I, "talk to her, get on her nerves, run up her mother's coffee bills and—that's all so far. I drive down to her place every other day as a rule, though sometimes I'm there every day. I go for walks in the garden with her, keep talking to her about my affairs and she tells me about hers, and from time to time she takes hold of this button and removes the fluff from the collar of my coat. I'm always covered in fluff, you know." Dr. Triletsky thinks her to be "a good girl" and Anna, too, thinks she is "a nice, clever little thing".

ANNA. What is she doing now?
DR. TRILETSKY. She reads and——

ANNA. —studies chemistry? (*Laughs.*)

DR. TRILETSKY. I believe so.

ANNA. What a sweet child! I like her with that little pointed nose of hers. She might become a good scientist one day.

DR. TRILETSKY. I don't think she knows what she wants, poor child.

And that, of course, is Mary's trouble. She is young and head-strong and in her predilection for science Platonov seems to divine the future bluestocking, which prompts him to be dis-agreeable to her whenever they meet. In Act I he insults her and in Act II he kisses her and calls her a pretty and original little beast, which makes her jump to the quite unwarrantable con-clusion that he is in love with her. The scene is interrupted by the entrance of Dr. Triletsky, whom Mary first adjures not to have anything to do with Platonov. When he refuses on the ground that Platonov is not only his brother-in-law, but also a friend of his, she replies: "All right, be friends with him. You all seem to think he is a second Hamlet, but I think he is a cad!" After she has gone, Triletsky tries to persuade Platonov to leave Mary alone, only to be told again that she is a fool and that he, Platonov, cannot stand fools. Triletsky—and here again the young Chekhov shows a remarkable insight into human nature—points out to Platonov that she is not a fool, but merely a victim of his dissatisfaction with his own life. "There are moments, my friend," he tells Platonov, "when one wants to hate someone, to take it out of someone, to make someone suffer for something one is ashamed of. So why not try it on with her? She's just the person for it. She is weak, timid, and quite stupidly trustful so far as you are concerned." But this fair analysis of his attitude towards Mary merely increases Platonov's irritation with her. He follows her into the house, kisses her again, but this time in the presence of the whole company, calls her a fool and pushes her on a table. This is too much even for the weak and timid Mary and she issues a summons against him. The summons rather amuses Platonov. He stops packing and writes at the back of it: "I kissed you because I felt irritated, but now I would kiss you as if you were a saint. I'm sorry I was so beastly to you. I am beastly to everybody. I'm afraid we shan't meet in court as I'm leaving tomorrow for good. I hope you will be happy and try your best to be at least fair to me. Don't forgive me!" The summons brings him back to reality. He is a realist and he knows that Sonia's idealistic attempt to save him is nothing but an illusion. "Sonia," he tells himself, "really believes in it. Blessed are they that believe." Now at least he is quits with Mary. "She'll make me an object of contempt in the whole country. And serves me right. It's the first time a woman has punished me. Usually, you're beastly to them and they fling themselves on your neck. Sonia, for instance. I was free as the wind and now I have to lie and—dream. Love! Amo, amas, amat![1] Got myself into a proper mess, I have. Ruined her and done myself a great service, too. (*Sighs.*) Poor Voynitsev! And Sasha? Poor child! How will she be able to carry on without me? She'll waste away and die. She's left me. Suspected the truth and left me with our child, without uttering a word. Gone away after that night. If only I could have said goodbye to her. . . ." But his reflections are interrupted by the arrival of Anna who comes to find out why he did not turn up that night and why he does not answer her letters. She wants Platonov to make it up with his wife since it is not her intention to be anything more than his mistress. He tells her that he is leaving for good, but refuses to say with whom. "Tomorrow I'm running away from here. I'm running away from myself. Don't know where. Running away to a new life! A new life! As if I didn't know what that new life will be like!" They drink (Anna, too, has a weakness for liquor) and he insists that she should leave him. But Anna cannot reconcile herself to the idea that she will not see him again and threatens that if he does go away, it will be with her.

But the moment Anna is gone, Platonov begins to wonder whether it would not after all be a good thing to go away with her for a fortnight so as to give Sonia time "to have a good rest and recover her strength". There is another knock at the door,

---

[1] Mary, in the third act of *The Three Sisters*, expresses her contempt for Kulygin's love in the same way.

and thinking it is Anna again, he laughs and goes to open it. But it is not Anna. It is Osip who has come to kill his rival. There follows a violent fight during which Osip produces a knife and is about to dispatch Platonov when Sasha runs in and saves him. (Chekhov has not yet managed to make his entrances and exits credible enough.) Sasha tells him that their child is ill, and Platonov tells her to take good care of him and asks her forgiveness for having hurt her. Sasha, who is thinking of his affair with Anna, asks him if "the intrigue" is finished. Platonov replies that there has been no intrigue but a kind of "stupendous absurdity". He assures her that it will be finished soon. "Sonia," he says, "will not be your rival for long." The news of his entanglement with Sonia comes as a terrible blow to her. "With Anna," she tells him, "it wouldn't have mattered much, but with someone else's wife? I didn't expect so mean an action from you!" To Sasha, the first deeply religious girl in a Chekhov play, this is the end. "Let me go," she cries. "I can't live with you!"

The last act of the play, which takes place in the study of the late General Voynitsev, begins ominously. After a desperate attempt by Sergey to persuade Sonia to return to him, Anna comes in to tell him that their estate has been sold. Looking out of the window she sees Osip's dead body lying near the well in the yard: he has been lynched by the peasants. Nemesis has overtaken both the old aristocracy and the man who battened on the common people, the man whose death is symbolic of the fate that awaits the new class of the Vengeroviches and the Bugrovs. Again and again in his plays Chekhov hints at such an end, but it is only in *Platonov*, a play which the censor's eye never saw, that he reveals his mind so clearly. The play then hobbles rather haltingly to its inevitable end. Platonov appears, looking very ill, has rather an inconclusive explanation with Sergey, dismisses Anna with the words, "And what are you, who are so fond of strong sensations, doing here?" and tells Sonia that he does not want any "new life". Sonia's reply is that she hates him and that she will not let it pass easily. Chekhov here piles horror on horror.

Triletsky appears and tells him that Sasha has taken poison. He
wants him to go to her as she is very ill. He agrees, but Sonia
again intervenes.

SONIA. You should have foreseen all that. I gave myself to you
without asking for anything. I knew that it might kill my
husband, but that didn't stop me. (*Goes up to Platonov.*)
What have you done to me? (*Sobs.*)

TRILETSKY (*clasps his head*). Good Lord! (*Paces up and down the
stage.*)

ANNA. Calm yourself, Sonia. Can't you see he's ill?

SONIA. How could he treat me so inhumanly? (*Sits down beside
Platonov.*) Don't you realise that my whole life is ruined
now? Save me, Platonov! It isn't too late. Platonov, it isn't
too late! (*Pause.*)

ANNA (*cries*). Sonia, what do you want? What can he say to you
now? Haven't you heard?

SONIA. Platonov, I ask you again. (*Sobs.*)
*Platonov moves away from her.*

SONIA. No? Very well. (*Kneels.*) Platonov!

ANNA. This has gone too far, Sophie! Don't dare do that! No
man deserves that a woman should go down on her knees
before him. (*Lifts her up and puts her in a chair.*) You—a
woman!

SONIA (*sobs*). Please, tell him—persuade him——

They take her away to her bedroom. Left alone, Platonov goes
up to the table and picks up a revolver.

PLATONOV. Hamlet was afraid of his dreams and I am afraid of—
life! What's going to happen to me if I go on living? I shall
be ashamed to face people. (*Puts revolver to his temple.*)
*Finita la commedia!* One clever cad less in the world!

But he does not shoot himself. At the last moment his nerve
fails him. He remains true to himself to the end. (In the first
version of *Ivanov*, too, Ivanov cannot face up to the act of self-
destruction: Chekhov makes him die of heart failure.) It is then
that Mary, who arrived earlier in order to tell Platonov that she
did not intend to go on with her court action, enters. Platonov

indulges in another love scene with her, but this time it is not to tease her so much as to tease himself by an act of self-castigation. Mary is once more taken in.

MARY. I see it all. I understand your position. It's Sophie, isn't it?

PLATONOV. Sophie, Zizi, Mimi—there are lots of you. I love you all. When I was at the university I used to try to help the women of the streets, in Theatre Square. Everybody was in the theatre, but I was in the square. I bought Raissa out. Collected three hundred roubles from the students and bought another one out, too. Shall I show you her letters?[1]

MARY. What's the matter with you?

PLATONOV. You think I've gone mad? No. It's only my fever. Ask Triletsky. (*Takes her by the shoulders.*) They all love me! All! Even if I insult them, they still love me. There was a girl—Mary her name was—I insulted her and pushed her on a table. She, too, loves me. But you're Mary, aren't you? I'm sorry.

MARY. What is wrong with you?

PLATONOV. Platonov is wrong with me. You love me, don't you? You do? Tell me frankly. I don't want anything. Just tell me whether you love me or not.

MARY (*puts her head on his chest*). I do. Oh, I do.

PLATONOV (*kisses her head*). They all love me. When I get well, I'll make a strumpet of you. Before I used to be kind to them, but now I'm going to make strumpets of them all.

MARY. I don't care. I don't want anything. You're the only man I want. I want no one else. Do anything you like with me. You're the only man I want. (*Cries.*)

PLATONOV. Now I understand why Oedipus tore out his own eyes! How base I am and how deeply conscious I am of my own baseness! Go away! It isn't worth it. I'm ill. (*Frees himself.*) I shall be going now. I'm sorry, Mary. I'm going mad. Where is Triletsky?

*Sonia enters and goes up to the table.*

MARY (*seizes Platonov's hand*). Sh-sh——

*Sonia picks up the revolver, fires at Platonov and misses.*

MARY (*placing herself between Platonov and Sonia*). What are you doing? (*Shouts.*) Help! Come here quick!

[1] In *Ivanov* Chekhov also refers to this rather idealistic solution of the problem of prostitution.

SONIA. Let me be. (*Runs round Mary and shoots Platonov point-blank in the chest.*)

PLATONOV. Wait, wait—— What are you doing?

The last scene dots the i's and crosses the t's of the situation. Anna refuses to believe that Platonov has been fatally injured and her last words after he dies are: "Platonov! My life! I don't believe it! You aren't dead, are you? My life!" Platonov's own last words are purposely couched in a minor key to heighten the tragic situation. Pointing to the old court messenger who comes in to tell him that Mary's summons has been withdrawn, he remembers the tip he promised him and says: "Give him three roubles." Mary collapses in a chair and weeps bitterly. Triletsky bursts out crying and exclaims: "Oh, the fools! They couldn't save Platonov!" And turning to his father, the old colonel, he advises him to go and tell Sasha that she'd better die now. The colonel himself decides that the tragedy is really due to his own "sins". He had killed so many of God's helpless creatures,[1] he had drunk, he had blasphemed, he had spoken ill of people, and now God had stricken him down. Sonia herself is not mentioned at all in the last scene except indirectly, Triletsky declaring that Platonov has shot himself and telling Voynitsev that it is now their duty to do their utmost to help his wife.

The crudities of the play are obvious. At the same time they are certainly due to Chekhov's inborn sense of drama and to his realisation of the paramount need of action on the stage. Even when, as in the first scene of the play, his characters are playing chess, they are always doing something. Their dialogue throughout the play is always charged with action: it is essentially a playwright's dialogue. On the other hand, the fact that no reference to the play is found in Chekhov's letters or writings seems to indicate that he was aware of the fact that it was not true to life. "Life as it is," therefore, became his watchword for a long time afterwards. His chief criticism of Ibsen many years later was that

---

[1] The first indication we have of Chekhov's condemnation of blood sports: later on he gave away some of his royalties from the performances of *The Seagull* to the Russian S ociety for the Prevention of Cruelty to Animals.

the characters in the great Norwegian's plays did not behave as people do "in life". Indeed, his chief reason for abandoning the plays of direct action was that the characters in such plays tended to become larger than life. When writing *The Wood Demon*, he formulated his new position in these words: "The demand is made that the hero and the heroine (of a play) should be dramatically effective. But in life people do not shoot themselves, or hang themselves or fall in love, or deliver themselves of clever sayings every minute. They spend most of their time eating, drinking, running after women or men, talking nonsense. It is therefore necessary that this should be shown on the stage. A play ought to be written in which the people should come and go, dine, talk of the weather, or play cards, not because the author wants it but because that is what happens in real life. Life on the stage should be as it really is and the people, too, should be as they are and not stilted."

In considering these often quoted remarks of Chekhov's, it is necessary to remember when it was that he first used them. It is obvious that a playwright who is as true to life as Chekhov wanted him to be must be an artist of quite exceptional genius. But would even such an artist be able to disregard completely those conventions of the stage which are inherent in the very art of dramatic expression? So far as Chekhov himself was concerned, his experience with *The Wood Demon* soon showed him that his formula required thorough revision. It took him seven years to evolve his own play of indirect action, and even then he found it impossible to dispense with the conventional pistol shot which occurs at the climax of all his plays except *The Cherry Orchard*. *Platonov*, then, first set Chekhov on the road as a reformer of the art of drama. But, as already pointed out, the play is significant as the repository of themes and characters he was to use in his later plays. *Ivanov*, *The Wood Demon*, *Uncle Vanya* and, particularly, *The Cherry Orchard* are directly derived from it, and even in *The Seagull* and *The Cherry Orchard* the *Hamlet* quotations are an echo of the *Hamlet* quotations in *Platonov*, except that in the two later plays their evocative implications are much more subtle. In *Platonov* it is Voynitsev, who at the end of Act II, just before Platonov goes to keep his appointment with Sonia, turns to Platonov and quotes Hamlet's lines to his mother—

Could you on this fair mountain leave to feed,

And batten on this moor?

Here the "poetic irony" is rather crude and is perceived only by Platonov, who is so struck by the appositeness of the quotation that, according to the stage directions, "he tears himself away and runs off", Voynitsev going out, too, with the words: "Ophelia! Nymph in thy orisons be all my sins remember'd."

Voynitsev appears in that scene accompanied by Nicolai Glagolyev, the spendthrift son of the old-fashioned rich land-owner. Nicolai is mainly a derivative character who goes back to the famous character in Fonvisin's eighteenth-century comedy, *The Brigadier*—the frenchified fop who intersperses his speech with French words and who despises everything Russian. It was Nicolai that Chekhov refashioned into Yasha in *The Cherry Orchard*. Yasha's favourite expression: "What ignorance!" is first used by Nicolai Glagolyev.

*Platonov* is also interesting as showing that what is commonly taken to be one of the characteristic features of Chekhov's great plays—the frequent use of pauses—is a device that Chekhov used as frequently, if not indeed more frequently, in his earliest play. It is merely another indication of Chekhov's inborn dramatic genius.

# 9

# *On the Highway*

THREE YEARS after his unsuccessful attempt to have *Platonov* performed on the Moscow Imperial stage, Chekhov again tried his luck with a play, but this time he was thwarted by the censorship. He had in the meantime established himself as a writer of amusing sketches, some of which, *The Surgery*, for instance, which he published in August, 1884, were really little comedies which could, and subsequently were, transported bodily to the footboards. He finished his new play in November 1884. In a letter to Nicolai Leykin, the editor of the Petersburg humorous weekly *Fragments*, on November 4th he wrote: "This week I am not sending you any stories, because I did not feel well all the time and, besides, I was busy: I have written some nonsense for the stage—a highly unsuccessful piece." The play, Chekhov's only naturalistic essay in play-writing, *On the Highway*, "a dramatic study in one act", is an adaptation of his story *In the Autumn*, which he had published in a Moscow magazine a year earlier. As with all his other adaptations, Chekhov lifted the dialogue practically without alterations from his short story, but he also enlarged the whole scope of the play, introducing several new characters, including the tramp Merik, who acts as the chorus to the action and is a direct successor of Osip in *Platonov*, a rebel who is deeply conscious of the social injustices of his time and becomes a robber from a sort of inverted sense of justice. The hero of the short story and the play, Semyon Bortsov, a rich landowner, takes to drink and becomes a dipsomaniac because he was deserted by his wife, with whom he was madly in love, on their wedding day, and then swindled by his brother-in-law of all his money. His real downfall, however, was due to what a peasant from his village called lack of "guts", but what was really an overdose of sensibility. Chekhov painted his portrait partly from life, having known just such a drunken, down-at-heel landowner by the name of Zabelin (he often addressed his younger brother Nicholai, a talented artist who indulged in heavy drinking bouts, by that name). The action of the story as well as of the play takes place late at night in a country pub in the autumn. The short story ends with the pawning by Bortsov of the gold locket with his wife's portrait for a drink. In the play, however, Chekhov contrives a meeting between Bortsov and his unfaithful wife, the curtain falling after a rather melodramatic attempt to murder her by Merik. In September 1885 Chekhov sent the play to the censor who refused to grant it a licence for public performances. The report of the censor has been preserved and is interesting as an instance of the mentality of the men on whom the fate of all Chekhov's plays depended. "The action of the play," the report states, "takes place at night in a public house on a country road. Among the various tramps and rogues who have come to the public house for warmth and shelter, is a down-and-out nobleman who implores the landlord to give him a drink on credit. From the conversation it transpires that the nobleman took to drink because his wife deserted him on their wedding day. By accident a lady seeks shelter from the rain in the public house, and the unhappy drunkard recognises her as his unfaithful spouse. One of the visitors at the public house, who sympathises with the drunken nobleman, rushes upon her with an axe, but he is held back. The dramatic study ends with this unsuccessful attempt on the lady's life. This gloomy and sordid play cannot, in my opinion, be allowed to be performed."

Except for the brief reference in his letter to Leykin, Chekhov never referred to his play again, and it was discovered in 1910, six years after his death, among his unpublished manuscripts.

The play is more remarkable as a dramatic study of the common people than as a personal drama of a good man brought low by human perfidy and ingratitude. It was Chekhov's only attempt to present the common people in a play, to give a faithful reproduction of their speech and to reveal their inborn humanity. The characters of the play include women pilgrims, peasants, a factory worker, and the tramp Merik who is actually its hero. When Bortsov is driven to desperation by the landlord's refusal to give him a drink, it is Merik who offers to buy him one.

MERIK. You won't get nothing from him, sir. A stingy beggar, that's him. Everybody knows it. Wait, I've got a five-copeck piece somewhere. We'll have a glass of vodka each—share and share alike. (*Fumbles in his pockets.*) Blast, can't find it nowhere. Thought I heard it jingling in my pocket not long ago. No, it isn't there. I ain't got one, sir. Seems it's just your luck, sir. (*Pause.*)

BORTSOV. I must have a drink or I shall kill someone or kill myself.
Lord, what am I to do? (*Looks at the door.*) Shall I go? Walk
out into the dark night and keep on walking?

MERIK. Well, what about you there? You, saintly pilgrims, why
don't you read him a little sermon? And you, too, landlord,
why don't you kick him out? He hasn't paid you for his
night's lodging, has he? Chuck him out! Why don't you?
Oh, everybody's so heartless nowadays! A man's drowning
and they shout to him, "Go on, don't take so long over it!
We can't stand watching you here for ever. We've got to
go to work!" They never think of throwing him a rope.
A rope costs money.

When Bortsov, having failed to get the landlord to accept his
torn hat and coat, at last offers him his gold locket and gets his
drink, a crowd gathers round the landlord to have a look at the
picture of the beautiful girl inside it. A peasant from Bortsov's
former estate then arrives and tells them the story of his old
master Merik seizes the locket and flings it on the floor with an
oath. Bortsov retrieves it, and lying down on the bench Merik
had quitted for him, mumbles words of endearment as he opens
it and gazes at the portrait of his unfaithful wife. A little later
Bortsov's wife, Mary, appears. The axle of her carriage has broken
as she is being driven past the public house, and while it is being
repaired, a place is made for her on the bench near her husband.
They recognise each other, and Mary utters a scream and rushes
to the middle of the room.

BORTSOV (*following her*). Mary, it's me—me! (*Laughs.*) My wife!
Mary! Where am I? Hey, there, a light!

MARY. Don't come near me! You're lying. It isn't you! It's
impossible! (*Covers her face.*) It's a lie! It can't be!

BORTSOV. Her voice—her movements. Mary, it's me! I'm drunk,
but I shan't be drunk much longer. Oh, my head! I feel
giddy. Good God! Wait, wait—I don't understand. (*Shouts.*)
My wife! (*Kneels at her feet and sobs.*)

MARY. Don't come near me! (*To her driver.*) Denis, let's go! I
can't stay here any longer!

MERIK (*jumps up and looks closely at her face*). The portrait! (*Seizes her by the hand.*) It's her! Look at her, all of you! It's the gentleman's wife!

MARY. Go away, you filthy peasant! (*Tries to free her hand from his grasp.*) Denis, what are you standing there like that for?
(*Denis and the landlord rush up to her and seize Merik by the arms.*)

MARY. This is a thieves' kitchen! Let go of my hand! I'm not afraid of you! Go away!

MERIK. Wait, wait, I'll let you go soon enough. Let me say something to you first. Just one word to make you understand— wait! (*Turning to the landlord and Denis.*) Go away, you yokels! Don't hold me! I shan't let her go until I've told her! Wait a minute! (*Slapping his forehead.*) No, God hasn't given me enough brains to think of the right word!

MARY (*wrenching her hand out of his*). Go away, you filthy drunkards! Come along, Denis. (*Going towards the door.*)

MERIK (*barring her way*). Just look at him once! Just once! Say something to him. A kind word. I entreat you in the name of the Lord!

MARY. Take this lunatic away from me!

MERIK. Then take this, damn you! (*Raises his axe.*)
*General consternation. All jump up noisily, uttering terrified cries. An old pilgrim stands between Merik and Mary. Denis pushes Merik out of the way and carries his mistress out of the public house. After that they all stand as if rooted to the ground. A long pause.*

BORTSOV (*waving his hands about in the air*). Mary! Where are you, Mary?

A WOMAN PILGRIM. Dear Lord, dear Lord. You've frightened me to death, you murderers! What a horrible night!

MERIK (*letting fall his hand with the axe*). Did I kill her or not?

LANDLORD. You ought to be thankful you're still a free man.

Merik staggers back to his bed, and the curtain falls as he lies down on it sobbing, and begging the people in the public house to have pity on him.

# 10

# Ivanov

AGAIN CHEKHOV has been deflected from representing "life as it is" by what he considered the first requirement of drama, namely, a series of highly effective climaxes in which emotion is expressed through action. His own climaxes, unfortunately, tended to become too stridently dramatic. Till now his heroes were extraverts who seemed to delight in screaming about their own insufficiencies. Platonov has seven soliloquies in each of which he turns himself inside out, laughing, crying, rushing about the stage, clapping his hands to his chest, shouting, clasping his head, pausing to ponder, and so on. It is, in fact, a part which would appeal strongly to a ham actor. The parts of Bortsov and Merik are no less clamant and shrill. Chekhov recognised these glaring faults (in his "vaudevilles" the comic situations acted as an effective check on them), and in his next big play he obviously tried his best to correct them. In the first flush of excitement after he had finished *Ivanov*, the play seemed to him so different from any of the plays he had written before that in a letter to his brother Alexander he declared: "This is the first time I have written a play." But very soon he became aware of the fact that he had gone too far in trying not to make it too "dramatically effective", and from 1887 to 1901 he kept revising the play, completely rewriting it in 1889 for its production in Petersburg. Altogether seven revised editions of the play are extant.

The first reference to the future *Ivanov*, which Chekhov himself is said to have often described as "a dramatic miscarriage", occurs in a letter to Maria Kisselev. "I have been twice to Korsh's Theatre," he wrote to her on September 13th, 1887, "and every time Korsh tried to persuade me to write a play for him. I replied:

With pleasure! The actors assure me that I am sure to write a good play because I know how to play on people's nerves. I replied: *Merci*. But of course I shan't write a play. I don't want to have anything to do with the theatre or with the public. To hell with them!" But in his letter to the novelist Nicolai Yozhov on October 5th he already announced the completion of the play. "My play is finished," he wrote. "If you haven't changed your mind and still want to help me, come tomorrow, Tuesday, at about 10 in the morning." The autumn and winter months of 1887–1888 were the most fruitful in the whole of Chekhov's literary career. "During the last season," he wrote to Pleshcheyev on September 15th, 1888, "I wrote *Steppe*, *Lights*, one play, two vaudevilles, a lot of short stories, began a novel, etc." *Ivanov* he finished in ten days. "I wrote the play quite unexpectedly after a conversation with Korsh," he told his brother Alexander in a letter on October 10th, 1887. "I went to bed, thought of a theme and wrote it. I spent a fortnight or rather ten days on it, for there were days during the fortnight when I did nothing or wrote something else. Of the merits of the play I cannot judge. It worked out suspiciously short. Everybody likes it. Korsh did not find a single mistake or fault in it so far as stage technique is concerned, which proves how good and sensitive my judges are. I have written a play for the first time—*ergo*, mistakes are unavoidable. The plot is complicated and not stupid. I end each act like a short story: all the acts run on quietly and peacefully, but at the end I punch the spectator on the nose. My entire energy has been concentrated on a few really strong and striking scenes, while the bridges that span these scenes are insignificant, dull and conventional. But nevertheless I feel pleased, for however bad the play may be, I have, I think, succeeded in creating a type which is of literary significance, and I have created a part which only such a talented actor as Davydov would undertake to play, a part in which an actor has room to move about and show his talent. . . . There are fourteen characters in the play, of whom five are women. I cannot help feeling that, with one exception, my women are not sufficiently realised." On October 21st, he was already able to tell Alexander that his play would be performed at Korsh's theatre either at the end of November or at the beginning of December and that he was getting eight per cent royalties on the gross receipts. He thought that the play would have a long run. "The praises showered upon it," he wrote, "as well as my hopes that it will turn out a good business proposition have raised my spirits a little. If the censorship does not pass it, which is not likely, I shall probably—no, I shall not shoot myself, but I shall be bitterly disappointed." Three days later[1] he again wrote to his brother about *Ivanov*: "Our modern playwrights stuff their plays exclusively with angels, villains and buffoons—go and find these elements in the whole of Russia! . . . I wanted to be original: there is not a single villain or angel in my play (though I could not resist the temptation of putting in a few buffoons). I have not found anyone guilty, nor have I acquitted anyone. Whether I have succeeded or not, I do not know. The play will most certainly be a success—Korsh and the actors are quite sure of that. But I am not so sure. The actors do not understand their parts, talk a lot of nonsense, insist on having parts for which they are in no way suited, but I am fighting them, for I am convinced that the play will be a failure if it is not cast as I want. If they refuse to do as I like, I shall withdraw the play to avoid being made a fool of. Altogether it is a troublesome business and a very unpleasant one, too. If I had known I shouldn't have had anything to do with them."

So far Chekhov was completely satisfied with his play. He had sat up discussing it with Davydov, who was to play the title part, till three o'clock one morning and he found that at least Davydov's conception of Ivanov was "just right". He found more. "If I am to believe such experts as Davydov," he wrote to Yozhov on October 27th, "I know how to write plays. It seems that I have written a perfectly finished piece instinctively, by a kind of sixth sense, without being aware of it myself and without committing one single stage error!" No wonder he was so carried away by

[1]It is important to note Chekhov's tremendous excitement at the thought that at long last a play of his will be performed, for it is the same kind of excitement that Treplyov feels and that plays so vital a part in the opening scenes of *The Seagull*.

his enthusiasm for Davydov's talents that he thought Davydov a very great artist indeed. He changed his opinion after he had seen Davydov play his part, but by that time he had also changed his opinion about the play itself. At the moment he felt sure that his play would be a failure because, with the exception of Davydov and another actor, the cast was poor. He even went so far as to ask Korsh's permission to withdraw the play, but, as he told Leykin in a letter on November 4th, "Korsh threw a fit".

The play was performed at Korsh's theatre on November 19th after only four instead of the promised ten rehearsals, and even those four rehearsals, Chekhov wrote to his brother on November 20th, were really two, the other two being only "tournaments in which the actors vied with one another in arguments and foul language. Only Davydov and Glama knew their parts; the rest relied on the prompter and on inner conviction". Chekhov left an amusing description of the first night of *Ivanov* in Moscow. "Act I," he wrote to his brother in the same letter: "I am behind the scenes in a small box resembling a prison cell. The rest of the family are in a stall box—in a state of trepidation. Contrary to expectation, I am cool and collected and not in the least excited. The actors are excited and tense and are crossing themselves. Curtain. Svetlov,[1] whose benefit night it was, enters. Lack of confidence, ignorance of his part and the bunch of flowers that is presented to him—all contribute to the fact that from the very first words I do not recognise my play. Kisselevsky (Prince Shabelsky), from whom I expected so much, did not utter a single sentence correctly. Literally not one. He just invented his own dialogue as he went along. In spite of this and the blunders of the producer, the first act was very successful. Many calls.

"Act II. A crowd of people on the stage. The guests. They don't know their parts, get all mixed up, talk nonsense. Each word they utter cuts me like a knife, but—O Muse!—this act, too, is successful. Everybody has to take a call. I am congratulated on the success of the play.

"Act III. They are not playing so badly. Terrific success. I have

[1] Svetlov played Borkin.

to take three calls, and while bowing to the audience Davydov keeps shaking my hand, while Glama, a la Manilov,[1] keeps pressing my other hand to her heart. Triumph of talent and virtue.

"Act IV, Sc. 1. Not bad. More calls. After which a very long and wearisome interval. The audience, who are not used to leaving their seats and going to the bar in the middle of an act, are protesting. The curtain goes up. Beautiful; through an arch the dining table can be seen (wedding). The orchestra plays a few flourishes. The best man comes out; he is drunk and therefore, you see, he has to clown and play the fool. Then Kisselevsky's entrance; a deeply moving poetic passage, but my Kisselevsky does not know his part, he is drunk as a cobbler, and the short poetic dialogue becomes boring and horrible. The audience does not know what to make of it. At the end of the play the hero dies because he cannot stand the insult he has suffered. The audience which is tired and has lost interest in the play does not understand this death (which the actors insisted on—I have another version). The actors and I are called out. During one of the calls booing can be heard, drowned by applause and the stamping of feet."

On the whole, the first night left Chekhov with a feeling of fatigue and disappointment. What pleased him, however, was that the play had provoked "a ferment in the theatre". No other play, it seems, had ever been known to arouse so many discussions. Chekhov was careful to point out to his brother on November 24th that the mere reading of the play would not explain the excitement in the theatre. "You will not find anything special in it," he wrote. But on the stage, as his painter brother Nicholas and his friends Franz Schechtel, the well-known Moscow architect, and Isaac Levitan, the famous landscape painter, assured him, "it was so original that they felt strange when they watched it. In reading, however, this is not noticeable."

The notices in the Moscow press were on the whole favourable, but certain papers, mostly the extreme conservative ones, damned it as "an essentially immoral" and "a highly cynical libel on contemporary life and men." In his letter to Davydov of

[1] A character in Gogol's *Dead Souls*.

December 1st, 1887, Chekhov himself summarised the opinion of his critics as follows: ("1) The play is written carelessly. From the point of view of technique it should be consigned to fiery gehenna. The dialogue is irreproachable. (2) There are no objections to the title.[1] (3) The idea that there is an immoral and highly cynical element in the play advanced by some critics provokes laughter and bewilderment. (4) The characters are delineated with sufficient sharpness of outline, the people are alive, and the life represented in the play has not been invented. I have heard no criticism or bewilderment expressed on that account, though I am being daily subjected to a most gruelling cross-examination. (5) Ivanov has been adequately drawn. Suvorin, however, is of a different opinion. He writes: 'I understand Ivanov very well, because I can't help feeling that I am myself an Ivanov, but the public, which every author has to keep in mind, will not understand him; it would not be amiss to give him a soliloquy'. (6) The majority find the scene between Ivanov and Sasha before their wedding in Act IV most illuminating from the point of view of the characterisation of Ivanov, and Suvorin himself is delighted with it.[2] (7) A certain tightness is felt in the play as a consequence of the large number of characters: this multiplicity

---

[1] Chekhov chose the quite ordinary Russian name of Ivanov to emphasise the fact that he meant his hero to be interpreted as a character who was typical of Russian life of that period.

[2] A curiously perverse judgment this, which can only be explained by Chekhov's excitement over the production of his play. In less than one year Chekhov himself was to alter this particular scene radically. In the first version of the play, Act IV is divided into two long scenes. The talk between Ivanov and Sasha takes place at the end of Sc. 1, and ends with Ivanov's sudden recantation and acceptance of his marriage to Sasha as a happy solution of all his troubles.

IVANOV (*kissing her*). I'm sorry if I've been such a nuisance to you. We shall get married today and tomorrow—to work! (*Laughs.*) My darling philosopher! I've been trying to impress you with my age, but when it comes to using your brains you're ten years older than I. (*Stops laughing.*) Seriously, darling, we're just like everybody else and we're going to be happy like the rest. And if we are to blame, then again we're not worse than the rest.

SASHA. Go, please, go. You're late.

IVANOV. I'm going, I'm going. (*Laughs.*) What a silly fool I am! What a child! What a rag of a man! (*Goes to the door and bumps into Lebedev.*)

LEBEDEV. Come here, come here. (*Takes Ivanov by the hand and leads him to the footlights.*) Look me straight in the eyes. Go on. (*Gazes at him intently a lomg time.*) Well, that's right, my boy, that's right. (*Embraces him.*) I hope you'll be happy, and forgive me my boy, for thinking badly of you. (*To Sasha.*) Look at him, darling, what a fine fellow! A real he-man—a lieutenant of the Guards. Come here, come here, you silly girl. (*Severely.*) Come here, I say.

(SASHA *goes to him.*)

of characters tends rather to blur the characterisation of Sarah
and Sasha, who have not been given enough elbow-room
and are therefore a little pale in places. And (8) the end of the play
does not transgress against truth, but is nevertheless 'a stage lie'.
It can satisfy the spectator only on one condition: given an
exceptionally good actor."

Act IV, Sc. 2 of the first version of the play, which takes place
shortly after the wedding ceremony, ends as follows:

Count Shabelsky asks Lebedev for some money in order "to
pay a visit to his wife's grave in Paris". At first Lebedev refuses,
but then he remembers the ten thousand he promised Ivanov and
decides that three or four thousand ought to be given to Shabelsky.
"You'll be able to have a good time in Paris for a whole year,"
he tells the Count generously, "and then you'll come back and—
who knows—you may find a grandson." At that moment Ivanov
comes in and asks his uncle "to cheer up and smile like me." He
goes on: "I'm happy and contented as I haven't been for a long
time. Everything is as it should be—normal—perfect. I've drunk
a glass of champagne (*laughs*) and now I feel as though the whole
world were whirling round for joy at my happiness." He notices
tears in his uncle's eyes, and learning that the old reprobate had
been thinking of poor Sarah, he pays his first wife the compliment
of calling her "a rare, splendid woman. Before she died," he
continues, "she forgave me everything and now I am sure she is
looking at us with her bright eyes and forgives us. She is resting
in peace in her grave now; we are alive, there is the band playing
in the next room, but the time will come when we, too, shall be
dead and people will say of me—he's resting in his grave. I like
this order in nature, though I must say I dislike nature herself.
(*Laughs.*) Everything seems so nice today. You, Paul," he turns to
his father-in-law, "are an honest fellow. I'm afraid I mustn't

---

LEBEDEV (*takes Ivanov and Sasha by the hands, looking round*). Listen to me. Don't worry
about your mother. If she doesn't want to give you the money, don't let her. You,
Sasha, are saying that you (*mimicking her*) don't want any money. Principles,
altruism. Schopenhauer. That's all stuff and nonsense. Now, listen to me. (*Sighs.*)
I've got ten thousand put away in the bank. (*Looking round.*) Not a soul in the house
knows it. They're your grandmother's. (*Letting go of their hands.*) Take it!
IVANOV. Goodbye! (*Laughs gaily and goes out*).

drink any more, but that's no reason why you, gentlemen, should not go and have a drink."

LEBEDEV. What about a drop of brandy, Count?

SHABELSKY. I don't mind if I do.

IVANOV. I can't drink myself, but I like to watch others drink. (*Rubbing his forehead.*) I'm very happy, to be sure, but I've been through such a terrible time and I feel as if I might be going to faint. My whole body seems to ache. (*Laughs.*) Come along . . .

Borkin comes in and puts another of his absurd propositions to Ivanov, but Ivanov merely laughs, tells him that he is a clever, capable young man and that he is sorry for their past misunderstandings. "We are all weak men," he says, "we are all to blame, and we are all in God's hands. Only men without charity or passions are wicked and strong." Lebedev tells him to stop talking like a German parson. "If we're going to drink, then let's start and not waste precious time."

The young widow Babakina comes in, is cold-shouldered by the old Count, and Ivanov, accompanied by his uncle and his father-in-law, disappears into the dining-room. There follows a long scene between Borkin and Babakina, at the end of which the two get engaged. After they have gone, Lvov comes in and delivers himself in a slightly abridged form of the soliloquy with which Chekhov opens the fourth act in the final version of the play. At the end of it, he turns to the open door of the dining-room and calls Ivanov a cad "in the hearing of everybody", an offence that, according to the conventions of the time, was equivalent to a challenge to a duel. Lvov's insulting words provoke "a commotion in the dining-room", and "Ivanov runs in, clasping his head; the rest come in after him."

IVANOV. Why? Why? Tell me why? (*Collapses on a sofa.*)

ALL. Why?

LEBEDEV. (*to Lvov*). For God's sake explain why you've insulted him? (*Clutches his head and paces the stage in great agitation.*)

SHABELSKY. (*to Ivanov*). For God's sake, Nicholas, don't pay any attention to him!

BORKIN. This, sir, is abominable. I challenge you to a duel!

LVOV. And I, sir, consider it beneath my dignity to talk to you, let alone fight with you. But I shall be pleased to offer satisfaction to Mr. Ivanov any time he likes.

SASHA (*comes in, swaying, from the dining-room*). Why? Why did you insult my husband? Ladies and gentlemen, I demand that he should tell me why!

LVOV. Madam, I didn't insult him without good reason. I came here as an honest man to open your eyes, and I ask you to listen to me carefully. I'll tell you everything.

SASHA. What can you tell me? What secrets do you know? That he was responsible for the death of his first wife? Everybody seems to know that. That he married me because of my money and because he does not want to repay his debt to my mother? That, too, the whole district knows. Oh, you paltry, cruel, worthless men! (*To her husband.*) Nicholas, let's go away from here. (*Takes his hand.*)

LEBEDEV (*to Lvov*). As the host here and the father of my son-in-law, I mean my daughter, sir——

(*Sasha utters a scream and falls on her husband.*)

(*All run up to Ivanov.*)

LEBEDEV. Good God, he's dead! Water! A doctor!

(*Sasha weeps.*)

ALL. Water! A doctor! He's dead!

Curtain.

II

*Ivanov*

CHEKHOV WAS certainly right in thinking that the end of *Ivanov* as performed in Moscow was "a stage lie". And he was a little too sanguine in stating that only an exceptionally good actor could make it credible to an audience. It may be doubted if even a genius would be able to hold the attention of an audience lying on a sofa in his death throes, while the other characters go on talking, and then expiring the moment his wife takes hold of his hand. In his anxiety to avoid any "dramatically effective" ending, Chekhov had rung down the curtain on a situation that was not only melodramatic but also absurd. What was his aim in writing *Ivanov*? As he later confessed, he had cherished the hope of summarising everything that had been written about the people who, faced with the political reaction in Russia in the eighties, had lost heart and had nothing to live for. By his play Chekhov wanted to put an end to all those writings. "It seemed to me," he declared, "that the Russian novelists and dramatists felt driven to depict this sort of dejected individual and that they all wrote instinctively without having any well-defined character in mind and without any definite views on the matter." But did *Ivanov* make the position of this type of person any clearer? "Not one man in the audience," he wrote to his brother Michael from Petersburg at the beginning of December 1877, "understood *Ivanov*." The whole play had now become "repugnant" to him. In a letter to Pleshcheyev on January 23rd, 1888, he referred to it as "my abortion *Ivanov*." But the fact remained that the play was a success and his friends in Petersburg seemed very excited about it and urged him to give it a trial on the Imperial stage. He had an offer from the producer of the Alexandrinsky Theatre who wanted the play for his benefit night. Chekhov therefore decided to re-write it. "I can't help thinking," he wrote to Suvorin in October 1888, "that if I write another fourth act, cut something out, and put in one soliloquy, which I've already got in my head, the play will be very effective. I shall have corrected it by Christmas and then I will send it to the Alexandrinsky Theatre." On December 18th he wrote to Suvorin that he had finished the new version of *Ivanov* and that it was being copied. The changes Chekhov introduced into the play were more radical than he had first intended to make them. In the first act the changes were comparatively few, merely some small alterations in the dialogue. The second act underwent a much more drastic revision. Whole scenes were entirely re-written, the dialogue was cut in some places and expanded in others, and the stage directions, too, were revised. In the third act Chekhov inserted Ivanov's long soliloquy; in the scene between Ivanov and Lvov he added at the end this motivation of Lvov's action (excised in the final version):

LVOV. . . . I used to like and respect people, but when I saw
    you——
IVANOV. I have heard that before.
LVOV. You have? Well, if that's so then you may as well know
    that I love your wife. I love her as much as I hate you. That's
    why I think I have a right to talk to you like that. When I
    first saw her sufferings, I couldn't stand it and—(*seeing Sasha
    who has entered in her riding habit*) now I hope we understand
    each other perfectly! (*Shrugs and goes out.*)

The scene between Sasha and Ivanov was also considerably enlarged.

But it was in the fourth act that Chekhov made his most drastic changes. The Moscow spectators and critics of *Ivanov* not only missed the whole point of the play, that is, Chekhov's wish to expose and put an end to the type of "whining hero" of the popular Russian novel and play, the man who had "no iron in his blood", but they had also imposed their own interpretation on it which was wholly at variance with Chekhov's intentions. To them Ivanov's heart failure at the end of the play was due to the slanders spread against him, culminating in the statement that he had got rid of his wife in order to marry a rich heiress, and in Lvov's public insult. To remove these misconceptions Chekhov recast the whole of the last act of the play. In a letter to Suvorin on December 19th, 1887, Chekhov wrote: "I have finished my 'Bolvanov' and am sending it to you together with this letter. . . . Now, I hope, Mr. Ivanov is much more intelligible. The finale does not satisfy me (except for the shot everything is dull and lifeless), but I comfort myself with the thought that its form is not yet final. I give you my word that I shall never write such rotten intellectual plays as *Ivanov* again."

Chekhov, of course, was right: the shot which kills Ivanov was the only improvement he had introduced in the second version of the play. And, unlike his later versions of this scene, the shot, which comes as an afterthought, is typical of Ivanov, the vacillating, helpless "rag of a man", the man without iron in his blood. But what worried his critics and, above all, Suvorin was that he had cut out Sasha at the end of Act IV. Chekhov at first insisted that that was as it should be. "Let the whole audience observe," he wrote to Suvorin on December 23rd, "that Sasha is not there. You insist that she should make an appearance. You say the laws of the stage demand it.   Very well, let her come, but what is she going to say? Such young ladies (she is not a girl, but a *young lady*) don't know how to talk and should not talk. The former Sasha could talk and was sympathetic, but the new one will only annoy the audience by her appearance. She could not very well fall on Ivanov's neck and say, I love you! for she does not love him and has confessed as much. To bring her on at the end one would have to alter her completely at the beginning. You say there is not a single woman in my play and that is what makes the ending so dull. I agree. Only two women could have appeared and taken Ivanov's part at the end: the Jewess and his mother. But as both of them are dead, there can be no question of that. An orphan had better stay an orphan and to hell with him."

On December 26th, however, Chekhov seemed willing to give in to Suvorin's arguments and bring in Sasha in the last scenes of the play. "If the play is to be put on," he wrote, "then I shall be glad to do as you say, but I shall give her hell, the slut!"

Four days later Chekhov again reverted to the character of Ivanov, which, it seems, had puzzled not only the Petersburg producer, but Suvorin himself. In his letter to Suvorin of December 30th, 1888, he gives a most circumstantial analysis of four of the leading characters of the play: Ivanov, Lvov, Sarah and Sasha. "Ivanov," he writes, "is a nobleman, a university man, and is not remarkable in any way; he is easily aroused, he is hot-tempered, prone to be carried away by some idea, honest and straightforward, like the majority of educated people of his class.

He used to live on his estate and was a member of the local agricultural board. What he did and how he behaved, what interested him and what aroused his enthusiasm can be seen from the following words which he addresses to the doctor (Act I, Sc. 5): 'Don't marry Jewesses, or neurotic females or bluestockings, don't wage war alone against thousands, don't tilt against windmills, don't make a habit of knocking your head against a brick wall. May the Lord preserve you from rationalised farming methods, modern schools, fervent speeches . . .' That's what his past life was like. Sarah, who had seen his rationalised farming methods and his other occupations, says to the doctor of him: 'He is a remarkable man, doctor, and I regret you did not know him two or three years ago. At present he is depressed and silent, he doesn't do anything, but before—oh, he was wonderful!' (Act I, Sc. 7). His past was wonderful, and this is true of the past of the majority of educated Russians. There is not, or at least there scarcely is a landed Russian gentleman or university man who at one time or another has not boasted about his past. His present is always worse than his past. Why? Because Russian enthusiasm possesses one specific quality: it is quickly followed by fatigue. A man who has only just left school assumes in his unbounded enthusiasm a burden he has not the strength to carry. He throws himself at once into the building of village schools, he tries to solve the peasant problem, he introduces rationalised farming, he subscribes to a liberal periodical, he makes speeches, he writes to the Ministry, he fights against evil, he applauds the good, he does not just fall in love with any woman, but always with bluestockings, neurotic females or even prostitutes whom he saves, and so on and so forth. But no sooner does he reach the age of thirty or thirty-five than he begins to feel tired and bored. He has barely had time to grow a decent moustache, but he already is saying authoritatively: 'Don't marry, old man. Listen to the voice of experience!' Or: 'What after all is liberalism? Between you and me, Katkov[1] is often right!' He is already willing to deny the usefulness of the agricultural boards, rationalised farming, science and love. My

[1] A well-known conservative editor and publisher.

Ivanov says to the doctor (Act I, Sc. 5): 'My dear fellow, you only finished your medical course last year. You're young and full of high spirits. But I'm thirty-five and I have a right to give you some advice.' This is the sort of tone these prematurely tired people use. Then, with an authoritative sigh, he tells you: 'Don't marry such or such a girl (see the quotation above), but choose something ordinary, something drab, something without bright colours, something nice and quiet. Generally speaking, try to live a conventional life. The drabber and more monotonous your background is, the better. My own life has been so wearisome— oh, so wearisome!'

"Overcome by physical fatigue and boredom," Chekhov continues his characterisation of Ivanov, "he does not understand either what is happening to him now or what was happening to him in the past. Horrified, he says to the doctor (Act I, Sc. 3): 'You're telling me that she will soon be dead and I feel neither love nor pity but a kind of emptiness, a kind of fatigue. To an outsider this would seem horrible, but I do not understand myself what is happening to me.' Finding themselves in such a position, people who are neither farsighted nor particularly honest with themselves usually put all the blame on their environment or enrol themselves among the misfits and the Hamlets and are content with that. Ivanov, however, is a straightforward man and he tells the doctor and the audience quite frankly that he does not understand himself: 'I don't understand . . . I don't understand. . . .' That he sincerely does not understand himself can be gathered from his big soliloquy in Act III, in which, speaking confidentially to the audience and laying his heart bare before it, he even bursts into tears!

"The change that has taken place in him insults his sense of decency. He looks outside for its causes and cannot find them; he then begins to look for them inside him, but all he finds there is a vague feeling of guilt. This is a Russian feeling. A Russian, if anyone in his family falls ill or dies, or whether he borrows or lends money, always feels guilty. Ivanov talks all the time of some sort of guilt of his, and this feeling of guilt grows with every jolt he gets. In Act I he says: 'I suppose I must be terribly guilty, but my thoughts are confused, my spirit seems to be paralysed by a kind of laziness, and I am not able to understand myself.' In Act II he tells Sasha: 'My conscience is tormenting me day and night, I feel that I'm deeply guilty, but I don't know what it is I am guilty of.'

"To his feeling of fatigue, boredom and guilt you have to add one more enemy. This is loneliness. If Ivanov had been a civil servant, an actor, a priest or a professor, he would have got used to his position. But he lives on his estate. He lives in the country. The people he comes across are either drunkards or gamblers or like the doctor. None of them cares for his feelings or for the change that has taken place in him. He is lonely. The long winters, the long evenings, the empty garden, the empty room, the grumbling Count, the sick wife . . . He has nowhere to go. That is why he is always worried by the question: what am I to do with myself?

"Now his fifth enemy. Ivanov is tired, and does not understand himself, but life is not concerned with it. It makes its lawful demands on him, and, willy-nilly, he has to solve his problems. A sick wife—one problem; a heap of debts—another problem; Sasha is throwing herself at him—a third problem. How he proposes to solve these problems must become clear from his soliloquy in Act III and from the contents of the last two acts. Such people as Ivanov do not solve problems: they are crushed under their weight. They are at a loss, they give up, they grow nervous, they complain, they do all sorts of stupid things, and finally, giving in to their flabby, unstrung nerves, they lose their footing and enrol themselves in the category of 'shattered' and 'misunderstood' people.

"Disappointment, apathy, nervous debility and a predisposition to fatigue are the inevitable consequences of over-excitability and such excitability is extremely characteristic of our youth. . . . This feeling of fatigue (Dr. Bertenson will confirm it) finds expression not only in whining or in the sensation of boredom. The life of a tired man cannot be expressed thus: ∿∿∿∿∿. It is very uneven. Tired men do not lose their ability to get highly excited, but their excitement does not last very long, and every period of excitement is followed by a period of even greater depression. Graphically it can be represented thus:

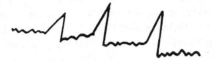

The downstroke of the graph, as you see, does not always follow the same inclined plane, but is different every time. Sasha tells Ivanov that she loves him. Ivanov shouts enthusiastically: 'A new life!' but next morning he no more believes in this new life than in a house-spirit (the soliloquy of Act III); his wife insults him, he is beside himself, he flies into a passion and retorts with a cruel insult. He is called a cad. As this is not enough to destroy his flabby brain, he gets excited and pronounces his own death sentence.

"Not to tire you out," Chekhov goes on, "I shall now take Dr. Lvov. He belongs to the type of the honest, straightforward, excitable, but also narrow-minded and plain-spoken man. About such men intelligent people say, 'He is a fool but he is not without a sense of honesty.' Anything resembling breadth of view or spontaneous feeling is alien to Lvov. He is a personified convention, a walking tendency. He looks at every phenomenon and every person through a narrow frame. He judges everything in a prejudiced way. If a man shouts, 'Make way for honest labour!' he worships him. And anyone who does not join in the shouting is a money-grubber and a scoundrel. He does not know any compromise. . . . In the theatre he saw the 'new men' on the stage, i.e. the moneygrubbers and the 'modern' man depicted by the new dramatists, 'men who make money'. He has got this so firmly into his head that when he reads *Rudin*, he invariably asks himself, 'Is Rudin a scoundrel or not?' He has been taught by literature and the stage to put the same question to every person he meets or reads about. . . . This question is important to him.

The fact that all men have faults does not satisfy him. Give him saints or scoundrels!

"He arrived in the country district already full of these preconceived notions. In every well-to-do peasant he at once saw a moneygrubber, and in Ivanov, whom he could not understand, a scoundrel. The man's wife is ill and he goes visiting a rich girl in the neighbourhood—isn't he a cad? He is obviously trying to kill his wife in order to marry a rich heiress.

"Lvov is honest and straightforward. He speaks his mind without prevarication and without sparing anyone's feelings. If necessary, he'll throw a bomb under a carriage, or punch a headmaster on the nose, or call someone a cad. Nothing will stop him. He never feels any qualms of conscience. Does not the fact that he is an honest and hardworking man entitle him to expose the 'dark forces' of society?

"Such people are necessary and in the majority of cases they are sympathetic men. To caricature them even in the interests of the stage is dishonest and serves no useful purpose. It is true a caricature is much sharper and hence more easily comprehended, but I'd much rather leave a portrait unfinished than spoil it.

"Now about the women. Why do they love Ivanov? Sarah loves Ivanov because he is a good man, because he is enthusiastic, brilliant and talks with the same fervour as Lvov (Act 1, Sc. 7). She loves him so long as he is enthusiastic and interesting, but when his face begins to become blurred in her eyes and his features lose their sharp outlines, she no longer understands him, and at the end of Act III she tells him so, frankly and bluntly.

"Sasha is a modern young lady. She is educated, intelligent, honest, etc. Among the blind the one-eyed is king, and that is why she shows a preference for the thirty-five-year-old Ivanov. He is better than the rest. She knew him when she was a little girl and watched his activities before he had become worn out. He is a friend of her father's.

"She is the type of female whom the males do not conquer by the brightness of their feathers, their fawning or their bravery, but by their complaints, their whining, their failures. She is a woman who loves a man at the moment of his downfall. The moment Ivanov loses heart, the girl is at his side. That was what she was waiting for. Dear me, has she not to fulfil such a grateful, such a sacred task? She will give new life to the fallen, she will put him on his feet again, she will make him happy. . . . She is not in love with Ivanov, but with that task of hers. Daudet's Argenton said: 'Life is not a love-story!' But Sasha does not know it. She does not realise that to Ivanov love merely means an unnecessary complication, another blow across his back. And what happens? For a whole year Sasha does her best to make a new man of Ivanov, but she fails to do so and he falls lower and lower."

That was what Chekhov wanted to express in his play. But did he? By that time it must have dawned on him that something had gone wrong. Otherwise his critics and the audience would not have misunderstood him so completely. There was, besides, a further complication. The famous actress Maria Savina wanted to play Sasha in the Petersburg production of *Ivanov*. "Savina," he wrote to the producer of the Alexandrinsky Theatre on January 8th, 1889, "has agreed to play Sasha, and yet Sasha's part is very weak and represents very poor stage material. When I wrote it about a year and a half ago I did not consider it important. But now, in view of the compliment Savina has paid to my play, I have decided to reshape this part radically." It was while revising the play for the third time that he realised how bad his second version of its last act was. The ending of the first version was preposterous, but the ending of the second version was even worse. To give Ivanov a long speech during which the other characters have nothing to do but listen to him and then make him shoot himself is a very clumsy piece of stage "architecture", of which Chekhov could not help but be aware. "Before," he wrote to Pleshcheyev on January 15th, 1889, "I did not think my play was of any particular importance and I looked upon it with condescending irony: there it was and to hell with it, as it were. But now that it is going to be performed at the Imperial theatre, I have realised how badly it has been made. The last act is amazingly bad. I have spent a whole week working on the play, writing different versions, making corrections and insertions; I have made a different Sasha, altered the fourth act beyond recognition, polished up Ivanov himself, and now I am so exhausted and sick of the sight of my play that I am ready to finish it with Kean's words: Give Ivanov a good thrashing—give him a thrashing!"[1]

Chekhov, besides, re-wrote the big scene between Ivanov and Sasha (Act III, Sc. 7), inserting passages which were meant especially for Savina and which he cut out in the subsequent editions of the play. For instance, after Ivanov's words: "Thanks to you the only people to be born into the world will be grumblers and lunatics," there followed this passage:

IVANOV. . . . Oh, what a funny child you are! What are you laughing at? You're much too young to set yourself up as my teacher or try to save me.

SASHA. Really, what a tone! I'm not really, am I?

IVANOV. Of course you are, you funny girl.

SASHA. Must you use this ironic tone?

IVANOV (*mimicking her voice*). I must.

SASHA. Very well, then. I know the sort of punishment you deserve. Move along, please! (*Pushes him from behind, then drags him along with all her strength by the hand.*) Come on, move along! Oh dear, what a clumsy man you are! Move along, Oblomov!

IVANOV. Not an inch! I am not the sort of man you can budge so easily, my dear child. Try harder if you like! Why don't you call your mother to help you? No, madam, I've plenty of strength left in me yet. Nothing can budge me from my place if I don't want to.

SASHA. Whew, I've no breath left—damn you!

IVANOV. And you are trying to save me! Oh, you blackeyed little idiot!

Again towards the end of the scene after Ivanov's words, "I always liked to discuss things, but never in my life did I say, 'our women are corrupt', or 'this woman has taken the wrong turning'. I was grateful and nothing more." there followed this little gay

[1] From the play by Alexandre Dumas fils.

interlude to give Savina a chance of displaying her acting abilities.

("Savina," Chekhov wrote to Suvorin on December 31st, 1888, "will be spinning round like a top, jumping on a sofa and reciting monologues. To make sure that the audience is not tired of Ivanov's constant moaning, I have depicted him in one act as merry and bright and Sasha, too, is merry and bright. This isn't unnecessary, is it? I think I've got it right. But how hard it is to be careful. I tremble at every word I write for fear of distorting Ivanov's character.")

IVANOV. . . . Oh, if only I could get over this horrible depression of mine! I'd be a real man then! Mind the train! (*Runs after Sasha.*) Puff-puff-puff——

SASHA (*jumps on a sofa*). Go away, go away, go away!

IVANOV. O frailty, thy name is woman! (*Roars with laughter.*) My sweet, what fun you are! And what a ridiculous fool I am! You know, there's a grey, gloomy and pathetic bird on the Dnieper, which lives in the rushes and moos despondently like a cow that's been shut up in a shed. I'm just like that. I sit hidden in my rushes for days on end, moaning and groaning and upsetting everybody. (*Moves away quickly.*) You'd better go, Sasha. We're behaving stupidly.

This passage, too, Chekhov later excised from the play.

It was the fourth act, however, that Chekhov revised most thoroughly. In the third version Sasha neither marries Ivanov nor gives him up. Chekhov had realised that the insult Lvov hurls at Ivanov was not a sufficient reason for Ivanov's suicide. He therefore shifted the dramatic centre of gravity to Ivanov's reluctance to go through with the wedding and, as a result, entirely re-shaped Sasha's part. Sasha now becomes a very forceful young woman who is determined to save Ivanov in spite of himself. It is because of the clash of two strong-willed characters that the final tragedy occurs.

The opening of the scene between Ivanov and Sasha (Act IV, Sc. 8) already shows the entirely different conception of the two characters:

## Second Version

IVANOV. My darling——

SASHA. You look upset. What's the matter?

IVANOV. Oh, my darling, listen to me. Forget that you love me, pay careful attention to what I'm going to say——

SASHA. Nicholas, don't frighten me! What's the matter?

IVANOV. I've just been dressing for our wedding. I looked at myself in the glass and I saw that my hair was going grey at the temples. Darling, we mustn't go on with it—while it isn't too late—we mustn't—we mustn't! (*Clasps his head.*) You're young, beautiful, pure. You have your life in front of you. And I—grey hair at my temples, a nervous wreck, a feeling of guilt, my past —I'm not a match for you!

SASHA (*severely*). Nicholas, what's the meaning of this? They've been waiting for you at the church for hours and you come here to moan. All this isn't new. I've heard it before and I'm sick and tired of it.

IVANOV (*takes her by the hand*). I love you too much, you're too dear to me, and I don't want to be a hindrance to

## Third Version

SASHA (*sternly*). What do you want?

IVANOV. I'm in a blind rage and I can't speak calmly. I've just been dressing for our wedding. I looked at myself in the glass and saw that my hair was going grey at the temples. Sasha, we mustn't go on with it! While it isn't too late we must put an end to this senseless comedy. You're young and pure, your life is in front of you, while I——

SASHA. All this isn't new. I've heard it a thousand times before and I'm sick and tired of it. Co to the church and don't keep people waiting for you.

IVANOV. I'm going home. Will you please tell your people that there isn't going to be a wedding. Explain it to them any way you like. It's time we acted sensibly. I've been playing Hamlet and you a highminded young lady long enough.

SASHA (*flaring up*). I resent your tone! I'm not listening to you.

IVANOV. And I'll go on talking as much as I like.

SASHA. What did you come here for? Your whining

| *Second Version* | *Third Version* |
|---|---|
| you. I shan't make you happy. I'm certain I shan't. Give me up before it's too late. That's the only honest and intelligent thing to do. I'm going home now. Will you please tell your people that there isn't going to be a wedding. Explain it to them any way you like. (*Paces the room agitatedly.*) Oh dear, oh dear, I can't help feeling that you don't understand me, darling. | has turned into mockery. IVANOV. No, I'm not whining any more. A mockery? Yes. I am mocking. And if it were possible to mock at oneself a thousand times more and make the whole world laugh with derision, I should have done it. I looked at myself in the glass and I felt as though a shell had burst in my conscience. I laughed at myself and I nearly went mad from shame. (*Laughs.*) |

At the end of this scene Chekhov still kept the incident with the gun, which in his subsequent revisions of the play he excised. In the final version Ivanov's last words before the entrance of Lebedev are: "I should have done what I meant to do," the phrase containing a hidden hint that he intended to kill himself. The same passage in the second and third versions is as follows:

| *Second Version* | *Third Version* |
|---|---|
| IVANOV. . . . If you hadn't agreed (to give me up), I should have—(*Takes a revolver out of his pocket.*) I brought it with me on purpose. (*Puts the revolver away.*) I should have killed myself rather than ruin your life. | IVANOV. . . . I should have done what I meant to do, and what I meant to do was—(*Shows a revolver and hides it again.*) I'd a hundred times rather kill myself than ruin your life. But I thought that you would listen to the voice of reason and—— |
| | SASHA. Give me the gun! |
| | IVANOV. I shan't give it you. |
| | SASHA. Give it me, I say! |

*Second Version*                          *Third Version*

IVANOV. I love you too much, Sasha, and I'm too angry with you to waste my time on silly talk. I ask you to give me up! I demand it in the name of justice and humanity!

The beginning of the last scene of the play corresponds to the final version of the play. But after Borkin's entrance and speech ending in the words: "You're a comical fellow!" Chekhov inserted these lines:

SASHA. Never mind, we shall be going together. (*Takes Ivanov's arm.*) Come along!

IVANOV. An energetic young woman! (*Laughs.*) You'd better send for a policeman.

Chekhov also changed Ivanov's reaction to Lvov's absurd outburst at the end of Act IV. Instead of Ivanov's melodramatic: "Why? Why? Tell me why?" followed by his collapse on the sofa of the first version and by his clasping his head in the second, we get the much more sensible line:

IVANOV (*coldly*). Thank you very much.

Again Sasha's reply to the doctor's insult is no longer hysterical: she passes the most damning verdict on Lvov's pose as an honest and "progressive" man. Her speech, in fact, led Chekhov to give Ivanov another fine dramatic line:

IVANOV (*laughing*). This isn't a wedding, but a parliament! Bravo! Bravo!

The last scene of the third version differs considerably from the final version.

*Third Version*                          *Final Version*

IVANOV. Where do you want me to go? Wait, I've something to say to them.

IVANOV. Where do you want me to go? Wait, I'll finish it all now. My youth has

### Third Version

SASHA. No, no, let's go.

IVANOV. Don't interfere with me! Listen, all of you! I shan't waste my time explaining to you whether I'm honest or not, clever or not, insane or not. It's impossible to convince everybody. But one thing I should like to ask you. If you should ever happen to meet a young man who is intelligent, enthusiastic and sincere, and see that he loves, hates and believes differently from anybody else, that he works and hopes for ten men, that he tilts against windmills, runs his head against a brick wall—if you should see that he has assumed so heavy a burden that his back is in danger of breaking—then say to him: "Do not be in a hurry to spend all your strength while you are young, but save it up for what is left of your life—get intoxicated with love and hate, suffer, be excited, but keep your head, for otherwise fate will punish you cruelly! At thirty you will already begin to suffer from a hangover and you will be an old man. You will

### Final Version

awakened in me. The old Ivanov has spoken. (*Takes out a revolver.*)

*Third Version*                    *Final Version*

wander about like a shadow, aimlessly, without faith and without love, and you won't know who you are or why you go on living. And love will seem nonsense to you, and caresses too cloying, and work will lose its meaning for you, and you will dismiss songs and fervent speeches as oldfashioned and vulgar. And wherever you go, you will carry your depression, your boredom and your hatred of life with you— and there will be no salvation for you—you will have perished beyond redemption." You can say that you've seen a man who at thirty-five was already worn out, disappointed, crushed by his little achievements and that you yourselves saw him overcome with shame and his pride wounded, and how he was misunderstood, disliked, and insulted, and how stupid his end was. How he was stifled with rage! But enough! I've said enough to you. I'm glad to have got it off my chest! My youth has

| *Third Version* | *Final Version* |
|---|---|
| awakened in me, the old Ivanov has spoken. Oh, I know how to end it all! | |
| SASHA (*utters a scream*). I know what he wants to do! Stop him! | SASHA (*utters a scream*). I know what he wants to do! Nicholas, for heaven's sake! |
| IVANOV. Who can stop me now? I've been going downhill long enough. Now the time has come for me to stop. High time I did! Get out of my way— all of you! Thank you, Sasha! Goodbye, Paul! | IVANOV. I've been going down-hill long enough. Now the time has come for me to stop. High time I did. Get out of my way! Thank you, Sasha! |
| SASHA (*shouts*). Nicholas, for heaven's sake! Stop him! | SASHA (*shouts*). Nicholas, for heaven's sake! Stop him! |
| IVANOV. Let me be! (*Runs to the other end of the stage and shoots himself.*) | IVANOV. Let me be! (*Runs to the other end of the stage and shoots himself.*) |
| *Sasha faints. General confusion.* | |
| Curtain | Curtain |

Ivanov's long monologue in the last scene of the third version Chekhov transferred in an abbreviated and slightly amended form to Act IV, Sc.10, the scene between Lebedev and Ivanov, in which Lebedev has only one line: "I don't understand anything."

Chekhov wrote *Ivanov* as an exposure of a literary character afflicted by an inner "emptiness" that reflected the general mood of disillusionment of the educated classes in Russia after the high hopes aroused by the liberal reforms initiated by Alexander II, and culminating in the liberation of the serfs in 1861. The play as a whole shows a great advance on *Platonov*. It is compact, its characters come to life the moment they enter the stage, and their indulgence in self-exhibitionism is not driven to the same extreme as in his earlier plays. It is still essentially a play of direct action:

everything of any dramatic importance happens before the eyes of the audience. Ivanov's suicide on the stage is indeed the weakest point of the entire play: dramatically it is a mistake because it presents the actor with a task that is impossible to carry out convincingly. The same can be said about the other curtains of the play. As a dramatist Chekhov was fully conscious of the importance of the curtains for bridging the inevitable gaps that arise in the spectator's mind as a result of the intervals between the acts. A curtain must be sufficiently effective to keep up the spectator's interest in the play and his feeling of suspense. Such "effectively dramatic" curtains, however, force the dramatist to subordinate the entire structure of the play to a single climax at the end of each act. In *Ivanov* each curtain is of this nature. To Chekhov this constraint on the playwright's art was becoming more and more burdensome. It prevented him from depicting life "as it is" and from representing that inner world of emotion of whose existence he was becoming more and more aware. He was beginning to loathe stridency of any kind, but in a direct action play like *Ivanov* he could not help being strident, much as he tried to damp down any violent outbursts of emotion in his subsequent revisions of the play.

Another weakness of the play arose out of Chekhov's desire to make an end of a stock *literary* character that was so common in the Russian novel and play of the eighties. In spite of his efforts to look at life in a completely detached way, there crept into his play a strong element of exposure which forced him to over-emphasise the purely "Ivanov" elements of the play. This made him depict Ivanov, in Suvorin's words, "ready-made" that is to say, to neglect the development of his character in the course of the play. Chekhov resented this criticism, perhaps just because it was incontrovertible. "If my *Ivanov*," he wrote to Suvorin on February 8th, 1889, "is not clear to everybody it is because its four acts were made by an unskilful hand and not at all because I took my hero 'ready-made'. Tolstoy's heroes are taken 'ready-made'; their past and their characteristic features remain unknown and are only guessed at from hints, but you would not claim that they did not satisfy you. The whole thing depends on the greatness of the author's creative gifts—*da liegt der Hund begraben*. The contours of my Ivanov have been outlined correctly. I began him as I should have done—my own feeling does not sense any untruth; it was the shading that went wrong, and because that is bad you suspect that the contours have gone wrong." But quite apart from the fact that Chekhov is wrong about Tolstoy's characters (if he had in mind Tolstoy's novels and not his plays), the great plays of his second period provide ample proof of an inner movement in the development of character in addition to the purely dramatic movement expressed in the external action of the play. Such inner movement, however, is absent in *Ivanov*.

*Ivanov*, which was first performed at the Alexandrinsky Theatre on January 31st, 1889, was a great success in Petersburg. "My *Ivanov*," Chekhov wrote to Maria Kisselev on February 17th, 1889, "is still a colossal success, a phenomenal success! In Petersburg there are at present two heroes: the nude 'Frina' by Semiradsky[1] and the clothed I. Both of us have created a stir."

The *Petersburg Gazette* explained "the enormous success" of the play ("a success which is rare on our stage") as due to "its accomplished dialogue, its vital truth expressed in action, its characters taken straight from life, and its far from conventional plot . . . By his sincerity, love of humanity and the force of his talent," the dramatic critic of the paper wrote, "the author arouses feelings in his audience which might otherwise have been stifled." Another critic declared significantly that the personality of Ivanov "is the expression of the mood that is at present prevalent among us and gives us the right to count Chekhov among those creative artists who know how to depict the inner physiognomy of an age". There were a number of unfavourable notices criticising the play for having too many unnecessary scenes, too much talk and too little movement, and, most extraordinary of all, because its social implications were not justified from the medical point of view. Chekhov himself was entirely satisfied with

[1] The painting "Frina at Poseidon's Feast in Eleusis" was one of five pictures exhibited by the painter H. I. Semiradsky at the Petersburg Academy of Arts on January 25th, 1889.

the reception of the play. "I did what I could and what I knew," he wrote to Leontyev on February 18th, 1889, "and hence I must be right. I received more praise than I deserved. Shakespeare himself never heard the kind of speeches I had to listen to. What more do I want? And if there are a hundred or so people in Petersburg who shrug their shoulders, grin contemptuously, foam at the mouth or lie hypocritically, I don't see any of it so that it cannot possibly upset me. In Moscow I meet lots of people every day and not one of them ever mentions *Ivanov*, as though I had never written such a play, and the success and ovations I earned in Petersburg appear to me now like some bad dream from which I am glad to have awakened."

But while outwardly calm and contented, Chekhov, who never allowed himself to be deceived by popular success, was already working on a play with which he hoped to challenge the accepted conventions of the stage by representing life "as it is", shorn of its dramatically effective trappings, but at the same time full of suspense and unflagging interest. "It is necessary," he observed, "that on the stage everything should be as complex and as simple as in life. People are having dinner, and while they're having it, their future happiness may be decided or their lives may be about to be shattered." The play he had in mind would also be radically different in spirit from his previous plays: it would no longer be a play of frustration. Chekhov, in fact, had now gone to the other extreme; he had decided to write a play with a happy ending.

# PART III

---

# Transition

# 12

# The Wood Demon

THERE were two valid reasons which prompted Chekhov to give up the play of direct action: its highly dramatic situations and its "theatrical" characters offended his sense of truth, and his wish to observe life in a detached way, without taking sides, tended to make his drama a drama of frustration. After *Ivanov*, however, he was beginning to feel that in addition to holding a mirror up to nature, a work of art must also have an aim that transcended the writer's wish to be a mere honest observer of life as he saw it. It was at this period that he fell for some years under the influence of Tolstoy's teachings, and *The Wood Demon* is essentially a morality play on Tolstoyan lines: it is not a play in which virtue triumphs over vice, but in which vice is converted to virtue. In this play Chekhov deals with the great theme of the reconciliation of good and evil by letting his vicious characters first defeat his virtuous ones and then realise the heinousness of their offence. At the same time, however, Chekhov wished to challenge the generally accepted view that stage characters ought to be "dramatically effective". He wished to show life on the stage as it really was and not as it was invariably contrived by the professional playwright. But, not surprisingly perhaps in view of the essentially "theatrical" nature of the main theme of *The Wood Demon*, what he finally produced was a revival of a romantic convention of a bygone age with all its incongruous crudities. And he did so chiefly because he failed to realise that the drama of indirect action he was attempting to write had its own laws which could be ignored only at the price of complete failure. When he discovered those laws, he transformed the crude melodrama he had written into a great stage masterpiece.

The first mention of The Wood Demon occurs long before Chekhov's second revision of Ivanov. In a letter to Suvorin, written on May 13th, 1888, Chekhov, in discussing his summer holidays in the Crimea, declared: "In the Crimea I shall start writing a lyrical play." Thus, long before he had actually begun writing The Wood Demon, Chekhov had announced his intention of breaking away from the generally accepted forms of the direct-action play. In the Crimea, however, Chekhov found it very difficult to write. In a letter to his sister, Mary, on July 22nd of the same year, he ruefully confessed: "It is much easier to fly up to heaven alive than write one line under the southern skies." The next mention of the play occurs in a letter to Suvorin on October 18th. It seems that he persuaded Suvorin to collaborate with him in the writing of the play and in his letter, written after receiving Suvorin's draft of the first act of the play, he reminds him of the "plan" they worked out together. Chekhov includes a list of characters, which later appeared under different names in The Wood Demon (most of them appeared seven years later in Uncle Vanya). The first of these characters, Alexander Blagosvetlov (the retired university don Serebryakov of The Wood Demon and Uncle Vanya), Chekhov describes in this letter as follows: "He is a member of the State Council, has been awarded the order of the White Eagle, and is in receipt of a pension of 7,200 roubles a year; his father was a priest and he was educated at a religious seminary. The position he had formerly occupied he obtained by dint of personal efforts. There is not a single stain on his past. He suffers from gout, rheumatism and ringing in the ears. His estate he acquired through marriage. He possesses a positive mind. He cannot stand mystics, dreamers, weak-minded religious maniacs, sentimentalists, and sanctimonious people. He does not believe in God and is accustomed to look upon the world from the point of view of practical work. Work, work, work, and the rest is just humbug and nonsense."

The remarkable thing about this first outline of the character and social position of Blagosvetlov is that, with the exception of the fact that the estate never passed into his hands, everything about him remains practically unchanged both in *The Wood Demon* and *Uncle Vanya*.

Blagosvetlov's daughter, Nastya (Sonia in *The Wood Demon* and *Uncle Vanya*), was to undergo several drastic changes during the transformation of the first play into the second. Her first description in the list of characters Chekhov sent to Suvorin reads as follows: "Nastya is a girl of 23–24. She has had an excellent education and is able to think. She is bored with Petersburg as well as with the country. She has never been in love. She is lazy, likes to take part in debates, reads books lying down; she wants to marry because she wants a change and because she is afraid to remain an old maid. She keeps saying that she can fall in love only with an interesting man. She would gladly have fallen in love with Pushkin or Edison and married him, but she would marry a good man only out of boredom; she would respect her husband and love her children. Having met and listened to the Wood Demon, she falls head over ears in love with him and is carried away by her passion to the point of physical suffering, to the point of being overcome by silly, senseless laughter. The gunpowder, which had got damp in the Petersburg tundra, dries up in the sun and bursts into flame with terrific force. The declaration of love I have in mind for her is absolutely phenomenal."

The first description of Vassily Volkov, who was later to become Uncle Vanya, though in *The Wood Demon* his name is George (in both plays his surname is Voynitsky, an echo of Voynitsev in *Platonov*), differs radically from his subsequent characterisations. It is, however, interesting as forming the crude ore out of which Chekhov later extracted one of his most pathetic stage characters. "Vassily Volkov," Chekhov wrote, "is the brother of Blagosvetlov's first wife. He manages the latter's estate (having squandered his own many years earlier). He is sorry he has been so honest. He did not expect that his Petersburg relations would show so little appreciation of his services. They do not understand him, they do not want to understand him and he is sorry he did not steal. Drinks Vichy and grumbles. Stands on his dignity. Makes a point of emphasising that he is not afraid of Generals.[1] Shouts."

The Wood Demon himself, who appears in the list under the name of Victor Korovin (in the play he appears under the name of Michael Khrushchov and in *Uncle Vanya* as Michael Astrov) is given this characterisation: "A landowner, aged 30–33, the Wood Demon. A poet and landscape painter, who is endowed with a strong feeling for nature. A long time ago, when he was still at school, he had planted a birch-tree in the garden of his house; when the tree was covered with green leaves and began to sway in the wind, rustling and casting a little shadow, his soul was filled with pride; he had helped God to create a new birch-tree, he was responsible for the fact that there was one more tree in the world! That was the beginning of his peculiar occupation. He does not embody his idea on paper or canvas, but on the earth, not with dead colours, but with living organisms. A tree is beautiful, but that is not enough: it has a right to live, it is as essential as water, the sun and the stars. Life on earth is unthinkable without trees. Forests influence the climate, the climate influences the character of the people, etc. etc. There can be no question of civilisation or happiness if trees are felled, if the climate is severe and cruel, and if people, too, are hard and cruel. The future is black. Nastya likes him not for his idea, which she does not understand, but for his talent, his passion, for the great sweep of his idea. What she likes so much about him is that his thoughts embrace the whole of Russia and that he is ten centuries ahead of his time. When he comes running to her father and beseeches him tearfully not to sell his wood for timber, she bursts out laughing with delight and happiness, for at last she has come across a man in whose existence she did not believe before when she recognised his features in her dreams and in novels."

Both in *The Wood Demon* and in *Uncle Vanya* Khrushchov or

[1] His brother-in-law, being a retired university professor, has attained the highest rank in the Russian Civil Service which is equivalent to that of an army general, and entitles him to be addressed as "Your Excellency".

Astrov is a doctor of medicine, a fact not mentioned in the first list of characters.

These are the characters mentioned in Chekhov's letter who were subsequently to appear in *The Wood Demon* and in *Uncle Vanya*. No mention is made of the bluestocking Maria Voynitsky, the mother of the professor's first wife and of Uncle Vanya, who does appear in *The Wood Demon* and *Uncle Vanya* as one and the same character. But the list contains three more characters who duly appear in *The Wood Demon* and two characters, a son of the professor and an old pilgrim, whom Chekhov did not include in either play. Anuchkin (Orlovsky in *The Wood Demon*) a "Tolstoyan" character whom Chekhov at first seemed to have considered rather important, is an old landowner who "regards himself as the happiest man in the world". He ascribes his good health to a sudden conversion he had experienced at a meeting of the local agricultural board: "Ten years earlier," Chekhov writes, "at a meeting of the agricultural board he felt a sudden urge to ask all those present for forgiveness and after that he felt happy and, being by nature subjective and possessing a strong social sense, he had come to the conclusion that absolute sincerity, like a public act of repentance, is the best remedy for every kind of illness."

The other characters mentioned in the list who appeared afterwards in *The Wood Demon* are Galakhov (Zheltukhin in the play), a rich landowner, and his sister Lyuba (Julia in the play). Chekhov first characterised Galakhov as an honest and sincere man who realised that the Wood Demon was a better man than he and admitted it openly. In spite of being a civil servant "to the marrow of his bones", he was a romantic, who wanted to marry for love and "is given to lyrical moods", but, adds Chekhov, "nothing comes of it." He wanted to marry Nastya (Sonia), but he looked on her only as "a good wife" and "a beautiful and intelligent girl". Julia (in Chekhov's first list of characters she is Volkov's, Voynitsky's, daughter) is the typical housewife. "Real housewives," Chekhov writes, "are never satisfied with whatever they happen to be doing, but always insist that their life is hard, that they have no time to rest and that nobody is doing anything, while they, poor things, work their fingers to the bone."

There was also to be a Mademoiselle Emily in the cast, an old Frenchwoman who, too, is "in raptures" over the Wood Demon. "We must show," Chekhov writes, "how these Wood-Demon gentlemen impress the ladies." The last sentence seems to indicate that Chekhov himself did not think a lot of his idealist hero.

A week later, in reply to Suvorin's refusal to collaborate with him on *The Wood Demon* and his remark that it would make a good novel rather than a play, Chekhov, who was still hoping to write a novel one day (his short story *The Steppe* was written as the opening chapters of a long novel), insisted that he meant it to be a comedy. But this time, he pointed out significantly, he was not going to think of the actors or the stage, but the literary quality of the play. "If the play turned out to be of literary importance," he wrote, "I should be thankful for that alone."

Chekhov found the writing of what he now called a "literary" play not so easy. In January, 1889, he again tried to persuade Suvorin to collaborate with him. "Let us write a second play in summer," he wrote to Suvorin on January 8th. "We have now caught the devil by the tail. We have acquired experience. I think my *Wood Demon* will be infinitely more subtle than *Ivanov*. Only it shouldn't be written in winter, not while there are people round you who are continually talking and not under the influence of the city air, but in summer when all that took place in the city in winter seems irrelevant and ridiculous. Never write a play in winter; don't write a single line for the theatre if you are not a thousand miles away from it." Which merely goes to show that the writing of *The Wood Demon* as a "lyrical" or a "literary" play was giving Chekhov more trouble than he had anticipated.

He was now busy revising *Ivanov* and he postponed the writing of *The Wood Demon* indefinitely, though he was still hopeful to have it ready for the theatrical season of 1890. Indeed, he was sure he would get as much as seven or eight thousand roubles in royalties for it. In March 1899, he seemed to have forgotten all about his idea that plays should only be written in mid-summer.

He now hoped to write the play either in May or in August. "Pacing about the room during dinner," he wrote to Suvorin on March 5th, 1889, "I composed three acts quite satisfactorily and outlined the fourth. The third act is so scandalous that when you watch it you will say, 'This was written by a very cunning and pitiless man!'" On April 17th, he told Suvorin that he had already started writing the play, but that it was working out "awfully tedious, something like *Nathan the Wise*". In May, however, he wrote to Suvorin that his *Wood Demon* "was taking shape". And in another letter a few days later, he wrote: "The first act of *The Wood Demon* is ready—believe it or not! It is not bad, though a bit too long. I feel much stronger than when I wrote *Ivanov*. The play will be ready by the beginning of June. . . . It is awfully queer and I cannot help feeling amazed that such queer things should emerge from under my pen. I am afraid the censorship won't pass it." By May he must have already changed the retired professor's name to Serebryakov, for writing to his brother Alexander on the 8th, he warned him that since he, too, was writing a play he'd better choose a pen-name, such as "Krushchov, Serebyakov or something of the kind". On May 14th he told Suvorin that his play was rather boring and mosaic-like, but it still gave him the impression of hard work. "My characters are quite new; there is no footman in the whole play, not a single comic character, and not a single widow.[1] There are only eight characters, and only three of them of secondary importance.[2] In general, I have tried to avoid anything that is unnecessary and I think I have succeeded in that. In a word, I am a clever fellow and no mistake. If the censorship doesn't knock me on the head, you are going to experience such a thrill in the autumn as you have not experienced even while standing on top of the Eiffel Tower and looking down on Paris." He was so sure of finishing the play and getting it accepted that a few days later he wrote to the secretary of the Society of Russian Playwrights and Composers to include *The Wood Demon* in the catalogue of new plays

[1] An indirect hint at the abundance of such theatrical characters in *Ivanov*.
[2] When finally completed the play had thirteen characters.

which was to be performed on the Imperial stage in the autumn. But almost immediately after he had posted that letter, he became so disgusted with what he had written that he decided to postpone the completion of the play indefinitely. "I hoped to write a comedy," he wrote to Leykin on May 22nd, 1889, "but have so far written only two acts, got fed up and put it away." And a week later, in a letter to V. Tikhonov: "I began writing a comedy, but I only wrote two acts and stopped. It is boring. There is nothing so boring as boring plays, and as I am not able to write anything now but boring things, it is best I let it rest for a while." He had, as a matter of fact, already promised the play to two leading actors of the Maly Theatre, who wanted it for their benefit nights. Notices of it had already been published in the papers. Yet in spite of that he "chucked it", as he wrote to Pleshcheyev on August 3rd. "I am sick of actors," he added, moodily. "To hell with them!"

In September he took up the play again, but this time he scrapped the two acts he had already written and began from scratch. He even invented a new description of the play: a comedy-novel. "I am writing," he told Pleshcheyev on September 30th, 1889, "a big comedy-novel and have already finished two and a half acts. After my last short story I find it very easy to write a comedy. In my comedy I am depicting good, healthy people, half of them sympathetic; it has a happy ending. The general tone —all-round lyricism. It is called *The Wood Demon*." He finished the play in October and wrote to Alexander Lensky, the producer of the Maly Theatre, about it. "If you find my play acceptable," he wrote, "I shall be delighted to be of service to you and shall be very flattered if my child sees the stage of the Maly Theatre. Your part is a very big one and, I hope, not an easy one. The parts I have in mind for Gorev, Sadovsky, Yuzhin, Rybakov and Muzil[1] are also good. The play will be performed in Petersburg on October 31st on a benefit night. I shall probably have to leave for Petersburg between the 25th and 28th of October. I don't particularly want to."

[1] All famous actors of the Maly Theatre.

Vain hopes of authorship! Lensky rejected the play as totally unfit
for the stage, and it was never performed in Petersburg for the same
reason. The play was passed by the censorship, but was rejected by
the Petersburg branch of the Dramatic and Literary Committee on
the ground that it was only "a dramatised short story". Chekhov
was understandably hurt by this decision, especially as his old
friend, the novelist Grigorovich, was a member of the Committee.
Grigorovich, it seems, spread the story that Chekhov had taken
Suvorin as his model for Serebryakov. Chekhov denied it
vehemently. "You are not in my play," he wrote to Suvorin on
October 17th, "though Grigorovich with his characteristic
'insight' seems to think the contrary. The play deals with a tedious,
selfish, wooden man, who has read lectures on art for twenty-
five years but does not understand a thing about art, a man who
makes people feel bored and depressed, who does not tolerate
laughter, music, etc., etc., but who in spite of it all is quite
extraordinarily happy." On October 21st he summed up the
reception of *The Wood Demon* in a short sentence. "My *Wood
Demon*," he wrote to Leontyev, "has flopped and bust."

What was the play like in the form in which Chekhov sub-
mitted it to the Moscow and Petersburg producers and to the
Dramatic and Literary Committee? It had thirteen characters
(including two peasants). These could be divided into four groups:
1) the Serebryakov ménage, consisting of the retired professor
himself, his beautiful young wife, Helen, who is a fine pianist,
his pretty twenty-year-old daughter by his first marriage, Sonia,
who possesses a very attractive soprano voice, the mother of his
first wife, Maria Voynitsky, and her thirty-seven-year-old son
George Voynitsky; 2) a rich landowner Leonid Zheltukhin and
his eighteen-year-old sister Julia; 3) Ivan Orlovsky, a well-
to-do landowner and his equally rich ne'er-do-well son Fyodor;
and 4) Michael Khrushchov (the Wood Demon), a landowner
who is also a qualified doctor, though he is too rich to practise,
and Dyadin (Telegin in *Uncle Vanya*), a landowner who has come
down in the world and now rents a water-mill from Khrushchov.
Of these characters, three—Serebryakov, Fyodor Orlovsky,

Zheltukhin—represent the forces of evil, three others—Helen, George, Ivan Orlovsky—represent the instruments of their eventual conversion, while Khrushchov and Sonia occupy a somewhat equivocal position between the two camps, not being directly involved in the actual persecution of the good characters by the evil ones, but not remaining exactly innocent onlookers of it, either. Dyadin, a type of saintly fool, plays the part of the fairy-godmother in the play: he is quite incapable of doing evil to anyone or indeed of thinking badly of anyone and whatever happens appears to him as "delightful".

The play also shows, though in an embryonic form, the complex triangular love entanglements which will become so characteristic a feature of Chekhov's first three indirect-action plays. There is one love triangle composed of Khrushchov, Sonia, and Zheltukhin, and another composed of Helen, Voynitsky and Fyodor. Sonia and Khrushchov are in love with one another, though for no reason that ever becomes apparent it takes four acts for their love to be sealed with a kiss, and Zheltukhin is also in love with Sonia. Voynitsky is in love with his brother-in-law's wife, though she, being a virtuous woman, does nothing to encourage his passion, and Fyodor, too, is in love with her. In the first act, which takes place in the garden of Zheltukhin's country house, the future conflict of the forces of good and evil is firmly outlined. It is at the beginning of this act that Voynitsky launches his attack on the old professor (most of his dialogue was later incorporated by Chekhov in *Uncle Vanya*), and it is here that the slander against Helen, which is to form so important a theme as the play develops, is first uttered by Zheltukhin. Voynitsky as well as Julia are overjoyed at the arrival of the Serebryakovs and go to meet them, leaving Fyodor and Zheltukhin.

JULIA (*utters a little scream*). Dear Sonia! (*Runs out.*)

VOYNITSKY (*sings*). Come let us meet them—come let us meet them! (*Goes out.*)

ZHELTUKHIN. How tactless people are! He lives with the professor's wife and he just can't keep it dark.

FYODOR. Who?

ZHELTUKHIN. George, of course. He was singing her praises so much before you arrived that it was really indecent.

FYODOR. How do you know she is his mistress?

ZHELTUKHIN. I'm not blind. Besides, everybody is talking about it.

FYODOR. Rubbish. At present she is nobody's mistress, but she will soon be mine. Understand? Mine!

Fyodor, a truly melodramatic Byron-cum-Lermontov character (in *The Three Sisters* he appears again in the guise of Solyony, but what a difference in the delineation of the two characters!), starts his attack on Helen's virtue immediately after the arrival of Khrushchov, who is greeted enthusiastically by everybody. Fyodor tells Khrushchov that he has just returned from the Caucasus where he owns two large estates.

KHRUSHCHOV. You're in love, of course?

FYODOR. That is something we ought to drink to, Wood Demon. (*Drinks.*) Gentlemen, never fall in love with a married woman. On my word of honour, I'd rather be shot clean through a shoulder or a leg, as I have been, than be in love with a married woman. It's such a confounded nuisance that——

SONIA. No hope at all?

FYODOR. No hope? Why, there's not a man in the world who need be unhappily in love. Unhappy love—sighing and moaning—that's just a lot of silly nonsense. All you have to do is to want something badly enough. If I don't want my gun to misfire it doesn't misfire. If I want a certain lady to fall in love with me, she will fall in love with me. That's how it is, Sonia, old girl. If I have my eye on a woman, she'll find it easier to jump over the moon than to get out of my way.

SONIA. You're a real terror, aren't you?

FYODOR. She won't get away from me. Never. I haven't exchanged three sentences with her, but she's already in my power. I only told her, "Madam, every time you look at a window, you must think of me—I want you to." And so she thinks of me a thousand times a day. And that's not all: every day I bombard her with letters.

HELEN. Letters are a very unreliable method. She may get them, but she need not read them.

FYODOR. Do you think so? Well, in all my thirty-five years I've never met a woman who'd have sufficient courage not to open a letter addressed to her.

To make the position even clearer than it is, Chekhov resorts for the first time to the aid of a rather transparent symbol. After Fyodor has proposed that they should go and have a game of croquet, Helen suddenly looks up at the sky and asks: "What bird is that?"

ZHELTUKHIN. A hawk.

FYODOR. Ladies and gentlemen, let's drink to the health of the hawk!

And at the end of Act I, after delivering herself of the "Tolstoyan" speech against the devil of destruction in people, which Chekhov kept almost without alterations in *Uncle Vanya*, Helen expresses her annoyance with Fyodor's impudent advances. "Tell Fyodor," she says to Voynitsky, "that I'm sick and tired of his impudence. It's revolting! To stare at me and talk aloud in the presence of everybody about his love for some married woman —how frightfully witty!"

But she does not suspect that her name is already being linked with the name of Voynitsky and that people are accusing her of an affair which is much more revolting than an affair with Fyodor would have been. She never takes Voynitsky's love for her seriously. It just bores her. In Act II, Sc. 5, she tells him so. "And," she adds, "tell your friend Fyodor that if he won't stop pestering me, I shall take appropriate measures." Voynitsky, who is drunk (he had been drinking with Fyodor), begins to kiss her hand, mumbling, "My darling! My wonderful one!" And it is at that moment that Khrushchov enters, and having of course heard of the rumours about Voynitsky and Helen, he immediately jumps to the conclusion that they are lovers.

KHRUSHCHOV. Your husband is asking for you.

HELEN (*snatches her hand away from Voynitsky*). Thank you! (*Goes out.*)

KHRUSHCHOV (*to Voynitsky*). Nothing is sacred to you! You and the dear lady who has just gone out should have remembered that her husband was once the husband of your sister and that a young girl lives under the same roof with you. The whole county is already talking of your affair. How disgraceful!

Khrushchov is afraid of Helen's malign influence on the pure and innocent girl he is in love with, and in the scene with Sonia (Act II, Sc. 9) it is obviously of Helen that he is thinking when he says, "A beautiful dress sometimes covers a soul so black that no make-up will ever be able to hide it."

Sonia, too, though in Act II, Sc. 10 (which is practically identical with the last scene of Act II of *Uncle Vanya*) she makes up her quarrel with Helen, suspects her of having an affair with Voynitsky, and in Act III, Sc. 6, she is convinced of it. She finds a letter from George to Helen in the garden and confronts Helen with it. Helen finds Sonia and Julia alone in the drawing-room and after greeting Julia, says to Sonia: "What is your father doing, Sonia? (*Pause.*) Sonia, why don't you answer me? I asked you what your father was doing. (*Pause.*) Why don't you answer me, Sonia?"

SONIA. You want to know? Come here—— (*Takes her aside.*) I'll tell you if you like. My heart is too pure today and I can't talk to you and go on hiding my thoughts from you. Here, take this! (*Gives her a letter.*) I found it in the garden. Julia, let's go. (*Goes out with Julia through door on left.*)

HELEN (*alone.*) What's this? A letter from George to me! But why should I be blamed for it? Oh, how cruel, how infamous! Her heart is so pure that she can't talk to me. How could she insult me like that? Oh, I feel giddy—I'm going to faint——

FYODOR (*comes out from door on left and walks across the stage*). Why do you always shudder when you see me? (*Pause.*) H'm . . . (*Takes the letter from her and tears it up.*) Throw this away. You must think only of me. (*Pause.*)

HELEN. What's the meaning of that, sir?

FYODOR. It means that if I have my eye on a woman she will never escape from my grasp.

HELEN. Not at all, it simply means that you're an insolent fool.

FYODOR. You'll wait for me in the garden by the bridge at half past seven tonight. Is that clear? I have nothing more to say to you. And so, my angel, till half past seven. (*Tries to take her by the arm.*)

                    Helen *slaps his face.*

FYODOR. That's a bit emphatic, isn't it?

HELEN. Go away!

FYODOR. As you wish. (*Goes and comes back.*) I'm moved. Let's talk it over peacefully. You see, I've experienced everything in the world. I've even eaten goldfish soup. But I've never yet either flown in a balloon or carried off the wives of learned professors.

HELEN. Go, please.

FYODOR. I shall be gone in a moment I've experienced everything. And that's made me so insolent that I don't know what I shall do next. I mean, I'm telling you all this because I want you to know that if you should ever want a friend or a faithful dog, you have only to come to me. I'm really moved.

HELEN. I don't want any dogs. Please, go.

FYODOR. As you wish. (*Deeply moved.*) All the same, I feel moved. Yes—moved. (*Goes out irresolutely.*)

Left alone, Helen delivers herself of another "Tolstoyan" speech in which she deplores the fact that instead of living peacefully together, young people should be behaving so disgustingly to one another that it almost seems that they will soon devour each other. There follows the big scene of the family council in which Serebryakov outlines his plan for the sale of the estate which does not belong to him. The part of the plot dealing with Serebryakov and his cunning scheme to possess himself of the fortune his wife left to their daughter, is practically identical with the main plot of *Uncle Vanya.* There are two important differences, though. George Voynitsky is ten years younger than Uncle Vanya. This makes his passion for Helen more liable to be misinterpreted. Secondly, his quarrel with Serebryakov during the family council ends tragically: he commits suicide. This tragic ending is necessary in the play since without it Serebryakov's change of heart in Act IV would not have occurred. Helen is present at the family council (Sonia is not), and her two short remarks: "George, I demand that you should stop! Do you hear?" and "If you don't stop, I shall go away from this hell this very minute! (*Screams.*) I can't stand it any more!"—Chekhov transferred with only the omission of a few words to *Uncle Vanya*. But her third remark is less forceful in *The Wood Demon*.

HELEN (*to her husband*). If anything like this happens again, I shall go away.

SEREBRYAKOV. Don't try to frighten me, please.

HELEN. I'm not trying to frighten you, but you all seem to have agreed to make my life a hell. I shall go away.

SEREBRYAKOV. Everybody knows perfectly well that you are young and I am old, and that you are doing me a great favour by staying here.

HELEN. Go on, go on——

It is then that Khrushchov appears and pleads with Serebryakov not to sell his wood for timber. Serebryakov calls him a lunatic and tells him to mind his own business. Khrushchov is furious. He had earlier (Act II, Sc. 9) been told by Sonia that his democratic feelings were outraged by his friendship with them, and she implied that he was ashamed to have fallen in love with "a girl who has been educated at a highclass finishing school and who has never been to a university". She had also made it clear to him that she regarded his views about the preservation of forests as an affectation, that, in short, she shared the general opinion of him as a crank. Now when Sonia tries to talk to him, he refuses to listen to her. "I was rash enough to fall in love here," he declares, "and that ought to be a lesson to me. Away from this stuffy hole!" Sonia bursts out crying and runs away. At that moment Helen comes in. She apologises to him for her husband's rudeness, tells him that she sympathises with him and respects him and offers him her friendship. Khrushchov, convinced that she is Voynitsky's mistress, snubs her. "Go away," he says. "I despise your friendship!" He goes out, leaving Helen stunned by the insult. "Why? Why?" she repeats Ivanov's cry after Lvov's public insult in the earlier versions of *Ivanov*. It is then that a shot is heard. Maria

Voynitsky staggers into the room and collapses in a dead faint.
She is followed by Sonia, Serebryakov, Orlovsky and Zheltukhin.
Sonia runs out and returns, shouting, "Uncle George has shot
himself!" They all run out except Helen.

HELEN (*moans*). Why? Why?
FYODOR (*in the doorway*). What's happened?
HELEN. Take me away from here! Throw me over a precipice!
    Kill me! Humiliate me! (*Falls into his arms.*)
FYODOR (*laughs harshly, imitating an operatic Mephistopheles*). Ha,
    ha, ha! (*An octave lower.*) Ha, ha, ha!
                    Curtain


# 13

# *The Wood Demon*

THE FIRST version of Act IV, like the end of Act III, is pure
melodrama. Not even in *Platonov* had Chekhov been so
dramatically strident. The action takes place outside the
water-mill Dyadin rents from the Wood Demon. Julia appears
and tells Dyadin that the professor and Sonia are living with her
and her brother. "Since George's suicide," she says, "they have
been afraid to live in their own house. The professor is dreadfully
depressed, he's got thin, and hardly ever opens his mouth. Poor
Sonia cries all the time and you can't get a word out of her. During
the day it isn't so bad, but at night they sit in one room till day-
break. They're terrified. They are afraid that George may appear
to them in the dark." Dyadin scoffs at their superstitions, "I
believe neither in ghosts," he declares, "nor in spiritualism." He
then asks Julia if they have heard anything about Helen, and
Julia tells him that Helen has run away with Fyodor. Dyadin
supplies some more information about Helen. It seems that the
servants and the peasants had seen Fyodor holding the unconscious

Helen with one hand while whipping the horses with the other, "driving like Phoebus in his chariot". But after driving for five miles, Fyodor stopped the horses and ran off to fetch some water for Helen. When he returned, Helen had vanished. He looked for her in vain, and "furious that his Don Juan plan had failed," played havoc in the cottage of a peasant and "blackened the eyes of his wife". "This," Dyadin adds, "is delightful!" Julia wonders whether Helen might not have committed suicide too, but Dyadin (in whose house Helen has taken refuge, though this does not come out till the end of the act) assures her that everything will end happily. Then Khrushchov enters, bringing some more disastrous news: a landowner in the neighbourhood has sold his woods for timber, Fyodor's father has contracted typhus and is dangerously ill ("I believe," Khrushchov adds to make quite sure that the old man's fatal illness, which is so important to the development of the plot, has not escaped the audience, "he has caught pneumonia, too"), and finally, Helen (as though the audience did not know) has run away with "that idiot Fyodor" and no one knows where she is. And that is not all by any means. It seems that Khrushchov too is afraid of seeing Voynitsky's ghost at night, for while visiting Orlovsky he was shown Voynitsky's diary from which it became clear that the whole story of Voynitsky's relations with Helen was "an odious slander". Julia confirms it: they, too, apparently have read poor George's diary.

KHRUSHCHOV. The illicit love affair between George and Helen which has been trumpeted all over the district seems to have been a libel. I believed it and I spread it along with the others. I hated, despised and insulted her! Why are you silent? Why don't you say something?

DYADIN. My dear Michael, I swear to you by the true Creator and by my eternal salvation that Helen is a most worthy woman. Gentle, highminded, truthful, sensitive and possessed of a soul which, fool that I am, I cannot find words to describe to you. (*Weeps.*) When it was vouchsafed to me to know her better, my soul was filled with indescribable bliss.

It is good to see physical beauty but to see spiritual beauty is a thousand times better.

Khrushchov then tells Julia that her brother is to blame for spreading the story about George and Helen. Julia bursts out crying and is taken into the house by Dyadin. Left alone, Khrushchov quotes some passages from George's diary. George, it seems, was quite sure that Sonia was in love with Khrushchov, which Khrushchov refuses to believe. "Even if there is some truth in it," he soliloquises, while mixing his colours (he had set up his easel and is about to paint a map of the district), "I mustn't think of it. It all began stupidly and it's sure to end stupidly. And, as a matter of fact, I did well to burn her photograph yesterday." He is interrupted by the arrival of Zheltukhin and Sonia. Zheltukhin goes off to join his sister, and Khrushchov tells Sonia about the map he is painting (this is the only incident that Chekhov used in *Uncle Vanya* when Astrov explains his map to Helen). He then asks her if she is happy, and is treated to a few more "Tolstoyan" sentiments.

SONIA. Now isn't the time to think of happiness.

KHRUSHCHOV. What else should we think about?

SONIA. Our present unhappiness has been caused by the fact that we were thinking too much of our happiness.

KHRUSHCHOV (*drops his saucer of paints*). I'm sorry.

SONIA. There's no evil without good. Our sorrow has taught me a lesson and now I realise how mistaken I was. We must forget our happiness and think only of the happiness of others. Our lives only consist of sacrifices.

KHRUSHCHOV. Of course.

SONIA. We must work for the good of all, we must help the poor, we must try to love those whom we do not love.

The last sentiment, however, is too much for Khrushchov. "All right, then," he says, "go and marry Leonid!" He goes on: "Mrs. Voynitsky's son has shot himself, but she still goes on talking about emancipation and looking for contradictions in her brochures. A misfortune has befallen you and you're consoling your vanity by thoughts of all sorts of sacrifices. . . . We go on doing what we ought not to do, and everything goes to wrack and ruin. I'd better be going——"

SONIA. They're coming here and I'm crying.

Julia, Zheltukhin and Serebryakov enter, followed by a maid with a picnic basket. George's death has wrought a wonderful change in the old professor. He declares that he is more to blame than anyone else and that he has been through so much since his brother-in-law's suicide that he could write a whole book "for the edification of posterity" on how people ought to live. He goes on: "I repeat, on the very next day after his suicide I was horrified by my own cruelty; I was surprised that I should have understood so little before and should have talked such a lot. Now I think it strange that I shouldn't have talked about anything to my wife except my gout and my rights and that I should have believed that that was as it should be. (*In a voice trembling with emotion.*) Of course it was my fault, not to speak of George who if——" Zheltukhin intervenes and reminds the professor that he has promised him not to speak of it again, and Dyadin, to dispel the atmosphere of gloom, asks him to read a poem. Zheltukhin is glad to oblige and recites a long poem by Nekrassov, describing a woodland scene and ending with the words, "You must love while you can—and God is your judge!" Still the tension persists, at least Zheltukhin says so, and Serebryakov indulges in a bit of psychological self-analysis. A strange feeling has come over him: he wants someone to say something insulting to him or wishes that he could fall ill. This provokes Khrushchov to a sudden outburst of self-accusation. He remembers Helen's appeal to him for his friendship and that he told her that he despised her friendship. He asks the professor of what use their work for humanity was if they had no pity in their hearts and if they went on destroying one another. "Did we do anything to save George? Where is your wife whom I insulted so inhumanly? Where's your peace of mind? Where's my love? Everything has been destroyed, everything has gone to wrack and ruin! Run all of you—shout at the top of your voices——"

They quieten him, and everybody settles down to enjoy their picnic, when Fyodor suddenly appears. At first Sonia mistakes him for George's ghost, but Khrushchov recognises him and asks everybody to ignore him. Fyodor, however, refuses to be ignored, and to everybody's astonishment, declares that he feels deeply hurt not to have been invited to the picnic. This is too much for Khrushchov. "Get out of here, you impudent cad!" he shouts at Fyodor, who challenges both Zheltukhin and Khrushchov to a duel. At that moment a peasant sent by Fyodor's mother appears with the news of Orlovsky's death.

FYODOR. Good Lord, and I—I haven't been home for a whole week. Poor father . . . (*In a penitent voice*.) Forgive me, all of you. I wanted to say something to you, professor, but I'm afraid it has escaped me. You were a friend of my father's— no, that's not it. I know: your wife is a saint. . . . (*Goes out with the peasant*.)

Everybody is again plunged into gloom, when suddenly Lensky's aria from *Eugene Onegin* is heard played on the piano and they realise at once that it must be Helen who is playing it.

KHRUSHCHOV. What's that? Is it Helen playing? Where is she? What does it mean?
DYADIN. This is delightful! She's in my house! She's been living here for the last fortnight. Michael, what joy! (*Shouts*.) Helen, my dear, come here! You needn't hide any longer!
SONIA. I'm sure it's Helen who's playing. It's her favourite aria.
KHRUSHCHOV. Where is she? (*Runs into the house*.)
SEREBRYAKOV. I don't understand—I——
DYADIN (*rubbing his hands*). One moment—one moment. This is the end of our troubles.

Helen appears, followed by Khrushchov who implores her to forgive him. Helen magnanimously kisses him on the head and tells him that henceforth they will be friends. Everybody surrounds her and there is a general exchange of kisses.

HELEN. All this time I suffered and thought no less than you. You have forgiven me and I have forgiven you, and we have all

become better. From now on, let's live in a new way. Let's
go home. I feel homesick.

DYADIN. This is delightful!

KHRUSHCHOV. I feel a different man now! I'm not afraid of anything any more. I'm happy!

SEREBRYAKOV. Let's go home, darling. Now I shall enjoy being
indoors.

HELEN. I sat at the window and heard everything. You poor
things! Come, let's go back quickly! (*Takes her husband's
arm.*) Let bygones be bygones. Mr. Khrushchov, come with
us.

KHRUSHCHOV. I'm all yours.

JULIA (*to her brother*). You, too, must ask her to forgive you.

ZHELTUKHIN. I can't bear all this excitement! It's sickening. Let's go
home—it's getting damp. (*Coughs.*)

HELEN. Sonia's laughing. Laugh, my dear! I, too, am laughing.
That's how it should be. Come along, Alexander! (*Goes out
with her husband.*)

ZHELTUKHIN. Let's go! (*Goes out with his sister and shouts behind
the scenes* "Alexey, my carriage!")

KHRUSHCHOV (*to Sonia*). When our hearts are pure, our eyes see
clearly. I see everything now. Come, my darling! (*Embraces
Sonia and goes out with her.*)

DYADIN (*alone*). They've forgotten me! This is delightful! This
is delightful!

Curtain.

In writing *The Wood Demon* Chekhov did his best to stick
to his new formula that in a play, as in real life, there should be
coming and going, eating and drinking, talking and playing
games, while the happiness or the ruin of the characters was taking
shape unbeknown to themselves. His characters eat and drink,
come and go, talk and make love, discuss important social
problems, and so on. But in spite of all that Chekhov never
succeeds in creating the illusion of real life on the stage. There is
not a single situation in which the characters act, or, at any rate,
appear to be acting, independently of the playwright. Their
entrances and exits may seem haphazard, but they actually occur
just at the moment Chekhov wants them to occur. The play, in

fact, is teeming with coincidences and *deus ex machina* situations.
A hawk flies across just when Helen looks up at the sky; Voynitsky
suddenly takes it into his head to write a compromising letter to
Helen and, quite unaccountably, leaves it lying about in the
garden for anyone to pick up; Fyodor turns up just at the right
moment for Helen to fall into his arms; a diary nobody has ever
heard of before turns up providentially to vindicate Helen's
character; an old landed gentleman of irreproachable character
dies just when his death might be calculated to produce the
greatest effect on his rake of a son, and so on. The action of the
play, in fact, is full of unlife-like, melodramatic touches, the
fourth act in particular being pure, undiluted melodrama. It was
the fourth act, indeed, that Chekhov set about revising immediately. He had sent the play to Suvorin and in reply to
his criticisms wrote on November 12th, 1889: "I knew myself
that the fourth act was no good at all, but I sent you the
play on the understanding that I should write a new act." In the
same letter he gave Suvorin the news that he had received an
offer for the play from M. Abramova, the owner of a private
theatre in Moscow, "on very good terms," adding, "If I decide to
accept her offer, I shall alter my play so much that you will not
recognise it." Alexander Lensky had written him earlier a long
letter in which he expressed the view that he (Chekhov) had no
respect for dramatic form which was much more difficult than
narrative form, and, he added, "you are too spoilt by success to
study dramatic form and learn to like it."

Nemirovich-Danchenko, who by that time had quite a few
dramatic successes of his own, agreed with Lensky, but he took the
view that Chekhov, though not despising dramatic form, had
little knowledge of it (none of them realised that what Chekhov
was trying to do was to create an entirely new dramatic form).
The main fault of the play, Nemirovich-Danchenko thought, lay
in the obscurity of its plot. The audience, he advised Chekhov,
must be able to get a clear idea of the essential points of the plot.
"This," he wrote, "is more important than any stage methods and
stage effects. But this is true of a work of fiction and of every work

of art." Still, Chekhov was determined to get the play produced and he sat down to revise it. The main revision he reserved for the fourth act, contenting himself with cutting down the dialogue in the first and third acts and leaving the second act unaltered. The end of the third act, however, he altered completely. Realising that Fyodor was too melodramatic a figure, he decided to bring Dyadin on at the end of the third act. The new version therefore ran as follows:

HELEN (*moans*). Why? Why?
DYADIN (*in the doorway*). What's the matter?
HELEN. Take me away from here! Throw me over a precipice, kill me, but don't let me stay here! Quickly, I implore you! (*Goes out with Dyadin.*)
Curtain

The fourth act Chekhov transformed from a melodrama into an idyll. It opens with Dyadin and Helen discussing the situation created by her running away from her husband. Dyadin is convinced that she will return, but Helen is not so sure. "I don't love my husband," she says. "I was so fond of the young people but they were unjust to me from first to last. Why then should I go back? You will say it is my duty. I know that perfectly well, but, I repeat, I must think it over." They hear somebody coming, and Helen retires to the house. Julia comes in and tells Dyadin, as in the first version, that Sonia and the professor are staying with her and her brother and that they are afraid that Voynitsky's ghost might appear to them in the dark. Chekhov omitted the lines about the professor feeling dreadfully depressed, losing weight and refusing to utter a word. The whole incident of Helen's abduction has quite naturally been cut out, which makes the scene between Dyadin and Julia considerably shorter.

The dialogue between Khrushchov and Dyadin has also been shortened. As there was no longer any need for the melodramatic conversion of Fyodor, it was no longer necessary to kill off his father, so that all the calamities that Khrushchov enumerates are Helen's running away from her husband, the sale of his wood by a landowner in the neighbourhood, and the third one: "I feel that I'm getting more stupid and more small-minded every day!" There follows the account of George's diary, Dyadin's panegyric on Helen being cut out because in the changed circumstances of her departure from home it was no longer needed. The scene between Khrushchov, Zheltukhin and Sonia is little changed. It is followed by the arrival of Serebryakov and the resurrected Orlovsky who are joined by Julia, Zheltukhin and Dyadin. This scene has been considerably cut, and the arrival of Fyodor in the next scene (Act IV, Sc. 8) quite understandably provokes no dismay of any kind. In re-writing it, Chekhov remembered his original characterisation of Orlovsky[1] and put in the account of his sudden conversion. Chekhov also added a naturalistic touch: the glow of a fire in the sky. Serebryakov in this scene is drawn with a much firmer hand than in the first version. When Orlovsky hints that he ought to "capitulate", Serebryakov replies: "Here we have a specimen of native philosophy. You advise me to ask forgiveness. But why? It is I who should be asked to forgive."

SONIA. But, Father, it is *our* fault.
SEREBRYAKOV. Is it? You're all, I gather, thinking of my relations with my wife. But do you really think that I'm to blame for what has happened? Why, that is really absurd. She has forgotten her duty and left me at a time when she should have remained at my side.

It is then that Khrushchov appeals to the professor to remember that they did nothing to save George. "Where is your wife whom we have all insulted?" he says. "Where is your peace of mind? Where is your daughter's peace of mind? Everything has been destroyed, everything has been ruined! You all call me a wood demon, but I'm not the only one. There is a demon in all of you. You are all walking in a dark forest. You are all groping your way in life. You all have just enough intelligence, knowledge and feeling to spoil your own lives and the lives of others." It is at this point that Helen comes out of the house (without a

[1] See page 125.

preliminary musical introduction this time) and sits down un-
noticed on a seat. Khrushchov goes on with his denunciation.

KHRUSHCHOV. I thought I was a man of ideas, a humane person,
but at the same time I refused to forgive people their smallest
mistakes. I believed the stories which were spread about
other people and I libelled them with the rest. When your
wife unsuspectingly offered me her friendship, I blurted out
majestically: "Go away! I despise your friendship!" This
is the kind of person I am. There's a demon in me. I'm
small-minded, stupid and blind, but you, my dear professor,
aren't exactly an eagle, either. And yet the whole country-
side, all the women, look upon me as a hero, as a progressive,
and you are famous throughout the whole of Russia. And if
people seriously regard a man like me as a hero, if they
seriously think that you are famous, it merely means
there aren't any heroes, that there aren't any talented people,
that there isn't anyone who could lead us out of the dark
forest, who could make good the damage we have done. It
merely means that there are no true eagles who have a right
to be famous.

SEREBRYAKOV. I'm sorry, but I didn't come here to enter into any
polemics with you or to defend my right to be famous.

ZHELTUKHIN. Don't you think, Michael, we'd better change the
subject?

KHRUSHCHOV. I haven't got much more to say and I'm going
anyway. Yes, I'm small-minded, but you, professor, aren't
an eagle, either. George, too, was small-minded if he didn't
find anything better to do than blow his brains out. All of
you are small-minded. As for the women——

HELEN (interrupting). As for the women, they aren't much better,
either. (Walks up to the table.) I left my husband, but do you
think that I did anything more sensible with my freedom? Don't worry. I shall come back. (Sits down at the
table.) I have come back.

The general bewilderment at her sudden appearance is interrupted by Dyadin's loud laughter and his usual exclamation:
"This is delightful!" He teases the professor with having abducted
his wife as Paris once upon a time abducted the beautiful Helen.

"There may not be any pock-marked Parises," he adds, "but there are more things in heaven and earth, Horatio, than are dreamt of in your philosophy!"

*Hamlet* seems to have been one of Chekhov's obsessions: he couldn't help bringing it in even if he had to make a grandiloquent ass quote the tritest passage from it.

The explanations which follow Helen's appearance convey very little to the spectator who, of course, has already seen Helen at the beginning of the act. But Serebryakov is true to type. When Helen offers her hand to him, he turns away.

HELEN. Alexander!
SEREBRYAKOV. You have forgotten your duty!
HELEN. Alexander!
SEREBRYAKOV. I don't want to pretend that I'm not glad to see you and I'm willing to talk to you but at home, not here. (*Walks away from the table.*)
ORLOVSKY. My dear chap! (*Pause.*)
HELEN. I see. So it means that our problem, Alexander, has been solved very simply: by remaining unsolved. All right, so be it. I'm an episodic figure and my happiness doesn't matter, it's a woman's happiness. Sitting at home, eating, drinking, sleeping and listening to your husband who goes on talking interminably about his gout, his rights, and his merits. Why have you all lowered your heads as if you're embarrassed? Come, let's have a drink! What does it matter?

Fyodor, who is deeply moved by Helen's speech (what a change from the Fyodor of the first version!), goes up to the professor and promises to give him his best team of horses if he will only say a kind word to his wife.

SEREBRYAKOV. Thank you, but I'm afraid I don't quite understand.
FYODOR. I see. You don't understand. One day as I was returning from a shoot I saw a long-eared owl sitting on a branch right in front of me. I took aim and fired. But nothing happened. The owl still sat there. I reloaded my gun and fired again. But he still sat there as cool as a cucumber. Just blinking at me.
SEREBRYAKOV. And who, pray, are you referring to?
FYODOR. The owl.

It is only now that they notice the glow in the sky. They are told that it is a wood that has caught fire, and Khrushchov runs off with the words: "I may not be much of a hero, but one day I shall be one! I shall grow the wings of an eagle, and no fire or devil will ever frighten me! Let the forests burn, I shall plant new ones! And though I am not loved, I shall love another!" This makes Helen exclaim, "What a fine fellow he is!" while Sonia demands to be taken home.

SONIA (*in great agitation*). Take me away from here! Take me away!
ZHELTUKHIN. I am at your service.
SONIA. Thank you, I'd rather my godfather took me home.
ZHELTUKHIN (*aside*). Damn it, all I get is insults!

Serebryakov feels a twinge in his left foot and braces himself to another sleepless night. Helen asks Dyadin to fetch her hat and coat and then tells her husband that she is ready to go home. His last words are almost identical with his parting words in *Uncle Vanya*. "Goodbye, gentlemen. I thank you for your delightful treat and for your pleasant company. A lovely evening, excellent tea—everything is fine, but I'm sorry to say I shall never accept your native philosophy and views on life. We must work, my friends. We can't go on like that. We must work. Yes. Goodbye!" (*Goes out with his wife.*)
Sonia, however, insists on remaining. She is in despair. Orlovsky offers her water, but she beseeches him to take her to the fire. At that moment Khrushchov returns and asks Dyadin for one of his horses.

SONIA (*recognising Khrushchov, utters a joyful cry*). Michael! (*She goes up to him.*) Michael! (*To Orlovsky.*) Go away, godfather, I have to talk to him. (*To Khrushchov.*) You said that you would love another—(*To Orlovsky.*) Go away, godfather. (*To Khrushchov.*) I'm different now. All I want is truth. Nothing but truth! I love you. I love you. . . . Yes, all I want is truth. Say something. Why don't you speak?
KHRUSHCHOV (*embracing her*). My darling!

But one happy ending did not satisfy Chekhov. He had another couple left on his hands and he had to marry them off, too. Fyodor and Julia enter and they all hide themselves. Fyodor's proposal of marriage is blunt. He feels that he has been roving about the world long enough and that it is time he changed his "mode of life". Would she marry him, meaning Julia.

JULIA (*embarrassed*). Well, you see, darling, first of all you must mend your ways—
FYODOR. Don't beat about the bush. Tell me straight.
JULIA. I feel ashamed. (*Looking round.*) Wait, someone might come and hear us. I think I can see Waffles looking out of the window.
FYODOR. I can't see anyone.
JULIA (*flings herself on his neck*). Darling!
  (*Sonia bursts out laughing. Orlovsky, Dyadin and Khrushchov roar with laughter, clap their hands and shout:*
  Bravo, bravo!*)
FYODOR. You frightened me. Where did you come from?
SONIA. Julia, darling, congratulations! Me, too! Me, too!
  (*Laughter, kisses, noise.*)
DYADIN. This is delightful! This is delightful!
                    Curtain

# 14

# *The Wood Demon*

The *Wood Demon* was performed for the first time in Moscow at Abramova's Theatre on December 27th, 1889. Chekhov therefore took only a month to revise it, and that probably accounts for the many loose ends in it. The character of Fyodor, in particular, lacks consistency. In the first three acts he is still the rampageous villain of melodrama, while in the fourth act he is shown as a man of irreproachable morals. He implores the professor to take his wife back, having apparently quite forgotten his own far from honourable designs on Helen's virtue. And this truly astonishing transformation has been brought about not, as in the first version of the fourth act, by the unexpected death of his father, but by a bout of drinking and gambling to the consequences of which he ought, one would have thought, to have become inured long ago.

The play was a failure. The critics condemned it unanimously for its blind copying of reality and mechanical reproduction of life! Chekhov was accused of having been carried away by his mistaken notion that events in the lives of his characters could be transferred to the stage just as if they had happened in real life. What no one seemed to have noticed was that Chekhov's attempt to reproduce "life as it is" made his play as unlike life as possible. Lacking the knowledge of the mechanics of the play of indirect action, he had to rely on the stale methods of the *deus ex machina* situation and the long arm of coincidence. Thus, the fire in the last act, unlike the fire in *The Three Sisters*, has no symbolic significance and was introduced simply because Chekhov wanted to get his central character off the stage. But Chekhov still hoped to be able to correct the more glaring mistakes of the play. In a letter from Petersburg to Fyodor Kumanin, the publisher of the Moscow journal *The Artist*, on January 8th, 1890, he wrote: "Please don't publish *The Wood Demon*. It is of no value whatever to *The Artist*: the Moscow public did not like it, the actors seemed to be embarrassed, and the newspapermen abused it. Send it back to me: it will be hardly noticed in *The Artist*, it will be of no use to anyone, and your two hundred roubles will be wasted. I repeat, my *Wood Demon* is of no value whatever to your journal. If you accede to my request, I shall be infinitely grateful and will write as many stories as you like for you. . . . I am asking you *seriously*. If you agree, let me know as soon as possible. If you don't, I shall be deeply hurt and unhappy, for this will deprive me of the chance of putting in some more work on the play. If it is already being set up, I shall be glad to pay your expenses, I shall throw myself into the river, I shall hang myself, do anything you like."

A month later he wrote to Pleshcheyev, who was at the time the literary editor of the Petersburg monthly *Severny Vestnik* (The Northern Herald): "I have just re-read my *Wood Demon*. This is what I have decided to do: I shall read it again, alter it, and send it to the *Severny Vestnik*. May your wish be fulfilled! I hope to send you the play about February 20th with this earnest request—if you don't like it, send it back to me and I shall destroy it." He sent it only on March 17th. In the accompanying letter to Pleshcheyev he wrote: "I am still hoping that, having read it, you will perhaps share my own doubts about the play which make me send it you with so much hesitation. Perhaps," he added, referring to the only two critics who had taken a favourable view of the play, "you will not be as indulgent as Merezhkovsky and Urussov and will draw a red line through my play." In the meantime the *Severny Vestnik* had to close down and Chekhov was glad to get his play back unpublished. Afterwards he refused to have the play performed or published. Writing to Urussov on October 16th, 1899, he declared: "Please, don't be angry with me: I can't publish *The Wood Demon*. I hate this play and I'm trying to forget it. Whether it is the fault of the play itself or of the circumstances under which it was written and performed on the stage, I don't know, but it would be a severe blow to me if it were dragged into the light of day and revived. Here you have an excellent example of the perversity of a parent's feelings!" But the truth was that by that time he had already mastered the technique of the indirect-action play. That is the real reason why he would have nothing more to do with *The Wood Demon*.

The process of Chekhov's gradual development from a writer of direct-action into one of indirect-action plays can perhaps be traced more clearly in his one-act play *On the Harmfulness of Tobacco*. Six different versions of the play are extant, covering most of his period as a playwright from 1886 to 1903. One of the most important of these versions, that of 1890, only came to light in 1948 and was published in 1949. It is, indeed, highly probable that Chekhov used this play, which after all is only an unimportant trifle, for his experiments in the new method of writing dramatic dialogue which depends for its main effect on inner rather than outer action. The first mention of the play is to be found in a letter to Victor Bibilin, a member of the editorial board of the Petersburg weekly *Fragments*, to which Chekhov contributed regularly at the beginning of his career. "I have just finished a monologue play *On the Harmfulness of Tobacco*", Chekhov wrote on February 14th, 1886, "which in my heart of hearts I meant to offer to the comic actor Gradov-Sokolov. But having only two and a half hours at my disposal, I have made a mess of this monologue and . . . sent it not to the devil but to the *Petersburg Gazette*. My intentions were good, but the execution was execrable." The comedy was published in the paper on February 17th and was later included in a revised form in Chekhov's first collection of stories, published in the same year. The last mention of the play is found in two letters Chekhov wrote to his publisher Fyodor Marx on October 1st and 16th, 1903. In his first letter Chekhov wrote: "Among my works which have already been sent to you is the play *On the Harmfulness of Tobacco* which I have included among those of my works which are on no account to be published. Now I have written an entirely new play under the same title of *On the Harmfulness of Tobacco*, retaining only the name of the character, and I am sending it to you for publication in Volume VII." In reply to Marx's inquiry whether, as the play was a new one, Chekhov would permit him to publish it first in his monthly magazine *Niva*, Chekhov wrote: "My play *On the Harmfulness of Tobacco* was written exclusively for the stage and, if published in a magazine, it might appear unnecessary and uninteresting. I should be glad, therefore, if you would not publish it in your magazine." In these letters Chekhov committed himself to two important statements. To begin with, he regarded the last version of the play as an *entirely new* play and this curious statement can only be explained by Chekhov's refusal to recognise a direct-action play as in any way similar to a play in which what matters is a character's inward reaction to the circumstances of his life and not the circumstances themselves. His second statement that his one-act comedy was meant exclusively for the stage shows that he regarded it as an *acting* copy, that is to say, as a play that could only be fully appreciated on the stage, and this is equally true about the plays of his last period which are all plays written exclusively for the stage. Chekhov realised very well that such plays must be acted quite differently. Indeed, he left two statements which show clearly enough the new kind of acting he had in mind for his indirect-action plays. "You must," Chekhov told the actors of the Moscow Art Theatre, "create a character which is entirely different from the character created by the author and when these two characters—the author's and the actor's—merge into one, you will get a work of art." Chekhov left the actors completely free to form their own conception of his characters, but at the same time he demanded that they should have a clear idea of his own conception of them, for it was only by a synthesis of the two different conceptions that the actors could create a work of art on the stage, that is to say, a character that was both true to the author and to themselves as artists. His second statement on the way in which his plays should be acted is to be found in his letter to Vsevolod Meierhold, written in January, 1900, at the time when Meierhold was still a member of the company of the Moscow Art Theatre. The acting he had in mind for his plays, Chekhov made it clear, did not mean rushing about the stage and expressing emotions by means of gestures. Strong emotion, he pointed out, should be expressed on the stage as it is expressed in life by cultured people, that is to say, not with one's hands and feet, but with the tone of one's voice and with one's eyes, not by gesticulating but by always keeping one's poise. And anticipating the usual reply that the conditions of the stage made such acting impossible, Chekhov insisted that no conditions justified a lie. A Chekhov play of the last period, there-fore, demands inner action from the actors, which does not mean that they should just sit about without doing anything except speaking their lines, a way in which unfortunately Chekhov's great plays are all too often "acted". It demands action of a very subtle kind, action that can only emerge after the complete fusion of the actor's conception of the character with the author's conception of it, an action which is both natural and expressive. The gradual development of these new methods of acting becomes evident from an examination of the stage directions of three versions of *On the Harmfulness of Tobacco*: in the first, belonging to the *Ivanov* period the actor is given 26 "dramatically effective" actions; in the second, belonging to the transition period of *The Wood Demon*, this number is reduced to 14, and in the third, belonging to Chekhov's last period, to 8.

The only character of the play is the elderly henpecked husband of the proprietress of a private boarding school for girls in a provincial city who bears the rather comic name of Nyukhin, the English equivalent of which would be Smelley. Chekhov left this name unaltered in all the three versions of the play, but he altered the Christian name of Nyukhin in the third version. In the first two versions Nyukhin bears the somewhat un- usual and ridiculous name of Markel; in the third version he is just an ordinary Ivan. Chekhov also altered the name of one of his daughters from (in Russian) the rather exotic Veronica to the more ordinary Barbara. Nyukhin is shown as delivering one of his usual highly moral lectures "in aid of charity" at the local club. In the first version he keeps interrupting his lecture with frequent asides which give the audience a glimpse into his private life; in the second, the lecture on the harmfulness of tobacco is practically cut out; in the third, nothing of it is left, the whole monologue being devoted to the story of Nyukhin's private life. The first version is entirely preoccupied with squeezing the last ounce of comedy out of a pathetically ignorant pedant lecturing on a subject he knows nothing about. We see nothing of the human tragedy of such a man: the "inner man" remains completely hidden from the audience and only his outer shell is paraded before it in all its gaudy absurdity. The second version is still trying to achieve its effect by exposing the ridiculous idiosyncrasies of the old man, Chekhov peppering his speech with such expressions as "in view of the fact that" and "in a manner of speaking", but towards the end of the play the "inner man" bursts out of its absurd shell and stands (metaphorically and almost literally) naked before the audience. The third version dispenses entirely with cheap external effects and reveals the "inner man" with all his manifold psychological subtleties.

The play falls naturally into four parts. Already in the introductory part the gradual shift from outer to inner action can be clearly perceived. Thus, in the first version Nyukhin has a violent attack of asthma, in the second this is watered down to an attack of the hiccoughs, and in the third (very characteristically) it becomes a mere nervous twitching of an eyelid.

In the second part of the play, which deals with the incident of the pancakes which the schoolgirls are to have for dinner, Chekhov again gradually eliminates all the crudities which in the first version made his character into a caricature of a man. In the second version Nyukhin is conceived in much more human terms, though he is still unnecessarily encumbered by his idiosyncrasies of speech. It is only in the third version that he really comes to life.

The third part of the play has been even more drastically revised by Chekhov. The first and second versions consist of two incidents, namely Nyukhin's attempt to advertise his wife's school, which seemed to have been part of his duties as a public lecturer, and the trick the girls played on Nyukhin by putting some caustic powder in his snuffbox. The second incident, which again is used by Chekhov for some obvious stage business, is completely cut out in the third version of the play. The first incident is not so fully elaborated in the third version, Chekhov preferring instead to emphasis the propensity of people to blame their failures on some quite absurdly irrelevant facts.

All the changes so far effected by Chekhov concerned mainly the removal of crudities of expression and characterisation so as to eliminate any coarse, unthinking laughter in the audience and to evoke its sympathy with his character. The number of Nyukhin's daughters is reduced from 9 to 7; his pomposity is no longer stressed; his ignorance is taken for granted and not alluded to in order to get a cheap laugh out of the audience; the fact that he himself is a tobacco addict is not made into a comic scene but is just hinted at by the direct statement: "I am a smoker myself:" and the sentence revealing the real pathos of Nyukhin's situation: "To my wife's daughters I always say, 'Children, do not laugh at something that is higher than laughter'" becomes in the second version "To my wife's daughters I always say, 'Children, do not laugh at me, for you don't know what I feel in my heart'", and is further refined to the more moving, direct and simple statement of fact, "I tell them, but they only laugh."

It is, however, in the last part of the play that Chekhov reveals to the audience the real tragedy of a man like Nyukhin, whose only desire is "to chuck everything" and "run from this silly and trivial life and—and to stop somewhere far, far away, in the middle of a field, and stand there like a tree beneath the wide sky and gaze all night at the bright and gentle moon, and to forget, to forget. . . ." The actual ending of the play is practically identical in the second and the third versions, but to make it really effective Chekhov removed from the last part anything that might interfere with the emotional reaction of the audience, such as Nyukhin's appeal to the young men to marry his daughters and even the comic surname of his sister-in-law which would have brought the wrong kind of laugh at the most vital moment in the play.

Chekhov's formula of "life as it is," as can be seen from the different versions of On the Harmfulness of Tobacco, has undergone a radical change in the course of time. The point he had made when writing The Wood Demon that "in life people do not shoot themselves, or hang themselves, or fall in love every moment" and that therefore on the stage, too, "people should come and go, have dinner, talk of the weather, or play cards" not because the author wanted it but because that was how things happened in real life, was based on a fallacy that he was to recognise very soon. For the things that ordinarily happen in life become drab and uninteresting on the stage. One might quite possibly come across a Nyukhin of the first version in real life, shorn no doubt of his music-hall trimmings, but one would never come across the Nyukhin of the third version, for no Nyukhin would be able to address an audience in such a way as to reveal the inner tragedy of his life in a dramatically satisfactory form. To reveal the inner substance of his characters on the stage, that is to say, to show them as they really are and not as they appear to be in real life, Chekhov had to go back to, and improve on, a type of drama that was not so much concerned with the highly dramatic events in the lives of its characters as with the effect those events had on them. This drama of indirect action is, in fact, much more complex in construction and more rigid in its adherence to the laws of the stage than the more common drama of direct action. Deprived of their "dramatically effective situations," the ability of such plays to hold the attention of the audience depends largely on a number of elements through which the functions of action are expressed. Most of these elements are present in Greek drama which is essentially a drama of indirect-action; others represent Chekhov's own contribution as an innovator in dramatic art. Together they provide a key both to a proper understanding of Chekhov's last plays and to the way they ought to be presented on the stage, if, that is, those responsible for their presentation are anxious to discover Chekhov's intentions rather than to follow their own fancies or "inspiration."

# PART IV

---

## Plays of Indirect Action

# 15

# *Basic elements*

THE DIFFERENT theories advanced by critics in and outside Russia to explain the nature of Chekhov's plays reveal a curious confusion of thought. This is mainly due to the inability to discover the general principles which, in Chekhov's own words, "lie at the very basis of the value of a work of art." The most common of these theories is that the plays are entirely devoid of action, plot, and subject-matter. Enough has already been said about the paramount importance of action in all Chekhov's plays. As for plot, it is not its absence but rather its complexity that distinguishes them, and the producer who fails to realise that simply cannot see the wood for the trees. Again, the plays of Chekhov are packed with subject-matter, each of them teeming with the most diverse themes dealing with the great problems of life, man's future, man's duty to society, and so on. Some critics, while admitting the presence of a well-defined plot in Chekhov's plays, seem to think that it only emerges in the last two acts. This leads them to the conclusion that one of the characteristic features of a Chekhov play of the last period is that its action does not centre round one chief character. But that is equally true of many direct-action plays, particularly those of Alexander Ostrovsky, the action of which does not revolve round one chief character.

None of these generally accepted views is therefore correct. There are, however, two more characteristic features of Chekhov's indirect-action plays that must be considered. The first concerns the difference between the dialogue of Chekhov's early plays and that of his late ones. The dialogue of the early plays is remarkable for the directness of its appeal to the audience, while in the late plays its appeal is indirect and, mainly, evocative. Take, for example, the opening scene of *Ivanov*. As the curtain rises Ivanov is discovered sitting at a table in the garden of his house reading a book. It is evening, and a lamp is burning on the table. Borkin, the manager of his estate, who has been out shooting, comes in with a shotgun, steals up to Ivanov and takes aim at him. Ivanov jumps up with a start.

IVANOV. What on earth are you doing, Michael? You made me jump. I'm upset as it is, and now you come along with your silly jokes. (*Sits down.*) Made me jump and looks as pleased as Punch about it.

BORKIN (*roars with laughter*). All right, all right—I'm sorry, old man. (*Sits down beside Ivanov.*) I'm hot. Covered fifteen miles in about three hours—upon my word, I have. I'm dead beat. Feel my heart—it's pounding.

IVANOV (*reading*). All right, later.

BORKIN. No, feel it now. (*Takes Ivanov's hand and puts it to his chest.*) Do you hear? Thump-thump-thump-thump. That means that I have a weak heart. I may die suddenly any minute. Will you be sorry if I die?

IVANOV. I'm reading—later——

BORKIN. No, seriously, would you be sorry if I died suddenly?

IVANOV. Don't pester me!

BORKIN. Please, tell me: will you be sorry?

IVANOV. I'm sorry you reek of vodka. That, Michael, is disgusting.

BORKIN (*laughs*). Do I? That's funny. . . .

Compare this with the opening scene of *The Seagull*, which also takes place in a garden in the evening. Again there are only two characters: Masha and Medvedenko, who have just returned from a stroll.

MEDVEDENKO. Why do you always go about in black?

MASHA. Because I'm in mourning for my life. I'm unhappy.

MEDVEDENKO. Why? (*Wonderingly.*) I don't understand. I mean, there's nothing the matter with your health, and even if your father isn't rich, he's not badly off, either. My life is much harder than yours. I only get twenty-three roubles a month, and I have my insurance deducted from that. But I don't wear mourning, do I? (*They sit down.*)

MASHA. Money's not everything. Even a pauper can be happy.

MEDVEDENKO. That's all very well in theory, but in practice it's quite a different matter. I have to provide for my mother, my two sisters, my little brother and myself, and all on a salary of twenty-three roubles. We have to eat and drink, haven't we? We have to get tea and sugar, haven't we? And tobacco? It's a problem all right.

MASHA (*glancing at the stage*). The play will be starting soon.

MEDVEDENKO. Yes. Nina will be acting in it, and the play itself was written by Konstantin. They are in love. Tonight their souls will unite in the effort to give expression to one and the same artistic idea. But your soul and mine have no common points of contact. I'm in love with you. I long for you so terribly that I find it impossible to stay at home. Every day I walk four miles here and four miles back, but all I get from you is cold indifference. Well, I can't say I'm surprised at it. After all, I have no money, and I have a family to support. What's the use of marrying a man who can't even provide for himself?

MASHA. That's not important. (*Takes a pinch of snuff.*) I'm touched by your love, but I can't return it—that's all. (*Holds out the snuffbox to him.*) Help yourself.

MEDVEDENKO. Thank you, I don't feel like it. (*A pause.*)

The difference between these two scenes is not that the first one is active and the second one inactive. As a matter of fact, the second one requires a great deal more acting than the first one. The difference lies mainly in the different impact on the audience: the impact of the first is direct and immediate, the impact of the second is indirect and evocative, that is to say, since the characters in the second play are introspective, they arouse in the audience an emotional mood which is identical with their own. In other words, while in Chekhov's early plays the dialogue is mainly dramatic, it is mainly evocative or poetic in his last plays. This evocative nature of his dialogue Chekhov obtains in many ways. In the opening scene of *The Seagull* (a play saturated with echoes from *Hamlet*), Masha's appearance in her black dress at once strikes the note that will be characteristic of the whole play, and especially of the conflict between Arkadina and Konstantine. In all his last plays Chekhov intensifies the evocative power of his dialogue by the prodigal use of literary echoes, random quotations from the Russian classics that he either works into his dialogue or quotes fully, references to Russian authors (for instance, Dobrolyubov), which his audience would immediately understand, snatches of folk songs, and so on. He did it also in his early plays, but much more rarely and with no attempt to create this identity of mood between the stage and the auditorium. Unfortunately, these evocative undertones in the dialogue are completely lost in the translation, with the result that an English version of a Chekhov play distorts the emotional reaction it is meant to set up in the audience, creating the impression that the characters express themselves so oddly because they are "Russians".

Chekhov's dialogue is therefore a very subtle instrument for evoking the right mood in the audience and in this way preparing it for the development of the action of the play. It is no longer the colloquial prose Chekhov used in his early plays and in *The Wood Demon*, but a prose that is highly charged with emotional undertones, or, in other words, a poetic prose. (It was Aristotle who pointed out that it was not the "verse" that made the poet but the "imitation", that is, the ability to create living characters on the stage.) But the evocation of a mood is not by itself sufficient to create that feeling of suspense in the spectator which will not only keep him interested in what is happening on the stage, but also help him to identify himself, indeed to merge himself, with the characters in the play. A much stronger stimulus is needed for that. The reader, Chekhov advised Leontyev as early as January 8th, 1888, must never be allowed to rest: he must be kept in a state of suspense. And if that is true of a reader of a short story, how much more is it true of a spectator in the theatre. Tension in an indirect-action play is, therefore, one of the main motive forces of action. In a Greek play it arose out of the spectator's knowledge of the main dramatic events in the story. The play was, in the main, a mere dramatisation of a well-known legend, and the spectator's interest was aroused even before the appearance of the actors on the stage: he was all agog to see how the playwright and the actors would interpret the characters of a story that was rich in dramatic events which he knew and in which he even believed. Chekhov had to invent another method to convey this tension to his audience at the very beginning of the play. He did it by showing one of his main characters in a state of high nervous tension, like, for instance, Konstantin in the opening scenes of *The Seagull* or Voynitsky in the opening scenes of *Uncle Vanya*. Failure on the part of the actor to convey this highly overwrought state of the character he is representing will destroy this feeling of tension with the result that the play as a whole will become dull and flat, and this fact alone is indeed responsible for the impression that Chekhov's plays are devoid of action and movement, both of which, as noted earlier, Chekhov esteemed above everything else in a dramatic work.

Another powerful impetus to action and movement is provided in an indirect-action play by the presence of "invisible" characters. In a Greek play it is mostly the gods who determine the fate of the characters. The presence of these "invisible" characters in a Chekhov play has been noted by many critics, who are merely content to record it as another characteristic feature of a Chekhov play. But what is the purpose of these non-existent characters? For instance, Nina's parents in *The Seagull*, Protopopov in *The Three Sisters*, and Mrs. Ranevsky's aunt and her Paris lover in *The Cherry Orchard*? In a play of direct action they would be allowed to take an active part on the stage, for they all occupy an important place in the plot and without them the final dénouement would be impossible. In an indirect action play, however, it is necessary that they, like the supernatural powers in a Greek play, should remain invisible, for their function is to supply a motive force for the action which is all the more powerful because the audience never sees them but is made to *imagine* them. (In *Ivanov* there are no such "invisible" characters and their presence in the play is indeed quite uncalled for.)

The main elements through which action is expressed in an indirect-action play are: the "messenger" element, the function of which is to keep the audience informed about the chief dramatic incidents which takes place off stage (in a direct-action play this element is, as a rule, a structural flaw); the arrival and departure of the characters in the play round which the chief incidents that take place on the stage are grouped; the presence of a chorus which, as Aristotle points out, "forms an integral part of the whole play and shares in the action"; peripetia, that is, the reversal of the situation leading up to the dénouement, which Aristotle defines as "a change by which the action veers round to its opposite, subject always to the rule of probability and necessity", and which is the most powerful element of emotional interest in indirect-action plays and their main instrument for sustaining suspense and arousing surprise; and, lastly, background which lends depth to such plays.

The messenger element is perhaps the most difficult one to manage satisfactorily as it tends to impede the action and divert the attention of the audience from it. Chekhov's first attempts to introduce it in *The Wood Demon* (it is absent in *Ivanov*) was far from successful. Take one small instance from the first and second versions of Act IV:

KHRUSHCHOV. . . . Twenty thousand sickening disasters! Shimansky has sold his forest for felling timber—that's one! Orlovsky is dangerously ill—he's contracted typhus and apparently pneumonia, too—that's two! Helen has run away with that ass Fyodor and no one knows where she is—that's three! Whether she's gone away somewhere or has poisoned or drowned herself—you can take your choice!

This becomes in the second version:

. . . Twenty thousand sickening disasters! Shimansky has sold his forest for felling timber—that's one! Helen has run away

from her husband and no one knows where she is—that's
two! I feel that I'm getting more and more stupid every day
—that's three!

Now, in the first and second versions the fact that some landowner by the name of Shimansky has sold his forest is of no
interest at all to the audience, since Shimansky does not take any
part in the action and has been dragged in by the scruff of the
neck to explain Khrushchov's annoyance. But there are plenty
of other reasons why he should feel annoyed. In the first version
the audience is kept in the dark as to Helen's fate and the news
of her disappearance is quite a legitimate use of the messenger
element, but in the second version Helen appears in the first
scene with Dyadin and Khrushchov's outburst is a bit of an anti-
climax. The news about Orlovsky in the first version would have
been a legitimate use of the messenger element if it were
not so obviously a *deus ex machina* trick. The audience knows
about Helen's abduction by Fyodor and her disappearance is
therefore a new development in the action of the play. But it knows
nothing at all about Orlovsky's illness, and this melodramatic
announcement of it is too transparently introduced in anticipation
of the no less melodramatic conversion of Fyodor at the end of
the play.

The messenger element must therefore concern itself strictly
with the action of the play and contribute to its development.
At the beginning of the play it serves the purely functional purpose of informing the audience about the events that have happened before the opening of the first scene, and at the end of the
play it helps to sustain and to satisfy the curiosity of the audience.
Chekhov's great art as a playwright is best revealed in the superb
way in which he handles the messenger element. In the opening
scene of *The Cherry Orchard* he reduces the narrative part to a
minimum, and yet the situation is immediately clear; nor does the
scene drag in the least: it is charged with tension and full of action:

*Enter* Dunya *with a candle and* Lopakhin *with a book in his hand.*
LOPAKHIN. The train has arrived, thank goodness. What's the
time?

DUNYA. Nearly two o'clock. (*Puts out the candle.*) It's daylight
     already.

LOPAKHIN. The train must have been at least two hours late.
     (*Yawns and stretches himself.*) And what a damned fool I am!
     Came here specially to meet them at the station and fell
     asleep. Sat down in a chair and dropped off. What a nuisance!
     Why didn't you wake me?

DUNYA. I thought you'd gone. (*Listens.*) I think they're coming.

LOPAKHIN (*listens*). No . . . I should have been there to help them
     with the luggage and so on. (*Pause.*) Mrs. Ranevsky has
     been abroad five years—I wonder what she's like now. She's
     such a nice person. Always so kind and so easy to get on with.
     I remember when I was a boy of fifteen my father—he used
     to keep a shop in the village in those days—hit me in the face
     with his fist and made my nose bleed. We'd gone into the
     yard to fetch something, and he was drunk. Mrs. Ranevsky
     —I remember it as if it happened yesterday—she was such a
     young girl then and so thin—took me to the washstand
     in this very room, the nursery. "Don't cry, little peasant,"
     she said to me, "it'll be all right by the time you get married."
     (*Pause.*) Little peasant! My father, it's true, was a peasant,
     but I go about in a white waist-coat and brown shoes, like a
     jackdaw in peacock's feathers! Mind you, I'm rich, I've
     got pots of money, but when you come to think of it, I'm
     just a plain peasant still. (*Turns over the pages of the book.*) I've
     been reading this book, but I couldn't understand a word of
     it. Fell asleep reading it. (*Pause.*)

DUNYA. The dogs have been awake all night—they know their
     mistress is coming.

LOPAKHIN. What's the matter with you, Dunya? You're in such
     a——

DUNYA. My hands are shaking. I'm going to faint.

The remarkable fact about *The Seagull* is that Chekhov dispenses with the messenger element in the first three acts altogether
and when he comes to use it in the fourth act he can afford to
take it at a more leisurely pace, for by that time the curiosity of
the audience has been sufficiently aroused and he runs no risk
of boring them. Still, he has to invent a special situation to make
it more acceptable: he has to send Dorn away to Italy so as to

THE SEAGULL, Moscow Art Theatre.
*Above:* First production, 1898. Act III: Arkadina (Knipper),
Sorin (Luzhsky)
*Below:* 1905 production. Act II: Masha (Savitskaya), Arkadina
(Knipper), Nina (Lilina), Dorn (Vishnevsky), Sorin (Luzhsky),
Medvedenko (Tikhomirov)

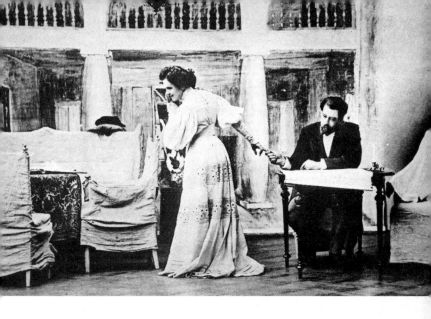

UNCLE VANYA, Moscow Art Theatre, first production, 1899.
*Left:* Act I: Marina (Samarova), Helen (Knipper), Astrov (Stanislavsky), Telegin (Artyom), Serebryakov (Luzhsky), Sonia (Petrova), Vanya (Vishnevsky)
*Above:* Act III: Helen (Knipper), Astrov (Stanislavsky)
*Below:* Act III: Helen (Knipper), Marina (Samarova), Sonia (Lilina), Serebryakov (Luzhsky)

THE THREE SISTERS, Moscow Art Theatre, first production, 1901.
*Above:* Act II: Vershinin (Stanislavsky), Kulygin (Vishnevsky), Irene (Litovtseva), Olga (Savitskaya)
*Below:* Act IV: Vershinin (Stanislavsky), Mary (Knipper), Olga (Savitskaya), Irene (Litovtseva)

IVANOV, Moscow Art Theatre, first production, 1904.
*Left:* Act I: Lvov (Moskvin), Sarah (Knipper)
*Above:* Act II: Sarah (Knipper), Ivanov (Luzhsky), Sasha (Tarina)
*Below:* Act III: Sarah (Knipper), Ivanov (Luzhsky)

THE CHERRY ORCHARD, Moscow Art Theatre, first
production, 1904. Stanislavsky as Gayev

make him ask all the right questions when the time comes for Konstantin to acquaint the audience with the highly dramatic events that have taken place in the interval between Act III and Act IV. Chekhov handles the scene with consummate skill.

Dorn, asked by Medvedenko which city abroad he liked best, replies that it was Genoa, and when again asked to give his reasons, he describes how when moving in the crowded streets of the Italian city he felt as though he became merged with the crowds and became one with them in spirit, which made him believe in the existence of the world soul Nina had acted in Konstantin's play. He then goes on, naturally enough, to ask where Nina is and how she is getting on.

KONSTANTIN. I believe she is quite well.

DORN. I was told she had been leading a queer sort of life. What did happen?

KONSTANTIN. Oh, it's a long story, doctor.

DORN. All right, make it short then. (*Pause.*)

KONSTANTIN. She ran away from home and went to live with Trigorin. You know that, don't you?

DORN. Yes, I know that.

KONSTANTIN. She had a child. The child died. Trigorin got tired of her and went back to his old attachments, as might have been expected. Not that he had ever really broken with his old attachments but, being the spineless character he is, he somehow contrived to make the best of both worlds. As far as I can gather, Nina's private life has turned out a complete failure.

DORN. And her stage career?

KONSTANTIN. Her stage career was an even worse failure, I believe. Her first appearance on the stage was at a holiday resort near Moscow. She then went away to the provinces. At that particular time I never lost sight of her, and for some months I used to follow her about wherever she went. She always took big parts, but her acting was crude, without a trace of good taste. She ranted and gesticulated wildly. Now and then she would utter a cry that showed that she had some talent or she would do a death scene really well—but those were only moments.

DORN. So she has some talent after all.

KONSTANTIN. I don't know. It's hard to say. I suppose she must have. I saw her of course, but she would not see me. I was never admitted to her hotel room. I realised how she felt and I did not insist on meeting her. (*Pause.*) Well, what more do you want to know? Later, after I had returned home, I used to get letters from her. Affectionate, intelligent, interesting letters. She never complained, but I couldn't help feeling that she was very unhappy, every line showing that her nerves were on edge. And her mind seemed a little unhinged, too. She always signed herself: "The Seagull". In Pushkin's *Water Nymph* the miller calls himself a raven, but in her letters she kept repeating that she was a seagull. Now she's here.

DORN. How do you mean—here?

KONSTANTIN. She's staying at an inn in the town. She's been there for the last five days. I nearly went to see her, but Masha has been there and it seems she won't see anyone. Medvedenko assures me that he saw her yesterday walking across a field about a mile and a half from here.

The scene is completely natural (and the messenger element does not lend itself so easily to naturalness) and it is punctuated with what Stanislavsky used to call "pauses of tragic action", that is to say, pauses during which Konstantin has to *act* and not just sit silent and look embarrassed, as, unfortunately, so many actors do. He has to make the audience aware of the agonies he has been through, and he has to convey it all, to quote Chekhov himself, "with his tone of voice and *with his eyes*".

The arrival and departure element is one of the most indispensable elements in an indirect action play. It introduces action of a purely external kind, fills the stage with noise and bustle, and provides the producer with inexhaustible opportunities for stage effects of the most varied sort. The whole action of the play, in fact, leads up to and centres round this element, and Chekhov took the greatest possible advantage of it. In *The Seagull* it provides him with a magnificent climax in the third act and helps him to heighten the suspense in the last. In *Uncle Vanya* it helps him to contrive a most moving anti-climax in the last act. In *The*

*Three Sisters* the entire action is built round it, and in *The Cherry Orchard* it gives him a fine dramatic opening and an ending of great poignancy. It is an element that is particularly welcome to producers who are incapable of dealing with indirect-action plays, and indeed it is the only element producers of Chekhov's plays have made full use of as a function of action.

The chorus element is another indispensable feature of the play of indirect-action. In Greek drama it was a special actor, or groups of actors, who gave expression to the moral and religious sentiments evoked by the action of the play. In the French pseudo-classical drama it was again a special actor who was entrusted with the task of passing a moral judgment on the characters, known in the Russian early pseudo-classical plays as the *raisonneur,* a somewhat tedious character spouting conventional moral sentiments. But quite often in a modern indirect-action play the rôle of the chorus is divided up between several characters, who stand apart from the main characters and are not directly involved in the action. In a Chekhov play, however, it is the characters themselves who provide the moral judgment on the action, and in it the chorus element therefore becomes an integral part of the whole play, as Aristotle urged the Greek playwrights to make it. His characters, as it were, assume the mantle of the chorus whenever their inner life bursts through the outer shell of their everyday appearance and overflows into a torrent of words. It is this spontaneous and almost palpable transmutation into speech of hidden thoughts and deeply buried emotions that is perhaps the most subtle expression of dramatic action in a Chekhov play. If not treated as such, it is liable to transform these flashes of self-revelation into static, isolated and disconnected statements of opinion. It is important to remember that no other great classical Russian playwright has employed this method of revealing the "inner man" of his character and that the notion, which is so common in England and America, that the Chekhov characters express themselves in such a way because they are "Russians" is entirely mistaken. Chekhov himself offered a very clear indication of his use of the chorus element in the opening scene of

*The Three Sisters*, a play in which it is predominant. Indeed, the scenery of the first act of the play was conceived by Chekhov in the form of a Greek theatre: he divided the stage into two parts separated by a colonnade, the front part representing a drawing-room and the back part a dining-room. There are six characters in the opening scene, divided into two groups, each keeping to its own part of the stage, the three sisters in front of the columns and Chebutykin, Tusenbach and Solyony behind the columns. Their dialogue, too, is conducted in a sort of strophe and antistrophe manner. (There is a strong admixture of the messenger element in the dialogue of the sisters.)

|  |  |
|---|---|
| *Strophe* | *Antistrophe* |

OLGA. It is just a year since father died—on this very day, the fifth of May—your birthday, Irene. It was dreadfully cold; it was snowing then. I felt as though I'd never be able to live through it and you were lying in a faint. But now a whole year has gone by and the thought of it no longer troubles us. You're wearing a white dress again, you look so radiant. (*The clock strikes twelve.*) Then, too, the clock struck twelve. (*Pause.*) I remember the military band playing at father's funeral, and they fired a salute at the cemetery. Though father was a General and a brigade commander, there were not many people at his funeral. It is true, it was

*Strophe*                          *Antistrophe*

raining then. Pouring with
rain and snowing.

IRENE. Why must you talk
about it?

 

 

*In the dining-room behind the columns, Baron Tusenbach, Chebutykin and Solyony appear at the table.*

OLGA. It is warm today—the
windows can be opened
wide—but the birch-trees
have not opened up yet.
It is eleven years since
father was given his
brigade and left Moscow
with us, and, I distinctly
remember it, the flowers
were in bloom in Moscow
just at this time—at the
beginning of May—oh, it
was so warm then, and
everything was drenched in
sunlight. Eleven years have
passed and I can remember
everything just as if we had
left Moscow only yester-
day. My goodness! When
I woke up this morning
and saw the bright sunshine
—saw the spring—my
heart leapt for joy, and I
felt such a longing to be
back home!

CHEBUTYKIN. The devil you did!
TUSENBACH. It's all nonsense,
of course!

*Mary, daydreaming over her
book, whistles a tune softly.*

OLGA. Don't whistle, Mary.

*Strophe*                                    *Antistrophe*

How can you! I suppose it's
because I'm at school all
day and then giving
lessons in the evenings
that I'm getting these
constant headaches and
these thoughts, just as
if I were old already.
And, really, all these four
years while I've been
working at school I've
felt as though my strength
and my youth were drain-
ing out of me drop by
drop. And one longing
only grows stronger and
stronger——

IRENE. To go to Moscow. Sell
the house, finish with
everything here and leave
for Moscow.

OLGA. Yes! To Moscow as soon
as possible.

*Chebutykin and Tusenbach
laugh.*

And the scene goes on till Tusenbach, clearly as a comment on
the plans of the sisters, though actually addressing Chebutykin,
says: "What nonsense you talk—I'm sick of listening to you."
The two groups then join and the action of the play really starts.
The end of the play, too, is composed entirely of a chorus scene
in which only the three sisters take part.

The most important element so far as the structure, the "architecture", as Chekhov called it, of a play of indirect-action is
concerned, is peripetia, the reversal of situation, which,
according to Aristotle, "arises from the internal structure of
the plot so that what follows should be the necessary or probable

result of the preceding action." Aristotle illustrates this element by a reference to *Oedipus* where, he points out, "the messenger comes to cheer Oedipus and free him from his anxiety about his mother, but by revealing who he (Oedipus) is, produces the opposite effect." This is the simplest and, no doubt, the most effective example of peripetia, but in Chekhov's plays of indirect-action this element assumes much more subtle forms. As it is so integral a part of the plot of the play, it will be discussed fully when the plays are analysed in detail.

The background element of a Chekhov indirect-action play consists of the realistic touches which lend actuality and intimacy to the life of the characters in it as well as of the not so easily defined literary undertones which lend a greater depth to it. These "literary undertones" may derive from an old story or a play by Chekhov himself or some other Russian playwright, notably Ostrovsky, or, as in *The Seagull* from *Hamlet*, which forms, as it were, an enigma variation in the symphonic score of the play: it is always present but only in one or two instances does it emerge clearly and unmistakably. For instance, in "the play within the play", which, as in *Hamlet*, comes to an abortive end because of the passions it arouses, or in the two quotations from *Hamlet*, which, as will be seen, are an essential part of the dramatic action of the first act, though they are usually omitted in a performance of the play on the English stage.

These are the main basic elements through which action is expressed in Chekhov's last plays. Where Chekhov's genius as a playwright, however, finds its most brilliant expression is in the entirely original form he gave to the indirect-action type of drama by a completely new and infinitely subtle combination of its basic elements, and in this sense Chekhov can be said to be one of the greatest innovators in modern drama.

# 16

# *The Seagull*

THE FIRST mention of his next play occurs in Chekhov's letter to Suvorin on March 31st, 1892. "When I start writing my play," Chekhov declared in that letter, "I shall want Ludwig Boerne's works. Where can I get them? Boerne is one of those clever fellows whom Jews and superficial people love so much." On the June 3rd of the same year Chekhov again referred to this play. "I have an interesting subject for a comedy," he wrote, "but I haven't thought of its ending so far. He who can invent new endings for a play, will start a new era. I can't get those endings right! The hero has either to get married or shoot himself. There is no other solution. The title of my future comedy is *The Cigarette Case*. I shall not start writing it before I have thought of an ending which is as tricky as the beginning. But when I have thought of an ending, I shall finish it in a fortnight." But he evidently could not think of the ending, for he did not mention the play again till January 10th, 1894, when he wrote to Suvorin that he hoped to write it in March. On February 16th he wrote to Suvorin: "This is what I want for my play if I am going to write it in the Crimea. Send me through your Moscow bookshop the works of Ludwig Boerne—that clever, frigid fellow. In my play I want to depict a gentleman who is always quoting Heine and Ludwig Boerne. To the women who love him he says like Insarov in Turgenev's *On the Eve*, 'Good morning, my wife in the eyes of God and men!' When left on the stage alone or with a woman, he gives himself airs, poses as a second Lassalle, a future president of the republic; in the company of men, however, he is silent and looks mysterious, and whenever he gets into an argument with them he becomes hysterical. He is of the Greek Orthodox faith, but he is dark-haired and his surname is Hinselt. He wants to publish a newspaper." In June and July he again referred to the same play, intending to write it "somewhere on the banks of Lake Como, or," he added, "even not write it at all, for this sort of thing can wait, and if it can't, then to hell with it".

Now, it is perfectly clear that the play Chekhov had in mind and that he tried in vain to write between 1892 and 1894 had nothing whatever to do with *The Seagull*. The point is important, for it shows that during those years he was still working out the technique of the new type of play that he was soon to write. And yet it is quite common to find Russian critics quoting the passage about the endings of plays as though it referred to *The Seagull*. Even as late as April 18th, 1895, that is to say, seven months before he sat down in the tiny hut on his estate in Melikhovo to write *The Seagull*, he declared in a letter to Suvorin: "I shall write a play, but not soon. I don't want to write dramas, *and I haven't thought of a subject for a comedy yet.*[1] I shall probably sit down to write a play in the autumn if I don't go abroad." On May 5th he promised his new play to Suvorin who had his own private theatre in Petersburg. "I shall write something strange," he told Suvorin. "I don't feel like writing for the Imperial theatre or for money. I have enough money to go on with and I can afford to write a play for which I shall get no money; but, of course," he was careful to add, as it turned out with good reason, "if my circumstances change, I shall sing a different tune."

Even in May, then, he had not yet thought of a subject for a play, though by that time he knew already that the play he was going to write would be "strange", that is, that it would be written in quite a different style from any of his previous plays and indeed from any other known play. Two months later something happened which provided Chekhov not only with the necessary impulse for the writing of *The Seagull* but also with the locale of the play without which the different pieces of the jigsaw puzzle he had in mind did not fit together. What

[1] My italics.

were those random pieces of literary and autobiographical material that Chekhov afterwards wove into the fabric of *The Seagull*? There was, first of all, his short story *A Boring Story*, written about six years earlier, in which, in addition to airing his ideas on literature and drama, he told the story of a stage-struck girl which is essentially similar to the story of Nina in *The Seagull*. It differs from Nina's story only in one point and that point is important to the understanding of the main theme of Chekhov's first indirect-action play. Katya, like Nina, went on the provincial stage. Like Nina, she fell in love, had a child by her lover, was jilted, and the child died. But unlike Nina, she left the stage and never returned to it. Why not? When her guardian, a professor of medicine who is the narrator of the story, asked her why she did not want to go back to the stage, she answered: "Do you want me to tell you the truth? All right, I will, if you wish. I have no talent! I have no talent and—and too much vanity! That's why!" She was, as she herself described herself, "a negative phenomenon". At the end of the story she follows the old professor to Kharkov. She comes to ask him what she ought to do with herself. "I can't live like that any more," she tells him. "I can't! For God's sake, tell me at once what am I to do? Tell me what am I to do?" But the professor can tell her nothing. She becomes hysterical. "Help me, help me!" she implores him. "I can't go on like this! . . . You're my only friend, I always looked on you as my father! You're intelligent, you're well educated, you've lived so long! Tell me what am I to do?" The old professor is moved by her tears, but all he can think of saying is that they should have breakfast. (She has arrived at the hotel early in the morning.) Katya smiles coldly, shakes hands with him, and goes away. And there the story ends. Katya's tragedy was that she had no talent or aim in life, that she did not know what to do with herself. Nina was different. She knew what she had to do because she had an aim in life and possessed real talent. It never occurred to her to leave the stage. Katya was rich, because her parents had left her a fortune. Nina was poor because her rich father had disinherited her. Yet in spite of that she carried on, for, unlike Katya, she possessed what Chekhov called "iron in the blood". It was to point this contrast, surely, that Chekhov used an identical set of circumstances in the lives of two of his heroines. He slightly altered a phrase he used in the same story and put it into the mouth of Trigorin to describe the sort of writer he was. In *A Boring Story* the old professor referred to the latest works of the writers of his day as "clever, high-minded, but not talented; talented, high-minded, but not clever, or, finally talented, clever, but not high-minded." Trigorin refers to his own writings in almost the same words as "charming and talented, but it's a far cry from Tolstoy!" (In his letter to Suvorin of November 25th, 1892, he already referred to these writers as "charming, talented".)

Chekhov went back to two of his other short stories for references in his play. Konstantin's reference to Trigorin's description of a moonlight night Chekhov took from his own short story *Wolf*. The lines Nina wanted Trigorin to look up were taken from his short story *The Neighbours*, though it was, of course, Lydia Avilov who first used them in her message to Chekhov: she had had the page and lines engraved on a watch chain pendant.[1]

Chekhov's letters also contain a great deal of material which he used in *The Seagull*. Before the performance of *Ivanov* in Petersburg he wrote to Suvorin: "The main thing so far as I am concerned, of course, is the money, but the details, too, interest me. For instance, I am amused at the thought that . . . all the dark-haired men in the audience will seem to be hostile to me and the fair-haired ones cold and indifferent." Trigorin uses the same words to Nina in describing his experience at a first performance of his play: "I have the odd feeling that the dark-haired people in the audience are my enemies and the fair-haired ones are cold and indifferent." There is again the famous incident with the woodcock he described in a letter to Suvorin on April 8th, 1892. He had accompanied his friend Levitan, the famous Russian landscape painter, on a shooting expedition. Levitan fired at a

[1] See *Chekhov in my Life*, by Lydia Avilov.

woodcock and winged it. The bird fell into a puddle. "I picked
it up," Chekhov wrote: "A long beak, large black eyes and
beautiful plumage. What was to be done with it? Levitan made a
wry face, shut his eyes and asked me in a trembling voice: 'Hit
it on the head, there's a good fellow.' I told him I couldn't do it.
He went on twitching his shoulders nervously, pulling a face and
asking me to kill the bird. The woodcock in the meantime kept
looking at us with surprise. I had to give in and kill it. There was
one beautiful creature less in the world and two fools went back
home and sat down to supper." This horror at the senseless
destruction of a beautiful bird he was later to make into one of
the most moving scenes in his play.

The first reference to Medvedenko, the village teacher in *The
Seagull*, can also be found in a letter to Suvorin. Describing his
visit to a village school, Chekhov wrote on November 27th,
1894: "The teacher gets 23 roubles a month, he has a wife and four
children and his hair is already grey although he is only thirty. He
is so crushed by his life that whatever you happen to be saying,
he turns the conversation to the subject of his salary. In his opinion,
poets and novelists must only write about the necessity of raising
the salaries of teachers; when the new Czar appoints his new
Cabinet, the salary of teachers will quite probably be increased,
and so on." It is interesting that in his notebook Chekhov describes Medvedenko as "a teacher, 32, with a grey beard."
Medvedenko's portrait, indeed, is a faithful copy of the teacher
described in the letter to Suvorin, except, of course, that at the
beginning of the play Medvedenko is still unmarried.

Another reference to a line Konstantin uses in Act IV of the
play can be found in a letter Chekhov wrote to the Russian
writer A. Zhirkevich on April 5th, 1895. He was criticising the
clichés Zhirkevich used in a short story he had sent to Chekhov
for criticism. "Now," Chekhov wrote, "only lady novelists
write 'the poster announced' or 'a face framed by hair'," the
exact expressions Konstantin crosses out as he reads through one
of his own stories in Act IV of the play.

In *The Seagull* one also gets glimpses of Chekhov's life in

Melikhovo. The avenue of trees where Konstantin puts up his stage in the first act is the fine avenue of trees in Chekhov's Melikhovo garden. The most popular game in Chekhov's family circle was loto. But, of course, the most intimate incident of Chekhov's Melikhovo life that left its mark on the play was the affair between Chekhov's friend, the novelist and playwright Ignatius Potapenko, and Lydia Mizinov, a friend of Chekhov's sister and a general favourite of the Chekhov family. Lydia, or Leeka as she was known to her friends, was a very jolly girl, a rather stout blonde, who possessed a great fund of natural gaiety, and whenever she came to Melikhovo "everybody," as Chekhov's younger brother Michael put it, "cheered up". Leeka fell in love with Chekhov, but finding that he did not exactly, to use another of Michael's expressions, "burn with passion for her", she transferred her affections to Potapenko. Now, as has already been explained, Chekhov took the Nina-Trigorin situation from *A Boring Story*, but in *The Seagull* Nina's lover is a novelist while in the short story Katya's lover was an actor. There is no doubt that in making this change Chekhov had the Potapenko-Leeka affair in mind, for in his first version of the play, which has not been preserved, the resemblance of Trigorin to Potapenko was so striking that Suvorin, to whom Chekhov sent the play, immediately spotted it. In his reply to Suvorin on December 16th, 1895, Chekhov wrote: "My play (*The Seagull*) has failed without seeing the footlights. If it really seems that I have put Potapenko in it, then it is of course impossible either to publish or to perform it." As his first version of the play, however, was only a rough draft, he soon eliminated the Potapenko idiosyncrasies from Trigorin's character.

By July 1895 Chekhov already possessed a large number of facts, both literary and personal, which he later incorporated in *The Seagull*. By October the play had already taken shape in his mind. What happened in between to make all these facts fit together and to set his creative genius ablaze so that he could finish the first draft of the play in about four weeks? Something must have occurred that moved him deeply and at the same time

supplied him with the one missing fact without which the play did
not hang together. What happened was that Chekhov's best
friend, the landscape painter Levitan, who suffered from fits of
depression all his life, attempted to commit suicide. Levitan was
at the time staying on the estate of a rich woman landowner in
what might be called the lake district of the province of Novgorod.
Her country house was near the banks of a large lake. Summoned
by a telegram, Chekhov immediately hurried off to his friend,
who fortunately was only slightly wounded, and discovered the
"fiendish" lake which provided him with the vital "seagull
theme". (The lakes in that district are not so very far from the
sea and there are undoubtedly many seagulls to be seen there.)
As Levitan's attempted suicide was naturally hushed up (in a
letter to Suvorin Chekhov merely wrote that he had been summoned "to a patient"), all sorts of fanciful stories arose about the
origin of the "seagull" theme in the play. One of these, particularly,
has gained currency because it is mentioned as a fact in Nicolai
Efros's well-known essay on *The Seagull*. Efros was the first
aesthete-critic to bury Chekhov's plays under a rubble-heap of
supersensitive impressions. His account of the origin of the "seagull" theme is characteristic. "Somehow or other," he writes,
"one summer Chekhov found himself on the estate of a rich
Petersburg civil servant in the province of Novgorod, on the
shores of a big lake, surrounded by a few more estates. Levitan, this
Chekhov of landscape painting, also stayed there. The lake, as in
*The Seagull*, was a 'magic' one. Love was in the air. In one love
affair, which almost ended tragically, Levitan was involved. This
had nothing to do with *The Seagull*. It was more of a Maupassant
type. But, all the same, this love affair, and particularly the environment in which it took place, the lake with the different
estates, etc., found its reflection in the play, having emerged in
Chekhov's mind, when, under different impressions and impulses,
*The Seagull* began to take shape. And so two currents have become
whimsically intermingled."

The whole story, of course, is "whimsical". Efros must have
heard rumours of Levitan's attempted suicide (he did not know

of his fits of depression or that at that time he was already suffering from an incurable heart disease). He had also heard of Levitan's somewhat complicated affair with the owner of the Novgorod estate and it was perhaps natural that he should imagine a love story of "a Maupassant type" with an "almost" tragic ending. He certainly got the dates hopelessly wrong. The "love in the air" bit, too, is pure fiction, in fact a "reflection" from Chekhov's play. Indeed, as Efros himself admits, Levitan's affair had nothing to do with *The Seagull*.

No less typical is the other apocryphal story Efros tells in the same essay. "With Levitan," he writes, "is undoubtedly connected the episode—one of the gems of the drama—which gives it its name. The painter, either on the Volga or in Babkino, for some unknown reason, impelled by a sportsman's high spirits, shot a seagull. Deeply grieved at this senseless act of cruelty, he swore never to go out shooting again and put the white seagull at the feet of Chekhov's sister with the words, 'I lay this vile deed of mine at your feet.' However, he went on shooting." There is not a scrap of evidence to support this story. The only incident that bears any resemblance to it is Chekhov's account of the shooting of the woodcock, which indeed Efros relates as "something analogical". Efros's story is full of vague and contradictory statements. It seemed to have happened either on the Volga or hundreds of miles away on the Babkino estate near Moscow.

Another version is supplied by Michael, who claims that Chekhov told him that Levitan had torn off the black bandage he was wearing round his head and thrown it on the floor during an explanation with his "lady." He then went out to the lake and returned with a shot seagull which he flung at her feet. It seems unlikely that Chekhov, who had only three years earlier been involved in a serious quarrel with Levitan for using some intimate details from the painter's private life in one of his stories, should have used two actual incidents in his play. Be that as it may, the fact remains that Chekhov was not staying at the Novgorod estate, as Efros asserts, but was summoned by telegram to Levitan's bedside. He remained there for less than a week and, after a short visit to Petersburg, was back in Melikhovo by the middle of July. But his short visit to the Novgorod estate with its big lake provided him with the missing piece of the jigsaw puzzle: now everything fell into its place and the play as a whole began to assume the complex form of human destiny inextricably bound up with the deep-rooted passions of its characters.

Chekhov began to write *The Seagull* in October, 1895. After telling Suvorin in a letter on October 21st, that he was planning to start building a new village school, he went on: "Just imagine, I am writing a play which I shall probably not finish before the end of November. I am writing it not without pleasure, though I am sinning terribly against the rules of the stage. A comedy, three female parts, six male, four acts, landscape (view of a lake); a great deal of talk about literature, little action, five tons of love." On November 2nd, he wrote to Suvorin: "My play is growing, but slowly. People constantly interfere with my writing. But I still hope to finish it in November. I have frequent headaches. No money." And on November 7th in a letter to the woman writer Shavrova: "I am writing a play for the Moscow Maly Theatre." Three days later he wrote to Suvorin again: "My play is progressing; for the time being everything is going on smoothly, but what will happen later, at the end, I don't know. I shall finish it in November. Pchelnikov[1] promised through Nemirovich to give me an advance in January (provided the play is accepted); so it may be worth my while to put off the production till next season. My palpitations have grown more frequent, probably because of the play. I fall asleep late and generally feel rotten, though on my return from Moscow I am leading an abstemious life in every way." On November 18th he wrote to Shavrova that the play was finished. "It is called thus: The Seagull. On the whole," he hastened to add, "I am rather an indifferent playwright."

In considering Chekhov's strictures on his new play and on himself as a playwright, one must bear in mind that he wrote them while engaged in the process of creation, at a time, that is, when he was hardly likely to form a proper judgment and when

[1] The manager of the Moscow office of the Imperial theatre.

the play was still no more than a rough draft. What the first version of *The Seagull* was like it is impossible to say, except perhaps from a few remarks in a letter to Suvorin on November 21st. It is usual, however, for critics to take these remarks to be Chekhov's opinion on the finished play. In his letter to Suvorin, for instance, he declares that he wrote the play against all the accepted rules of the stage, which is true enough, but he adds that he began it "forte" and finished it "pianissimo". Chekhov goes on to say that he was more dissatisfied than satisfied and that, on re-reading the play, he was again convinced that he was not a dramatist. That is undoubtedly true if, as is likely, he meant by a dramatist a writer of direct-action plays. The whole letter, how-ever, was prompted by his feeling of dissatisfaction with the first rough draft of the play.

*The Seagull*, as is abundantly clear from the quoted passages, was written in a feverish rush, in a state of high tension, and con-sidering that its dramatic style was entirely new, it is not surprising that Chekhov should have failed to produce a finished master-piece at once. Indeed, he warned Suvorin in the same letter that he was sending him only "the skeleton of the play, which will be altered a million times before the next season".

After Suvorin's criticism of the play and especially his remark about Trigorin's resemblance to Potapenko, Chekhov sat down to revise it. He must have spent about three months on its revision. In a letter to his brother Alexander on March 8th, 1896, he wrote: "I am busy with the play. I am altering it." On March 15th he sent it to the censorship. He received the play back on August 11th, the censor underlining several passages which he wanted altered. Most of these passages related to Konstantin's attitude to his mother's relations with Trigorin, the censor demanding that Konstantin should not comment on them at all and should not even seem to be aware of them. Chekhov cut out one or two sentences, but the censor was still not mollified. However, Pota-penko, who was conducting the negotiations with the censor on behalf of Chekhov, succeeded in getting the play passed for the stage after making a few more small alterations in the text. The play was put on at the Alexandrinsky Theatre on October 17th and its failure has now become an historic example of how a play can be killed by people without understanding and vision. The chief blame for its failure must be borne by the producer of the Alexandrinsky Theatre, E. Karpov, whom Chekhov met for the first time in 1888 and whose play he had characterised in a letter to Suvorin as "incompetent rubbish" and "a travesty of life". That the fate of a play like *The Seagull* should be placed in the hands of a man like Karpov merely emphasises the utter helplessness of the playwright in those days. Karpov later tried to justify himself by publishing a long account of his production of *The Seagull* and, as was to be expected, putting all the blame on the management of the theatre. His apology, however, contains a very interesting description of Chekhov's behaviour at the rehearsals of the play (there were only nine rehearsals, Chekhov being present at five of them, beginning with the fourth). "Chekhov," Karpov writes, "winced at every false note uttered by the actors and at their conventional intonations. In spite of his inborn shyness, he often stopped the actors in the middle of a scene and explained to them the meaning of some phrase, interpreted the characters as he conceived them, and all the time kept saying, 'Above all, avoid theatricality. Try to be as simple as possible. Remember that they are all ordinary people'."

The play was first published in 1896, in the December issue of the Moscow monthly *Russian Thought*. Chekhov made a great number of cuts in the published text, while restoring the cuts made by the censor. A few of these cut out bits of dialogue are interesting as throwing a light on Chekhov's conception of some of the minor characters. For instance, at the end of Act I Masha says of herself: "Mother brought me up like a fairy princess living in a flower. I can't do anything." In Act II after Arkadina's reference to Maupassant's story, the dialogue went on:

MEDVEDENKO. I've never read it.
DORN. You only read what you don't understand.

MEDVEDENKO. I read any book I can get.

DORN. You read Buckle and Spencer, but you have no more knowledge than a night watchman. As far as you know the heart may be made of gristle and the earth may be held up by whales.

MEDVEDENKO. The earth is round.

DORN. Why do you say it with such diffidence?

MEDVEDENKO (*hurt*). When you have nothing to eat, it makes no difference to you whether the earth is round or square. Leave me alone, please.

Polina's jealousy, too, is given more prominence in the first acting version of the play. At the beginning of Act II, after the stage direction: *Nina appears in front of the house: she is picking flowers*, the dialogue between Dorn and Polina went on as follows:

POLINA (*to Dorn, in an undertone*). Have you been with Irene all morning again?

DORN. I have to be with somebody.

POLINA. I'm tormented by jealousy. I'm sorry. You must be tired of me.

DORN. No, not at all.

POLINA. Of course, you're a doctor and you can't avoid women. I realise that. But please understand it makes me feel awful all the same. Be with women, if you must, but at least don't let me notice it.

DORN. I'll do my best.

And in the last act, after Dorn breaks into the room:

POLINA (*entering after him*). You never took your eyes off her! I ask you, I implore you by all that you hold sacred, not to torture me. Don't look at her. Don't talk to her for hours.

DORN. All right, I'll do my best.

POLINA (*pressing his hand to her bosom*). I know my jealousy is foolish and senseless, and I'm ashamed of it myself. You must be tired of me.

DORN. No, not at all. If it makes it easier for you to talk, then go on talking.

When reprinted in book form in 1897, Chekhov thought it advisable to submit to the demands of the censorship and alter those passages in the play which might cause it to be banned. He therefore changed Konstantin's words in Act I from "because her novelist might like Zarechnaya" to "because she is not acting but Zarechnaya". And his words, " . . . but she smokes, drinks, lives openly with that novelist", were changed to: " . . . but she lives a senseless sort of life, and is always running about with that novelist". In Act III Konstantin's words, "But why, why does that man stand between you and me?" were altered to: "Only why, why are you under the influence of that man?" And Arkadina's words: "What nonsense! I'm taking him away today myself. You may not like our intimacy, but you're a clever and intelligent person and I have the right to demand that you should respect my freedom", were altered to "What nonsense! I've asked him myself to leave today". In Konstantin's reply, the initial sentence was consequently also cut, namely, "I respect your freedom, but please don't deny me my freedom to think what I like of this man." Arkadina's words, "I shall take him away at once and she will love you again," were altered to, "He's going at once and she will love you." Konstantin's characterisation of Trigorin—"Now he only drinks beer and can love only elderly women"—was cut out.

The text of the play was further revised by Chekhov in 1901, but the only major alteration he made was the cutting out of the line: "Nina (shudders). Please, don't——" after Trigorin's words in Act II: ". . . Then a man comes along, sees her and, having nothing better to do, destroys her, like the seagull there."

The last edition of the play to be published during Chekhov's lifetime appeared in 1902 without any more alterations.

# 17

# The Seagull

THE MOST remarkable thing about *The Seagull* is that in it Chekhov has achieved a complete synthesis of theme and character, and that the action of the play flows logically and naturally out of the interplay of the themes and characters upon each other. So complete is this synthesis that an illusion of real life is created, while in fact nothing could be further from reality than the events that happen in this play, or the situations out of which Chekhov so cunningly contrives its climaxes. Where in life would one come across such an absolute agglomeration of love triangles as in Chekhov's comedy? There is the Nina-Konstantin-Trigorin triangle and, since Arkadina is Trigorin's mistress, the Nina-Trigorin-Arkadina triangle. Then there is the further complication of Masha's hopeless love for Konstantin, which creates another, if not real, then potential triangle: Masha-Konstantin-Medvedenko. Finally, as though this were not enough, we get the Polina-Dorn-Shamrayev triangle. And yet the love theme does not play any important, or any decisive part in the play: it is an ancillary theme introduced to give point to the comic elements in the play, though it is not the main comic element in it by any means. "Sex," Chekhov wrote to Suvorin in January 1900, "plays a great role in the world, but not everything depends on it and not everywhere is it of decisive importance."

And, perhaps it may be as well to dispose here of the charges of amorality or even immorality which have been brought against Chekhov at one time or another for presenting so many unconventional love entanglements in *The Seagull*. Discussing *Dr. Pascal* by Zola in a letter to Suvorin on November 11th, 1893, Chekhov found that there was something intrinsically wrong about the hero of Zola's novel. "When I have diarrhoea at night," he wrote, "I usually put a cat on my stomach and it keeps me warm like a hot compress. Clothilde, or Abishag when ministering to King David, is the same sort of cat. Her earthly lot is to keep an old man warm, and nothing more. What an enviable lot! I am sorry for this Abishag, who never composed psalms but was probably purer and more beautiful in the sight of the Lord than the wife of Uriah. She is a human being, a human personality. She is young and she quite naturally craves for youth, and one has, excuse me, to be a Frenchman to make of her a hot water bottle for a white-haired Lothario with the spindly legs of a cock in the name of goodness only knows what. I feel sorry that Pascal and not someone younger and more vigorous should have made use of Clothilde; an old King David who becomes exhausted in the arms of a young girl is like a melon touched by night-frost that still hopes to ripen—every vegetable has its day. And what nonsense it all is! Is sexual virility a sign of real life or health? All thinkers were already impotent at the age of forty, while savages at ninety still keep ninety wives. Our serf owners kept their procreative powers and got their young serf girls with children right up to the moment when, in their old age, they died of heart failure. I am not moralising and I daresay my own old age will not be free from attempts 'to draw my bow', as Apuleius puts it in his *Golden Ass*. To judge from a human point of view, there is nothing wrong about Pascal's sleeping with a young girl—that's his own private business; what is wrong is that Zola should have thought it necessary to commend Clothilde for having slept with Pascal, and it is wrong that he should have called this perversion love."

What then is the main comic element in the play, or, to put it another way, why did Chekhov call his play a comedy? *The Seagull* is usually interpreted on the stage as a tragedy (a misinterpretation which Stanislavsky was the first to impose on the play), and yet Chekhov always referred to it as a comedy; indeed it never occurred to him to call it anything but a comedy. Did Chekhov not know the difference between a comedy and a tragedy? "I don't want to write dramas,"[1] he told Suvorin only a few months before sitting down to write *The Seagull*, "and I haven't thought of a subject for a comedy yet." Here Chekhov clearly differentiated between the one type of play and the other. The difficulty obviously arises from the ending of the play. Konstantin shoots himself—Konstantin is one of the main characters of the play—therefore the play must be a tragedy. For does not a tragedy end in the death of its hero? And does not a comedy always have a happy ending? At least, that is the generally accepted idea.

Incidentally, what Chekhov thought of a happy ending in its conventional sense can be gathered from his letter to Suvorin on April 13th, 1895, that is, only about six months before he began his work on *The Seagull*. Discussing the happy ending of a novel by Henryk Sienkiewicz, the famous Polish historical novelist, Chekhov declared that its aim was "to lull the bourgeoisie in its golden dreams. Be faithful to your wife," Chekhov continued with his analysis of the happy ending, "read the prayer book with her, make money, love sport—and you have nothing to worry about in this world or the next. The bourgeoisie loves so-called 'positive' characters and novels with happy endings very much, for they enable it to find consolation in the thought that it is possible to amass a fortune and keep your innocence, to be a wild beast and happy at one and the same time."

The answer to the puzzle why Chekhov called *The Seagull* a comedy will be found when one considers the implications of the peripetia element in the play, which comes in the inner development of the characters of the protagonists—Konstantin and Nina —and has nothing whatever to do with their unhappy love affair, as it is generally assumed by those (and that is practically every producer) who, in spite of Chekhov's unmistakable intentions, regard the play as a tragedy. In Konstantin's case it deals with his most powerful passion—his desire to become a great writer; in Nina's case it deals with her strongest passion—her desire to

[1] In Russian literary usage a distinction is drawn between a comedy, a drama, i.e., a play of a serious character, and a tragedy.

become a great actress. The whole play, in fact, deals with one of the most important problems in art—what makes a creative artist?

The symbolism of the play expressed in the "seagull theme" applies only outwardly to Nina. In all Chekhov's great plays there are two distinct planes of perception: the realistic and the symbolic. At the end of Act II Trigorin tells Nina as he catches sight of the dead seagull that it has given him a subject for a short story: "A young girl has lived in a house on the shore of a lake since her childhood, a young girl like you; she loves the lake like a seagull, and she's as free and happy as a seagull. Then a man comes along, sees her, and, having nothing to do, destroys her like the seagull there." There is a pause at the end of his speech, and in the earlier versions of the play, as already pointed out, Chekhov filled that pause with a sudden premonition that comes over Nina:

NINA (*shudders*). Please, don't.

Chekhov took that line out perhaps because it seemed to him a little too transparent a hint of what was going to happen, but as Nina has already made up her mind to run away with Trigorin and become an actress, the dreadful premonition of disaster that comes over her is very natural when one takes into account her sensibility, and it *must* come out in that pause. ("To me," Chekhov repeatedly said, "Nina's part is everything in the play.") As her love affair with Trigorin draws to its inevitable end, the image of the dead seagull begins to prey on her mind. Her premonition becomes an obsession. She signs her letters to Konstantin: "The seagull," and Konstantin, who knows nothing of the scene between her and Trigorin in the second act, naturally concludes that her mind has become unhinged. But the whole point of the play is Nina's struggle to overcome her obsession and her triumph in the end. It is here that the element of the reversal of the situation comes to the fore. At the beginning of the play, Nina, who is to be the sole performer in Konstantin's "advanced" play, is very excited about her coming appearance on the stage, hoping to impress Arkadina, a famous actress, and, above all, Trigorin, a celebrated novelist and playwright, whose writings she admires and with whom, in fact, she is already in love. Her girlish affair with Konstantin bores her. It is she who perceives the hollowness of his pretensions and tells him so, and it is with unconcealed reluctance that she allows him to kiss her. This kiss must reveal to the audience in a flash the nature of her true feelings for Konstantin, while her second kiss in the third act is her first *real* kiss, and must reveal to the audience that so far as she is concerned her love for Trigorin is not just a young girl's "crush", but the real thing. When the moment of Nina's appearance on the stage comes, her utter inexperience and nervousness practically kill Konstantin's play even before Arkadina's unfortunate interjection, after Dorn had taken off his hat to mop his brow. Nina's total inexperience of the stage is of vital importance if we are to appreciate the change in her acting of the opening of Konstantin's play in the last act, and believe in her, as Chekhov undoubtedly wants his spectators to, as a future great actress. Chekhov was very careful to point out to Kommissarzhevskaya, the great Russian actress who played Nina at the Alexandrinsky Theatre, that "Nina is a young girl who finds herself for the first time on a stage, who suffers from stage fright and is very nervous". In the fourth act Nina comes back an entirely different person from the inexperienced girl of the first three acts. A complete reversal of the situation has occurred: Nina has become an actress and is well on the way to becoming a great actress. In her last long speech she is still haunted by the spectre of the seagull. "I'm a seagull," she goes on repeating. "No," she immediately declares, "that's not it!" And at last the spectre is exorcised for good, and her speech becomes confident and sure. "I'm different now," she says. "I've become a real actress. I enjoy acting. I revel in it. The stage intoxicates me. On it I feel that I'm peerless. But now, while I've been here, I've been walking about a lot and thinking— thinking—and feeling that the powers of my mind and spirit are growing stronger every day. Now I know, now I understand, my dear, that in our calling, whether we are writers or actors, what matters is not fame, nor glory, nor any of the things I used to dream of. What matters is knowing how to endure. Know how to bear your cross and have faith. I have faith and it doesn't hurt me so much any more. And when I think of my calling I'm no longer afraid of life."

On the realistic plane, therefore, the "seagull" theme personifies Nina's tremendous spiritual struggle against adversity and her final triumph over it. But on the symbolic plane it is a poetic way of expressing the very common fact of life, namely, the destruction of beauty by people who do not see it and are not aware of the terrible crime they commit: Konstantin shoots down the seagull because he is so blinded by his own unhappiness that he does not think of what he is doing, his selfishness making him kill a beautiful bird in order to frighten Nina with the threat that he, too, would shoot himself; Trigorin nearly ruins Nina's life just because of a passing infatuation, a selfish whim; Arkadina tramples on and utterly destroys the spark of genius in her son because she is quite incapable of appreciating it.

It is here that the "seagull" theme becomes closely interwoven with another important theme in the play: the "Hamlet-Gertrude" theme, or one might call it the "mother fixation" theme. Here again it is the peripetia element that brings it to the fore. In the first act Konstantin talks very confidently, and indeed almost hysterically, of the new forms that he is going to introduce in art. Here he is undoubtedly voicing Chekhov's own ideas, and indeed the whole play is an example of the new forms of dramatic expression Chekhov himself was introducing. In criticising "the modern theatre" as "compounded of prejudice and dead convention", Konstantin again merely voices Chekhov's views. "What we want is new forms, uncle," Konstantin says to Sorin. "We must have new forms. If we can't get them, I'd much rather have nothing at all." Where Konstantin differs from Chekhov is that he stakes everything on the new forms. Dorn, who is deeply impressed by his play, tells him at the end of Act I that he did not object to his taking a subject out of the realm of abstract ideas. "A work of art," Dorn says, and here he, too, surely voices

Chekhov's views, "ought to express some great thought, but—" and this is the real point Chekhov wants to drive home—"there must be a clear and definite idea in every work of art—you must know why you are writing—if not, if you walk along this picturesque road without any definite aim, you will lose your way and your talent will ruin you." Thus, at the very beginning of the play Dorn already foresees the disaster towards which Konstantin is heading. But Konstantin, too, at last realises that new forms in art are not everything. In the last act—and this is where the reversal of the situation comes in—Konstantin becomes more and more convinced that, as he says, "It isn't old or new forms that matter; what matters is that one should write without thinking of any forms at all, and that whatever one has to say should come straight from the heart." And in reply to Nina's confident assertion that she is no longer afraid of life because she has faith and believes in her calling, Konstantin sadly confesses his complete lack of faith in anything: "You've found your road," he says, "you know where you are going, but I'm still whirled about in a maze of images and dreams without knowing what it is all about or who wants it. I have no faith, and I don't know what my calling is." What a change from the almost deliriously confident Konstantin of the first act! What a complete reversal his ambitions and hopes have suffered after he has put them to the test of practical experience as a writer! Chekhov has here invested a purely literary theme with the attributes of high drama, but the outcome of this dramatic conflict, so far as Konstantin is concerned, possesses the ludicrous attributes of comedy rather than the noble attributes of tragedy. If Konstantin had really been what he is so often assumed by critics to be, namely, a writer of genius who, but for an unhappy love affair, would have lived to be acknowledged as such, then the play, in spite of the rather paltry theme of a genius brought to ruin because he was crossed in love, might have been a tragedy. But Konstantin is not a genius, nor would he have ever become one. Chekhov was absolutely clear about that. "Treplyov," he wrote down in his note-book, "has no definite aims and that has led to his destruction.   His talent is his undoing. He tells Nina in the final scene—you have found your road, you are saved, but I am done for." In other words, it is the realisation that he is a failure that drives Konstantin to suicide and not at all Nina's rejection of him. His unhappy love affair never leads to death: he tries to commit suicide after the second act, but he only wounds himself. And a failure who runs away from life is not a subject for tragedy. Chekhov would never have accepted Aristotle's definition of comedy as aiming at representing men as worse and tragedy as better than in actual life. Such a definition would indeed have meant to him an intolerable falsification of the high purpose of art. But he might very well have agreed with Aristotle's more precise definition of comedy as "an imitation of characters of a lower type who are not bad in themselves but whose faults possess something of the ludicrous in them". The play's sad ending moves us deeply because it has been contrived by a dramatist whose motto was, "A writer must be humane to the marrow of his bones," but the whole idea of Chekhov's comedy would be distorted if we were not at the same time aware that there was a strong admixture of the ludicrous in Konstantin's death. It is different with Nina: there is nothing ludicrous about her, but then she does not kill herself.

But—and it is here that the "seagull" and the "Hamlet-Gertrude" themes become interwoven—if Konstantin is a failure, it does not mean that he has no talent, "You are a talented man," Dorn tells Konstantin at the end of Act I. "You must go on writing." What destroyed Konstantin's talent was his "mother fixation". Chekhov does not describe the past life of any other character in the play, not even Nina's, only Konstantin's. In Act III in the scene between Arkadina and Konstantin, we get a glimpse of Konstantin's childhood, ending in his words "during these last few days, mother, I've loved you as tenderly and as dearly as I used to love you when I was a little boy." His obsession with his mother is quite abnormal: it alternates between outbursts of extreme love and extreme hatred. Whatever he does, there is always the thought of his mother at the back of it. The whole aim of his life seems to be to convince his mother that he is a genius. The terrific tension of the first act, after the quiet opening scene, is due entirely to this deep-seated conflict of his with the woman to whom he is neurotically attached. What is at the bottom of this conflict? It seems to go back to Arkadina's marriage. She had married beneath her. She was a member of the aristocracy, and her husband belonged to the despised artisan class: he was, as Konstantin, into whom the phrase must have been dinned by his mother, tells Sorin (who, surely, knew all about it), "a Kiev artisan, though a famous actor". Arkadina, who, as Chekhov explained to the actress who took her part at the Alexandrinsky Theatre, was "a foolish, mendacious, self-admiring egoist," must have felt this "humiliation" of her marriage very much, for in Act III when she can't think of anything else to call her son, she calls him "a Kiev artisan". Konstantin was therefore branded in her eyes from his very birth: she would all her life be saddled with a son who was not "a born gentleman".

This attitude to her son must have produced a feeling of great tension between them: even as a child Konstantin must have become aware of the hidden contempt his mother had for him. This contempt darkened his whole life and was responsible for all his failures, including his failure to finish his course at the university: that was his way of revenging himself on his mother. In Arkadina, on the other hand, her son's failure merely increased her conviction that Konstantin was a "nonentity". This mixture of intense love and intense hatred is wonderfully brought out in the scene between Arkadina and Konstantin in Act III. Konstantin is jealous of her relations with Trigorin, and the remarkable thing is that it is not Nina but his mother he is jealous of. The scene starts quietly enough: both of them are overflowing with affection for one another, and it is his great affection for his mother that makes him exclaim: "Why, oh, why, mother, are you so much under the influence of that man?" Arkadina replies calmly enough: "You don't understand him, Konstantin. He's one of the most honourable men I've ever known." This curious appraisal of Trigorin's character is too much for Konstantin. Two strong motives combine to make him lose his temper: his hatred of Trigorin for turning Nina's head and his hatred of him for being his mother's lover. He taunts Trigorin with being a coward.

KONSTANTIN. Yet when he was told that I was going to challenge him, his honourable character did not prevent him from playing the coward. He's leaving. What an ignominious flight!

ARKADINA. What nonsense! It was I who asked him to leave.

KONSTANTIN. One of the most honourable men you've ever known! Here you and I are almost quarrelling over him and he's probably somewhere in the drawing-room or the garden laughing at us, cultivating Nina's mind, doing his best to convince her finally that he is a genius.

Now this was a very shrewd blow: he not only taunted his mother with not being able to keep her lover, but suggested almost in the same breath that the man she was so much in love with was not the genius she held him to be. It is, however, the second challenge that Arkadina takes up.

ARKADINA. You seem to enjoy saying all sorts of disagreeable things to me. I respect him and I'd thank you not to speak badly of him in my presence.

KONSTANTIN. And I don't. I know you'd like me to think he's a genius, but I'm sorry, mother, I don't like telling lies: his books make me sick.

It is now Arkadina's turn to deliver a shrewd blow: Konstantin indeed left himself wide open to an attack on his most vulnerable spot.

ARKADINA. You're jealous. Mediocrities who cherish absurdly grand ideas about themselves usually turn up their noses at men of real genius. Very comforting, I'm sure!

The scene that follows must have occurred between mother and son a hundred times before, but never before could it have been so violent, for now Nina's affair with Trigorin has added fuel to the flames of their ancient enmity.

KONSTANTIN (*ironically*). Men of real genius! (*Angrily.*) I've got
    more genius than any of you, if it comes to that! (*Tears the
    bandage off his head.*) You, the dealers in stale ideas, have
    usurped the supremacy in art and you think that it's only
    what you do yourselves that is real and legitimate. Every-
    thing else you stifle and suppress. I don't acknowledge your
    authority. I don't acknowledge you or him!

ARKADINA. Decadent!

KONSTANTIN. Go back to your precious theatre and act there in
    your contemptible, third-rate plays!

ARKADINA. I've never acted in such plays. Leave me alone.
    You're not even capable of writing a miserable farce. You
    Kiev artisan, you! Parasite!

KONSTANTIN. Miser!

ARKADINA. Tramp!

And, as always, this scene ends in Konstantin's complete
collapse: he sinks into a chair and cries. But his mother is still
boiling with rage, and it is just when her anger reaches its highest
point that she utters the terrible word that is always at the back
of her mind: it comes welling out with dead conviction from
somewhere deep, deep inside her:

ARKADINA. Nonentity!

One can almost hear her hiss the word out. It is the end.
Konstantin is utterly beaten and he becomes again a helpless child,
fawning on his mother, who wipes his tears and does her best to
comfort him.

How deep his preoccupation with his mother was is perhaps
best shown in his amazing last utterance after Nina's departure
and before he goes out to shoot himself.

KONSTANTIN (*after a pause*). I hope no one sees her in the garden
    and tells mother about it. It's sure to upset mother!

His last thought is not for Nina, but for his mother!

In the first act, too, it is only his mother that he really wants to
impress with his play. Nina's objections he brushes away as of no
consequence whatever. His attraction to her is purely physical.

When Nina tells him that there are no living people in his play (a criticism repeated by Trigorin in Act IV about Konstantin's stories, which shows how little progress there was in his work), he replies contemptuously: "Living people! Life has to be represented not as it is, nor as it should be, but as we see it in our dreams!"

Here Chekhov, too, brands Konstantin as a decadent, for there could be nothing further from Chekhov's thoughts than presenting life as it appears in one's dreams. To him the important thing then was to present life "as it is" and as it should be. Konstantin's play is Chekhov's parody—a parody by a genius—of the decadent drama that was just then beginning to be fashionable in Russia, and it was just because such plays were becoming fashionable that it was taken seriously and that Chekhov's instructions about Nina's acting the play were disregarded.

But Konstantin's excitement in the first act is not really due to his desire to impress his mother, but to his knowledge that, whatever he did, he would never succeed in impressing her. Arkadina, too, knows of course of her son's desire to impress her, and she does her best to show him that she is not going to be impressed by turning mockingly to him and reciting Queen Gertrude's lines—

> O Hamlet speak no more;
> Thou turn'st mine eyes into my very soul;
> And there I see such black and grained spots
> As will not leave their tinct . . .

The unconscious aptness of the quotation is amazing just because it means something quite different from what Shakespeare meant—it does not describe Gertrude's feelings towards Hamlet, but it does describe Arkadina's feelings towards her own son. Konstantin is quick to catch the hidden meaning of the quotation, which completely escapes Arkadina herself, or she would not have used it, and turns viciously on his mother and her lover, again fitting Shakespeare's words to suit the present occasion—

Nay, but to live
In the rank sweat of an enseamed bed,
Stew'd in corruption, honeying and making love
Over the nasty sty.

The fine opportunities for real acting which such a scene presents are obvious enough, but they can only be used if the terrific tension in the preceding scenes between Konstantin and Sorin and Konstantin and Nina is conveyed and the true relationships between Konstantin, Arkadina and Nina firmly established. Konstantin's smouldering excitement is the real key to the whole action of the first act and it is aptly expressed in Dorn's last words: "How overwrought they all are!"

Curiously enough, Trigorin, who is the central figure of the two chief love triangles in the play, stands apart from the main action. He is fought over, but he does not do any fighting himself. This is due to the fact that he only appears on the realistic plane of the play. He and, especially, his position as a writer are so important to the whole development of the plot that the play as a whole is often distorted because the producer or the actor playing Trigorin either misinterprets his character or does not have a very clear idea about his standing in the literary world. The first thing to bear in mind is that he is what might be called "a writer of eminence." It is that that arouses Konstantin's contempt, and it is that that explains the tremendous respect both Arkadina and Nina feel for him. And their love for him is so strong just because he is such a weakling, for this arouses their motherly instinct. A great man and such a baby! All this is well brought out in the scene between Arkadina and Trigorin in Act III.

ARKADINA. . . . You're so gifted, so clever. You're the best of all our modern writers. You're Russia's only hope. You have so much sincerity, simplicity, freshness and healthy humour. With one stroke of your pen you can catch what is typical of any person or landscape. Your characters are so alive. Oh, no one can read you without delight!

And this, of course, is quite true. Nina, too, bears witness to it. "His stories are so wonderful!" she tells Konstantin in the first act.

What is wrong with Trigorin then? Why did not Chekhov himself consider him a good, let alone a great, writer? What was wrong with him both as a man and as a writer was that, to use Chekhov's phrase again, he had no "iron in his blood". This, as has already been noted, Chekhov considered as the glaring fault of the writers of his day. Trigorin belonged to the class of writer who, as the old professor points out in *A Boring Story*, "have not the courage to write as they want to" and who for this reason alone are not "creative artists". It was Trigorin, as he himself confesses to Nina, who, in the old professor's words, "purposely covered page after page with descriptions of nature for fear of being suspected of tendentiousness". He was the sort of writer who, as Chekhov wrote to Suvorin on November 25th, 1892, that is only three years before *The Seagull* was written, "depicts life as it is", but whose writings "are not permeated by a consciousness of an aim", an aim which "makes the reader feel not only life as it is but also life as it should be". In fact, Trigorin as a writer is in a way a reflection of Chekhov as a writer during the period when he, too, had cultivated complete detachment as an aim in itself. It is not without significance that the description of the moonlight night, which Konstantin so admires, was taken out of a story Chekhov wrote in 1886, that is to say, during that very period. Chekhov indeed endows him with many autobiographical features, such as his passion for fishing, and many others already referred to. What is so important is Trigorin's *outward* appearance. He is often represented on the stage as a smartly dressed man (an unfortunate result of Stanislavsky's entire misconception of Trigorin's character in the Moscow Art Theatre production of *The Seagull*), but as Chekhov went to the trouble of explaining, "he wore check trousers and his shoes were in holes". He did not even know how to smoke a cigar properly! He was entirely oblivious of his appearance, and this Nina must have found particularly attractive about him; for she was used to seeing smartly dressed men at her father's house, and it was this "bohemianism" of Trigorin and the whole Arkadina set that attracted her, perhaps just because of her father's dislike of it. Trigorin in England today would have worn a pair of old flannels and a dirty old tweed jacket.

Chekhov also left another description of Trigorin's habits which is characteristic of his entire lack of self-consciousness. "His fishing rods," he told Kachalov, who for a short time also took the part of Trigorin in the Moscow Art Theatre production of the play, "are home-made, you know, all bent. He makes them himself with a penknife. His cigar is a good one, perhaps even a very good one, but he never removes the silver paper from it." Then, after a moment's thought, Chekhov added: "But the chief thing is his fishing rods." These remarks sounded like riddles to the actors, but they are essential to an understanding of Trigorin's character: his utter disregard of the social conventions, and his complete indifference to what people might say about him. It is the complete absence of vanity in Trigorin's character that must be conveyed to the audience, for it helps to explain a great deal of Nina's love for him. It also explains the sincerity of his writings.

Of the remaining three male characters in the play, Shamrayev is the only "theatrical" personage in the play. A cuckold has always been a figure of fun on the stage, and Shamrayev is no exception to the rule. He is another type of a rascally manager of an estate that is familiar from Chekhov's earlier plays. Dorn, on the other hand, is one of the most endearing stage doctors Chekhov has given us. His ruling passion is humanity. He is proud of being a good doctor. "Ten or fifteen years ago," he tells Polina, "I was the only decent obstetrician in the whole county." His success with the ladies never turned his head. He suffers Polina's outbursts of jealousy with philosophic calm. Altogether life has taught him the wisdom of not expecting too much of it. He is always humming some snatch of a song. He is quickly moved by suffering. He is entirely disillusioned about the nostrums with which doctors ply their credulous patients and his usual prescription is Valerian drops, a mild sedative popular in Russia. As a doctor he reminds one strongly of Chekhov himself. Humane but not sentimental, sensitive but always keeping his compassion within the bounds of reason. He looks on life with a sober eye and accepts death like a true philosopher. He brushes away Sorin's complaints of being a failure with the sensible remark that he could not have been such a failure since he had reached one of the highest ranks in the Civil Service which entitled him to be addressed as "Your Excellency", and all through the play he refers to him goodhumouredly as "His Excellency". He demands a "serious attitude to life". For a man of sixty like Sorin to grouse about his health or his lost opportunities is "sheer folly". He deprecates Sorin's drinking and smoking because "after a cigar and a glass of wine" he is no longer Sorin, but Sorin plus someone else. "Your personality becomes blurred," he tells Sorin, "and you think of yourself as you would of a third person—as he." He is the only well-balanced character in the whole play and Chekhov uses him to set off the nervous tension of the others.

In the earlier version of the play Chekhov seemed to have experimented with another element of the indirect-action play, the element Aristotle calls "recognition", which is so characteristic of Greek drama. In the scene between Dorn and Masha at the end of the first act, Dorn suddenly discovers that Masha is his daughter. This new development would undoubtedly have strengthened Dorn's inner link with the other characters and would have given Chekhov a very dramatic curtain. But the new theme did not contribute to the inner development of the plot and it was not mentioned again in the other acts. Nemirovich-Danchenko, to whom Chekhov sent a copy of the play and with whom he discussed it afterwards, advised him either to cut it out entirely or to develop it further. Chekhov cut it out. And, no doubt, Dorn's aloofness, which is so important to the action of the play and to the consistency of his character, would have been gravely imperilled by such an unexpected development. Above all, he could not have kept his head as he does at the end of the fourth act if the man his daughter was so desperately in love with had shot himself.

Masha's unhappy love affair is on quite a different plane from Nina's just because there is nothing in Masha that can compare with Nina's intense striving for self-realisation in art. Masha, like her mother Polina, sees the whole aim of her life as being the mistress of the man she loves. But for that, life is a desert to her. When Arkadina, who, stingy and stupid egoist though she is, is a great actress (there is no reason in the world why great actresses should not be stingy and stupid egoists), tells Masha at the beginning of Act III that it is hard work that makes her feel so young, Masha replies, "And I always feel as though I'd been born ages ago. I drag my life behind me like an endless train, and very often I have no desire at all to go on living." And that is the trouble with Masha: she has nothing to live for, so she wastes her life. She drinks and takes snuff (Chekhov actually met a young girl of Masha's age who was addicted to snuff-taking) because she is in constant need of stimulants; she marries Medvedenko because it makes a change; she does not care for her child because it requires too much attention and effort; she lets her mother plead with Konstantin for her because even her sense of human dignity has become blunted. Polina merely expresses Masha's views when she says to Konstantin in Act IV: "All a woman wants is that a man should give her a kind look." And what is the cause of this searing emptiness of soul? Again, though on quite a different plane, Chekhov drives home the lesson that people who have nothing to live for are doomed to a life of constant disappointment and unhappiness. They are a nuisance to themselves and to everyone else. And that seems to be the leitmotif of *The Seagull*.

# 18

# *Uncle Vanya*

CHEKHOV COMPLETED *Uncle Vanya*, his second indirect-action play, before the end of 1896. He must have started working on it soon after the final revision of *The Seagull*. In December, 1896, he wrote to Suvorin, who was publishing a special edition of his plays, to send him the proofs of *Uncle Vanya*. "Two big plays," he wrote on December 2nd, "have still to be set up in print: *The Seagull*, which is known to you, and *Uncle Vanya* which is not known to anyone in the world." This is the first mention of the play in his correspondence. On December 7th he wrote: "Please, make sure that *Uncle Vanya* is printed first . . . After I have read it through, I shall be able to decide whether it is good enough to be made into a short novel. Oh, why did I write plays and not short novels? I've lost good plots, lost them irretrievably, and disgraced myself into the bargain." Chekhov was, of course, referring to the failure of *The Seagull* on the stage of the Alexandrinsky Theatre in Petersburg, after which, as he wrote to Nemirovich-Danchenko on November 20th, 1896, he "flew out of Petersburg like a cannon-ball, according to the laws of physics." But his regret that he did not write the two plays as short novels ought to dispose once and for all of the still widely held view that his plays are merely dramatised novels. In fact, neither in construction nor in execution do they bear the slightest resemblance to novels.

*Uncle Vanya* is of course an adaptation of *The Wood Demon*, but Chekhov always maintained that it was an entirely new play, and so it is in spite of the fact that the second and third acts of two plays are practically identical. For what did Chekhov do? He took one of the main themes of *The Wood Demon* and built an entirely different play round it. What must have struck him

forcibly when he exhumed *The Wood Demon* six years after he
he had decided to bury it for good was that the dramatic relationships in that play were all wrong, mainly because they did
not develop naturally, but were mostly contrived by the playwright
himself. Now that he had mastered the technique of the indirect-
action play he could see clearly why it was so. The action, for one
thing, did not unwind itself *inevitably* because it lacked the
elements through which it is expressed in a play which depends
for its final effect on the inner workings of the minds and hearts
of its characters. The messenger element was most grossly
mishandled; the chorus element was submerged in a flood of
irrelevant detail because the playwright was too anxious to *copy*
life instead of *creating* it; the most vital peripetia element was not
there at all, so that the dramatic movement of the play did not
follow one single line of development, thus creating a most
chaotic impression and resulting in a most unconvincing ending.
Only the Serebryakov-Voynitsky incident seemed to hang
together, and even that came to an abrupt end by Voynitsky's
suicide. The play had therefore to be first of all disencumbered of
all irrelevant matter and its action firmly based on the peripetia
element. All unnecessary characters had to be dropped. Fyodor
Orlovsky, that highly melodramatic villain of the first version
and highly unconvincing penitent of the second, had to go. So
had his father. Julia, who married Fyodor in the finale of the
second version, had, logically, to be excised too. And her brother,
who anyhow did not seem to fulfil any useful function, had also
to be dropped. Of the characters which remained, Serebryakov,
Helen and Voynitsky formed a strong emotional team, and it was
round them that the action of the new play would revolve. Now,
if the action of the play was to be built round the Serebryakov-
Voynitsky incident, then obviously it would be Voynitsky and
not Khrushchov who would become the central figure of the
dramatic action. That being so, it was first of all necessary that the
Voynitsky of the new play should be a much older man than the
Voynitsky of the old one, for that would emphasise the tragedy
of his wasted life. He must be at least ten years older, that is, 47

instead of 37. The title of the play had to be changed: instead of
*The Wood Demon*, standing for Khrushchov, it would have to be
given a title which would convey the most typical traits of the
character of the older Voynitsky. His christian name in the first
play was Yegor, standing for George, by which second name in
its French form he was generally spoken of by the other characters
in the play. But Uncle George would not convey anything of the
mild and inoffensive character of the man, who at the age of 47
saw through the brainless pedant he had worshipped as a great
thinker and scholar and fell desperately in love with that worthy's
young and beautiful wife, only at the crucial moment to bungle
both his love affair and his revolt against the professor. He would
have to have an ordinary name, such as Ivan, used moreover in its
diminutive form of Vanya—Uncle Vanya, in fact, or, to give it
its equivalent in English–Uncle Johnnie. A man of 47 who could
never outgrow his childish pet name. Uncle Johnnie does not
commit such a desperately final act as suicide; instead he fires at the
professor twice and misses. This vital change in the plot at once
supplied Chekhov with the peripetia element of the new play:
the whole action now centred round the reversal of the situation
as it existed at the beginning of the play.

When Astrov asks Uncle Vanya at the beginning of Act I how
long the professor and his wife are going to stay, he gets a most
definite reply:

VOYNITSKY (*whistles*). A hundred years. The professor has decided
    to stay here for good.

Even after Uncle Vanya's quite unexpected outburst in Act III,
Serebryakov is still determined to stay put, for he has nowhere
else to go: he can't afford to live in town on his pension, and,
besides, he sponged on his country relatives even before he
retired from the university and he is certainly not going to give
up his claim to be kept by them now.

SEREBRYAKOV. Now, this is really going a bit too far! Take that
    madman away! I can't live under the same roof with him! He
    is always there (*points to the middle door*), almost beside me.

Let him move into the village or to the cottage in the grounds,
or I will move myself, but stay in the same house with him
I cannot.

When his wife, Helen, for reasons of her own, tells him that
they had better leave at once, the professor does not pay any
attention to her. He is still furious with Uncle Vanya for having
put a spoke into his plan for robbing his own daughter and
throwing her, her uncle and her grandmother ("the old fool",
as he uncharitably describes this most faithful of his followers)
into the street. "The numskull!" he splutters against poor Uncle
Vanya. It is indeed quite obvious that the retired professor of fine
arts never dreams of leaving the comfortable mansion which he
has filled with his perpetual groaning ever since his arrival. Uncle
Vanya has to fire at him twice before it dawns on him how very
unwelcome his presence really is. At the end of the play, then, we
get a complete reversal of the situation: the professor, who has
settled in the Voynitsky's country house for good, leaves with
his wife for Kharkov, and they leave in such a hurry that they do
not even take their things with them. The peripetia element is
here treated in its simplest form, and the more simple its form,
the more dramatic the climax it brings about.

But there still remained Khrushchov (the wood demon), Sonia,
Serebryakov's daughter of his first marriage and the legal owner
of the estate, and Dyadin, the Arcadian miller who sees everything in roseate hues, and they all had to be fitted into the new
play. (Voynitsky's "highbrow" mother presented no difficulties
since her only reason for being there at all was to act as a constant
reminder of the great respect in which the professor was held
before the scales fell from Uncle Vanya's eyes, and that reason
was as valid for *Uncle Vanya* as for *The Wood Demon*.)

Dyadin appears in the new play under the name of Telegin,
a sure sign that Chekhov meant him to be quite a different character, as, indeed, he is in spite of the fact that his nickname remains Waffles. In *Uncle Vanya*, for one thing, he takes no part
in the external action at all. His social position, too, has been

reduced: he lives on the charity of the Voynitskys whose estate he once owned and in whose household he acts as a general facto- tum and clown. But he has a very important part in the inner movement of the play, having been cast by Chekhov for the part of the chorus whose comments on the action heighten the dramatic tension just because they often are so naïve and wrongheaded. Externally, he forms a kind of counter-part to Serebryakov: both of them are spongers, both live in a make-believe world, and both are quite incapable of forming a sane judgment of their position or of the people on whom their very existence depends. But intrinsically they are poles apart: the gulf that separates them is that between good and evil. Serebryakov's selfishness and vanity make him quite impervious to Sonia's appeals for mercy, as becomes all too evident at the end of Act III; Telegin, on the other hand, is the very personification of mercy and selflessness, as is clear from his short account of his life in Act I (an echo, by the way, of Bortsov's life story in *On the Highway*). The same parallelism of good and evil also exists, as will be seen presently, between Helen and Sonia.

Already at the beginning of the play Telegin helps to arouse the spectator's feeling of suspense in two short passages of dialogue he is given by Chekhov. A storm is any moment about to break— literally and metaphorically—over the outwardly peaceful country house. The feeling of tension is conveyed immediately Uncle Vanya comes out of the house, immaculately dressed but with a crumpled face, and sits down heavily, muttering to himself. "Yes," he says, and after a short pause repeats his enigmatic affirmative: "Yes . . ." He sees it all now: the absurd pretensions of the old impostor of a don and his own wasted life. When the old nurse becomes worried about the tea getting cold before the professor's return, he calms her brusquely: "Here they are— here they are—don't get so excited." Serebryakov, Helen, Sonia and Telegin enter and are invited to have tea by Uncle Vanya (it is, of course, essential that the actor taking the part of Uncle Vanya should at this point convey the meaning of his two enigmatic yes's to the audience by his openly ironic attitude to the professor, strengthened by the contrasting attitudes of the rest); but the professor, who has a real genius for giving people unnecessary trouble (he is convinced that he is conferring a great favour on them) asks for his tea to be taken to his study as he has "something to do". He is followed into the house by Sonia and Helen, and Uncle Vanya immediately launches his attack on "our eminent scholar".

VOYNITSKY. It is hot and close, but our eminent scholar walks about in his overcoat and goloshes, wearing gloves and carrying an umbrella.

ASTROV. Which means that he takes good care of himself.

VOYNITSKY. But how lovely she is! How lovely! I've never seen a more beautiful woman.

TELEGIN. Whether I drive through the fields or take a walk under the shady trees in the garden, or look at this table I experience a feeling of indescribable bliss! The weather is enchanting, the birds are singing; we all live in peace and harmony—what else do we want?

The question could not have been more inept, for except Telegin himself, the old nurse and Uncle Vanya's mother, there is not a single character in the play who does not want something else. Telegin's idyllic picture, indeed, is immediaely torn to shreds by Uncle Vanya's vitriolic attack on the professor. Telegin says nothing at first, but it would be a mistake to suppose that his silence is inactive: he can be seen squirming in his seat at the inexplicable and to him quite outrageous outburst against so eminent a man. When, however, Uncle Vanya goes so far as to suggest that Helen is an immoral woman because she is faithful to her husband, he can hold out no longer.

TELEGIN (in a tearful voice). Vanya, I don't like to hear you talk like that. Really, you know, anyone who is unfaithful to a wife or husband is a disloyal person and will betray his country, too!

This amazing non sequitur enrages Uncle Vanya who turns on Telegin with the words: "Waffles, dry up!" But Telegin does not dry up: where his sense of moral values is concerned, he is not so easily daunted. The short account he gives of his unhappy marriage is merely another comment on the action of the play: he has lost his happiness but not his pride (a wonderfully characteristic touch this in a man who has been reduced to the state of a despised "toady", as the village shopkeeper calls him), but Uncle Vanya has lost both his happiness and his pride, and it is the loss of his pride that must be most galling to a man who, like Uncle Vanya, has worked hard all his life, proud in the belief that by paying off the mortgage on the estate and by sending Serebryakov his regular allowance he was helping the cause of the intellectual advancement of his country.

In the great scene of the family council in Act III Chekhov gives Telegin a few lines which indicate quite a new departure in his use of the chorus element. In *The Wood Demon* Dyadin comes in only towards the end of the scene. After Serebryakov's words, "I fail to understand what you are so excited about. I don't say that my plan is ideal. If all of you should find it unacceptable, I will not insist on it," Dyadin comes in in a frock-coat, white gloves and a wide-brimmed top-hat (one can hardly imagine Telegin dressed up like that). The dialogue then goes on as follows:

DYADIN. How do you do, ladies and gentlemen? I'm sorry to come in without being announced. I shouldn't have done so, I know, but I hope you will excuse me as there was not a single servant in your hall.

SEREBRYAKOV (*embarrassed*). I'm very glad to see you. Please, take a seat.

DYADIN (*bowing*). Your Excellency, ladies and gentlemen, my intrusion into your domains has a double aim. First of all, I came here to pay my homage to you, sir. Secondly, I should like to invite you all, seeing the weather is so lovely, to undertake an expedition to my part of the country. I inhabit a water-mill which I lease from our mutual friend the Wood Demon. It is a poetic and secluded spot where at night you can hear the splashing of water-nymphs and in the day——

VOYNITSKY. Just a moment, Waffles—we're discussing business. Wait a little—later——

In *Uncle Vanya* Telegin is present during the whole of the family council scene; in fact, Serebryakov wants him there because he is quite sure that he could rely on Telegin's support should Uncle Vanya become difficult. But throughout the first half of the scene Telegin is silent, and it is only after Serebryakov's words, which in *The Wood Demon* are Dyadin's cue to enter, does he make this apparently irrelevant little speech (he never uses the stilted dialogue which in *The Wood Demon* conceals rather than reveals his character):

TELEGIN (*looking embarrassed*). I've always had a great reverence for learning, sir, and, if I may say so, my feelings for it have a certain family connexion. I mean, sir, that my brother Grigory Ilyich's wife's brother, Konstantin Trofimovich Lacedaemonov, as you perhaps know, was an M.A.——
VOYNITSKY. Just a moment, Waffles, we're discussing business. Wait a little—later——

As the stage direction quite clearly indicates, Telegin is fully aware of the iniquity of the professor's proposal and feels it his duty to intervene on Uncle Vanya's behalf, but he is too overawed by Serebryakov's eminence to speak his mind plainly. He therefore at first tries to ingratiate himself with the professor by expressing his reverence for learning, but the roundabout way in which he does it exasperates Uncle Vanya who shuts him up. His apparently irrelevant little speech, however, is much more relevant than it might appear. His words indeed contain an unconscious criticism of everything Serebryakov stands for. The strange name of his brother's brother-in-law—Lacedaemonov— is surely meant by Chekhov to indicate the particular field in the world of art that is Serebryakov's speciality—ancient Greece, and more particularly the artistically arid Sparta is a hint at the aridity of the learning of the "dried-up biscuit", as Uncle Vanya calls the professor, and the rather remote relationship by marriage of the M.A. suggests the same kind of remote relationship between Serebryakov and Uncle Vanya. Telegin's little speech as a whole, in fact, is meant to bring out the grotesqueness of the professor's standing both as an art critic and scholar and as a claimant to the Voynitsky estate. But it also reveals in a flash the "inner man" in Telegin—his fairness, his humility and his utter absurdity.

This use of the chorus element by Chekhov both as a comment that throws into relief the dramatic situation of a scene and as an exposure of the "inner man" of the speaker is one of the most characteristic features of *The Three Sisters*, but in *Uncle Vanya*, too, the same method is used with shattering effect in the last act—Astrov's words as he contemplates the map of Africa. It is a fatal mistake, as has already been pointed out, to suppose that this is the way "Russians" usually talk. It is only Chekhov's way of delineating character and heightening the tension of a scene.

# 19

# *Uncle Vanya*

THE SCENE preceding Voynitsky's hurried departure in Act III of *Uncle Vanya* is practically identical with the same scene in Act III of *The Wood Demon,* and yet in *The Wood Demon* Voynitsky shoots himself, while in *Uncle Vanya* he first fires at the professor behind the scenes and then runs in after him and fires at him again. Here are the two versions of this scene in the two plays:

|  *The Wood Demon*<br>(2nd version) | *Uncle Vanya* |
|---|---|
| SEREBRYAKOV. What do you want from me? And what right have you to speak to me like that? If the estate is yours, take it! I don't want it. | SEREBRYAKOV. What do you want from me? And what right have you to speak to me like that? If the estate is yours, take it! I don't want it. |

| *The Wood Demon*<br>(2nd version) | *Uncle Vanya* |
|---|---|
| ZHELTUKHIN (*aside*). Now the fat's in the fire! I'd better make myself scarce. (*Goes out.*) | |
| HELEN. If you don't stop, I shall go away from this hell this very minute! (*Shouts*) I can't stand it any longer! | HELEN. I shall go away from this hell this very minute! (*Shouts.*) I can't stand it any longer! |
| VOYNITSKY. My life's ruined! I'm gifted, I'm intelligent, I have courage. If I'd had a normal life, I might have become a Schopenhauer, a Dostoevsky. I'm talking nonsense. I'm going off my head. Mother, I'm in despair! Mother! | VOYNITSKY. My life's ruined! I'm gifted, I'm intelligent, I have courage. If I'd had a normal life, I might have become a Schopenhauer, a Dostoevsky. I'm talking nonsense. I'm going off my head. I'm in despair! Mother! |
| MARIA (*sternly*). Do as Alexander tells you! | MARIA. Do as the professor tells you! |
| | SONIA (*kneeling down before the nurse and clinging to her*). Darling nurse! Darling nurse! |
| VOYNITSKY. Mother, what am I to do? Never mind, don't tell me! I know myself what I must do! (*To Serebryakov.*) You will remember me! (*Goes out through middle door.*) (*Maria goes out after him.*) | VOYNITSKY. Mother, what am I to do? Never mind, don't tell me! I know myself what I must do! (*To Serebryakov.*) You will remember me! (*Goes out through middle door.*) (*Maria goes out after him.*) |

In *The Wood Demon* Voynitsky's departure is followed by three scenes. In the first, between Khrushchov and Serebryakov, Khrushchov comes to expostulate with the professor against the sale of his wood for timber. They quarrel, and Serebryakov, followed by Orlovsky, retires to his study. Next comes the scene between

Khrushchov and Sonia, who, according to the stage direction,
"has been listening at the keyhole" throughout the preceding
scene. Khrushchov tells Sonia that after his short acquaintance
with her what will remain in his mind will be her father's gout
and her own remarks about his democratic ideas. Sonia bursts out
crying and goes out. Khrushchov, left alone on the stage, exclaims, "I've been rash enough to fall in love here and I hope this
will be a lesson to me! Out of this stuffy hole!" But just then
Helen comes in, apologises to him for her husband's rudeness
and offers him her friendship. Khrushchov rebuts her with the
words, "I despise your friendship!" He goes out, leaving Helen
stunned by this unprovoked insult and moaning, "Why? Why?"
It is then that the shot is heard behind the scenes.

In *Uncle Vanya* the departure of Voynitsky is followed only by
a short scene in which Sonia makes her moving appeal to her
father to be merciful and reminds him of the long nights Uncle
Vanya spent translating books for him and copying his papers.
Helen, too, demands that Serebryakov should patch up his
quarrel with Uncle Vanya. Serebryakov agrees. After all, he
realises very well that unless he succeeds in placating Uncle Vanya,
he and his wife will be doomed to a life of privation. He goes out
to talk it over with Uncle Vanya and is followed by Helen,
leaving Marina, the nurse, trying to calm the distraught Sonia.
It is then that the shot is heard behind the scenes, followed by a
scream from Helen.

| *The Wood Demon* | *Uncle Vanya* |
|---|---|
| (*Maria comes staggering in and collapses in a faint on the floor.*) (*Sonia comes in and rushes out through the middle door.*) | SEREBRYAKOV (*runs staggering in looking terrified*). Stop him! Stop him! He's gone mad! |
| (*Serebryakov, Orlovsky and Zheltukhin run in.*) | (*Helen and Voynitsky struggle in the doorway*). |

| *The Wood Demon* | *Uncle Vanya* |
|---|---|
| SEREBRYAKOV. ⎫ What's<br>ORLOVSKY. ⎬ the<br>ZHELTUKHIN. ⎭ matter? | HELEN (*trying to snatch the revolver away from him*). Give it to me! Give it to me, I tell you! |
| (*A scream is heard from Sonia; she comes back and shouts:*)<br>SONIA. Uncle George has shot himself!<br>(*Runs out through the middle door, followed by Serebryakov, Orlovsky and Zheltukhin.*)<br>HELEN (*moans*). Why? Why?<br>DYADIN (*in the doorway*). What's the matter?<br>HELEN (*to Dyadin*). Take me away from here! Throw me over a precipice, kill me, but don't let me stay here! Quickly, I implore you! (*Goes out with Dyadin.*) | VOYNITSKY. Let go of me, Helen! Let go of me! (*Freeing himself, he runs in and looks for Serebryakov.*) Where is he? Ah, there he is! (*Fires at him.*) Bang! (*Pause.*) Missed him! Missed him again! (*Furiously.*) Damn it! Damn it! (*Bangs the revolver a few times against the floor and sinks exhausted in a chair.*)<br>HELEN. Take me away from here! Take me away—kill me—I can't stay here, I can't.<br>VOYNITSKY (*in despair*). What have I done! What have I done!<br>SONIA (*softly*). Darling nurse! Darling nurse! |
| Curtain | Curtain |

Voynitsky's words before he rushes out of the room being identical in *The Wood Demon* and *Uncle Vanya*, the spectator may be justified in assuming that in the second play, too, Voynitsky has rushed out to commit suicide. Terribly distracted as he is, Uncle Vanya might for all we know have at first been intending to do that when he ran out to fetch his revolver. But the moment Serebryakov entered his office, he changed his mind and fired at his enemy. At the end of Act III of *Uncle Vanya*, then, Chekhov piles surprise on suspense and achieves a dramatic climax that is infinitely more effective than the curtain of the third act of the second version of *The Wood Demon*.

# 20

# *Uncle Vanya*

O F THE two remaining characters in *The Wood Demon* Khrushchov and Sonia had obviously to play an important part in *Uncle Vanya*. Khrushchov, in particular, having lost his leading position in the new play and having nothing whatever to do with its main plot, had to be given a sufficiently *intimate* connexion with it to justify his importance in the development of the action. In *The Wood Demon* he is a rich landowner, who dabbles in medicine, "a landowner", as his description in the list of characters states, "who has finished his course at the medical faculty", with a bee in his bonnet—the preservation of forests which has become such an obsession with him that he has embarked on a campaign to substitute peat for wood as fuel. This obsession is regarded even by Sonia as a mania. "He is always thinking and talking about his woods, he plants trees," Sonia says in Act II of *The Wood Demon*, "and of course there is nothing wrong about that, but on the other hand it is quite possible that it is just madness." In *The Wood Demon* he is in love with Sonia, who is just a silly society miss, and the dénouement of the play revolves entirely round the trivial happy ending of their love affair. That love affair, with its absurd, man-made complications, was not only artistically false, but also dramatically unconvincing. It had to go. And it is interesting that in refashioning the characters of Khrushchov and Sonia for his new play, Chekhov left a number of "sign-posts" in the new play to emphasise the entire difference in their conception. Khrushchov becomes Astrov, and here perhaps the symbolism of the different names is not without significance: *khrushch* in Russian means a cock-chafer, which is so destructive to vegetation (a rather rough way of emphasising by contrast the wood demon's mania for preserving the trees), and

Astrov no doubt indicates the deep idealistic streak in the character of the poor country doctor (in the list of characters Astrov is simply stated to be "a doctor") in the new play. Khrushchov is generally considered a crank, a "wood demon", which in Russian demonology is an irresponsible, Puck-like creature. Astrov, whose name suggests the idealist, is a man whose idealism is respected by everybody, and above all by Sonia. Even Voynitsky is never sarcastic about Astrov as he is about Khrushchov in *The Wood Demon*. This changed attitude to Astrov is best seen in the way Chekhov has altered a speech by Voynitsky in Act I of *The Wood Demon*, cutting out that part of it which is outspokenly sarcastic and giving most of the rest of it, describing Khrushchov's great expectations from the preservation of the forests, to Sonia, in whose mouth it no longer sounds derisory but is convincing.

| *The Wood Demon* | *Uncle Vanya* |
|---|---|
| VOYNITSKY. And everything I've so far heard you say in defence of the forests is old, not serious and tendentious. I'm awfully sorry, but I have good reason for saying this, for I know all your speeches almost by heart. For instance— (*Raising his voice and gesticulating as though imitating Khrushchov.*) You, O men, destroy the forests, which adorn the earth, teach man to understand the beautiful, and instil in him a feeling of awe and respect. Forests temper the severity of the climate. Where the climate is less severe less energy is wasted on the | SONIA. Dr. Astrov is planting new forests every year, and he has already been awarded a bronze medal and a diploma. He does his best to prevent the destruction of the old forests. If you listen to him you will agree with him entirely. He claims that forests adorn the earth, that they teach man to understand the beautiful, and instil in him a feeling of awe and respect. Forests temper the severity of the |

| *The Wood Demon* | *Uncle Vanya* |
|---|---|
| struggle with nature, and that is why man is also milder and more affectionate there. In countries where the climate is mild, the people are beautiful, supple and sensitive, their speech is refined and their movements graceful. Art and learning flourish among them, their philosophy is not gloomy, and their relations with women are full of refinement and nobility. And so on and so forth. All this is charming, but it is so little convincing that you will, I hope, allow me to go on heating my stoves with logs and building my barns of wood. | climate. In countries where the climate is less severe, less energy is wasted on the struggle with nature and that is why man there is milder and more affectionate; the people there are beautiful, supple and sensitive, their speech is refined and their movements graceful. Art and learning flourish among them, their philosophy is not so gloomy, and their relations with women are full of refinement and nobility. |
| | VOYNITSKY *(laughing)*. Bravo, bravo! All this is charming, but not convincing, and so *(to Astrov)* allow me, my friend, to go on heating my stoves with logs and building my barns of wood. |

But it is not the attitude of the other characters to him as much as his own attitude to himself that distinguishes Astrov from Khrushchov. In *Uncle Vanya* Astrov looks back on a life of selfless devotion to humanity. Unlike Khrushchov, he takes his medical practice seriously. He is terribly overworked. He is on his feet from morning till night. He has not had one free day, he tells the old nurse at the beginning of the play, during the ten years he has known her. He is ageing, though he is only in his late thirties.

His feelings have become blunted. "There's nothing I want, there's nothing I need, there's no one I love," he tells his nurse.

"There's no one I love"—there at the very start of the play the difference between Khrushchov and Astrov is firmly established. To make Astrov's connection with the main plot of the play as intimate as possible, it is not with Sonia that he had to be in love but with the woman Uncle Vanya himself was so desperately in love. Chekhov had to provide a strong motive for this drastic change in the plot. The motive was Astrov's passion for beauty of form, for external beauty. "I don't love anyone," he tells Sonia in Act II, "and I don't think I shall ever love anyone. The only thing that still exerts the strongest possible appeal on me is beauty. I just can't remain indifferent to it. If, for example, Helen wanted to, she could turn my head in a day." It is true that Astrov, the idealist, is fully aware of the importance of spiritual beauty. "In a human being," he tells Sonia a little earlier, "everything ought to be beautiful: face and dress, soul and thoughts." Nor is he blind to Helen's shortcomings. "She is very beautiful," he tells Sonia, "there's no denying it, but, after all, all she does is eat, sleep, go for walks, fascinate us all by her beauty and—nothing more. She has no duties, other people work for her—isn't that so? And an idle life cannot be a pure one." But in spite of this realisation of Helen's true nature, he is helpless against her bodily beauty. That is something he cannot resist.

What is the consequence of this fundamental change in character which makes Astrov quite a different man from Khrushchov? The consequence is that Sonia, who was a beautiful girl in *The Wood Demon* could not possibly be beautiful in *Uncle Vanya*. And Chekhov has again put up unmistakable "signposts" of this important change. In her soliloquy in Act II Sonia exclaims: "Oh, how awful it is that I am not beautiful! How awful! And I know that I'm not beautiful. I know it, I know. Last Sunday, as people were coming out of church, I heard them talking about me, and one woman said: 'She is so good and generous, what a pity she is not beautiful.' Not beautiful . . ." And at the beginning of Act III, Sonia begins her talk with Helen about Astrov with the bare statement: "I am not beautiful." To Helen's quick, but scarcely sincere, objection that she has beautiful hair, Sonia replies: "No! (*Looks round so as to glance at herself in the mirror.*) No! When a woman is not beautiful, she is always told, 'You've got beautiful eyes, you've got beautiful hair'."

This, then, is the contrast on which the sub-plot of the play is built up: Helen represents bodily beauty, and Sonia represents spiritual beauty, and the line of demarcation between the two is drawn with unmistakable clarity by Chekhov. Helen, like her husband, is evil because she is always thinking of herself. In her scene with Sonia in Act III, it is of herself that she thinks when she proposes to talk things over with Astrov.

HELEN (*musing*). He's a strange man. Do you know what? Let me talk to him. I'll do it carefully. I'll just give him a hint. (*Pause.*) Now, really, how much longer do you propose to remain in uncertainty? Please!

But she does not "do it carefully". Far from just giving Astrov "a hint", she opens her "interrogation" with brutal frankness:

HELEN. What I want to talk to you about is my stepdaughter Sonia. Do you like her?
ASTROV. Yes, I respect her.
HELEN. But do you like her as a woman?
ASTROV (*not at once*). No.
HELEN. Just one thing more and I've done. Haven't you noticed anything?
ASTROV. Nothing.
HELEN (*takes him by the hand*). You don't love her, I can see it from your eyes. She is unhappy. Please, understand that and— stop coming here.
ASTROV (*gets up*). I'm afraid I'm too old for this sort of thing. And, besides, I haven't the time for it. (*Shrugging his shoulders*) When indeed could I? (*He is embarrassed.*)

Helen is not only brutal about Sonia's feelings towards Astrov; she introduces a condition which would have appalled Sonia— she demands that Astrov should never see her again. Astrov himself confesses that if he had been told about it two or three

months before, that is, before he met Helen, his reply might have
been different. It was therefore only Helen who prevented his
friendship with Sonia from developing into something more
intimate. And having confessed as much, Astrov immediately
realises the true reason for Helen's "interrogation". It was not
Sonia at all she was concerned about. Her pity for "the poor girl",
as she calls Sonia in her soliloquy, was a mere pretence. "You're
a sly one!" he tells her, as he looks into her eyes and wags a
minatory finger at her.

HELEN. What do you mean?
ASTROV (*laughing*). A sly one! Suppose Sonia is unhappy, I'm
    ready to admit it, but what is the real meaning of your inter-
    rogation? (*Preventing her from speaking, quickly.*) Please, don't
    look so surprised, you know perfectly well why I'm here
    every day. My sweet beast of prey, don't look at me like
    that, I'm an old hand at this sort of game—you can't deceive
    me.
HELEN (*perplexed*). A beast of prey? I don't understand anything.
ASTROV. A beautiful, fluffy weasel. You must have your victims.
    Here I've been doing nothing for a whole month, I've
    dropped everything, I seek you greedily, and you're awfully
    pleased about it, awfully. Well? I'm conquered, and you
    knew all about it without your interrogation. (*Folding his
    arms and bowing his head.*) I submit. Here I am—eat me up!
HELEN. You've gone off your head!
ASTROV (*laughs through his teeth*). You're shy, aren't you?
HELEN. Oh, I'm much better and more worthy than you think! I
    swear to you!

And so the scene goes on, Helen caught out and trying her best
to get out of a situation which has turned out much more
dangerous than she had expected, and Astrov determined to make
her play the game according to his own rules, till—till Uncle
Vanya appears with that idiotic bunch of autumn roses which he
had promised to bring her "as a sign of peace and harmony" at the
beginning of the act.

Astrov, the idealist, is helpless against "the gorgeous woman",
as he calls Helen, although he realises very well that his life would

be ruined if she were to leave her husband and go away with him. But Helen, too, realises it, and she prefers to stick to her husband, with whom she is unhappy and whom she swears that she did not marry from any interested motives, but because she was attracted to him as a famous man—Sonia seems to have thought otherwise at first—for with her husband she is safe. Always it is herself she thinks of first.

In Act IV Astrov realises that very well. Stanislavsky at first completely misinterpreted the last scene between Astrov and Helen. He wanted Astrov to talk to Helen like "a passionate lover", but Chekhov immediately objected to this distortion of Astrov's real feelings. "This is wrong, absolutely wrong!" he explained in a letter to Olga Knipper, who played Helen, on 30th September, 1899. "Astrov likes Helen, she appeals to him strongly because of her beauty, but in the last act he knows already that nothing will come of it, that Helen is going away from him for ever—and he speaks to her in this scene in the same tone as he speaks of the heat in Africa, and he kisses her simply because this seems to be the only thing to do. If Astrov acts this scene passionately, he will ruin the whole mood of Act IV— quiet and languid."

It is in this scene that Astrov pronounces the final verdict on Helen. "You and your husband," he tells Helen, "have infected us all with your idleness. I became infatuated with you and I have done nothing for a whole month, and in the meantime people have been ill and the peasants have been grazing their herds in my newly planted woods—so that wherever you and your husband go, you bring destruction everywhere."

Serebryakov would, of course, have been amused even by the suggestion that he was idle. Was it not his constant admonition to everybody to do "something useful", something, that is, of real importance? And did not everybody, including Uncle Vanya before the arrival of the Serebryakovs, accept it as a matter of course that the work he was doing was important? To impose upon the whole world in so shameless a fashion requires a great deal of luck, and Professor Serebryakov is lucky. "He is

always complaining about his misfortunes," Uncle Vanya tells
Astrov, "though as a matter of fact he himself is extraordinarily
lucky." Work to Serebryakov means chewing over other people's
views on art, and he works hard at it. His whole life has been devoted to it. He is the type of university don that is unfortunately
all too common, and it is significant that when *Uncle Vanya* was
put on for the first time by the Moscow Art Theatre the professors of Moscow University took strong objection to the play.
"The attitude to *Uncle Vanya* of the professors of the Moscow
branch of the Dramatic and Literary Committee," Nemirovich-
Danchenko wrote to Chekhov on November 28th, 1899, "is
interesting because of its quite incredible stubbornness. Storo-
zhenko added this note in a business letter to me: 'I am told *Uncle
Vanya* is a great success in your theatre. If this is truer then you
have performed a veritable miracle.' But," Nemirovich-Danchenko goes on, "as professors do not believe in miracles, they
are saying this sort of thing in their common rooms: 'If *Uncle
Vanya* is successful, then it can only mean that the Moscow Art
Theatre is a disreputable theatre'." And in another letter to
Chekhov Nemirovich-Danchenko wrote: "I believe I have already written to you that when Serebryakov says in the last act,
'You must work, my friends, you must work!' the audience
quite perceptibly grins, which redounds to the honour of
our audiences. But this the Serebryakovs will never forgive
you."

In contrast to the idleness, uselessness, and, above all, lack of
courage of Serebryakov and Helen, is the useful work performed
by Uncle Vanya, Sonia and Astrov, and, what is no less important
to a proper appreciation of the play, their tremendous courage.
This is indeed one of the principal themes of the play. Nothing,
surely, shows this more clearly than Sonia's deeply moving
speech with which the play ends and which Rachmaninoff set to
music. Sonia has seen her whole life ruined by Helen, and yet it
never occurs to her to blame her stepmother, for she is the personification of spiritual love. Uncle Vanya's life, too, has been
wasted by the old professor, "that old soap-bubble," as Uncle

Vanya calls him, but his hatred has brought him only desolation.
All Sonia thinks of is how to inspire Uncle Vanya with her faith
and courage. When he turns to her with the desolate cry, "My
child, I feel so wretched! Oh, if only you knew how wretched I
feel," her reply is that there is nothing to be done about it and
that life has to be carried on. They have to go on living. They have
to bear patiently the trials that fate may have in store for them.
They must work for others so that when the time comes for them
to die, they will die without a word of complaint in the full consciousness that they have done their duty to their fellow-men and
that they will find their reward in the life to come. Sonia is deeply
religious and it is natural for her to seek consolation in a brighter
future beyond the grave. But it would be a mistake to interpret
that as an admission of a frustrated life. Nothing in Sonia's last
speech justifies the generally accepted view that she regards her
future life with Uncle Ványa as a life of frustration. On the
contrary, it is now that her dream of a happy married life has been
shattered that she can wholly devote herself to a life of service to
her fellow-men. Unfortunately, the last words Sonia uses as a
refrain to her speech—the last chord of a beautiful musical
composition (it is delivered to the accompaniment of a guitar)—
can only be translated as "we shall rest", the verb "to rest" in this
particular context having the definite implication in English of
"eternal rest" or "death". But the Russian verb does not bear any
such implication. Here we are dealing with one of those "literary
echoes" which Chekhov uses with telling effect to evoke the
right mood in the audience. The verb was used by the Russian
poet Lermontov in his lovely translation of Goethe's lyric *Ueber
allen Gipfeln ist Ruh'*. Lermontov translated the last line of this
lyric—*Ruhest du auch*—literally: *otdokhnyosh ee ty*, "you, too, will
rest", which evokes a much more serene mood than the English
verb would in the same context. There is, besides, a feeling of
finality in the sound of the English monosyllable as compared
with the Russian trisyllabic—*otdokhnyom*, ending in a long drawn
out consonant, suggesting not the horror of the rest in the grave,
but a serene and happy rest after a task well and truly done.

The principal theme of *Uncle Vanya*, therefore, is not frustration, but courage and hope. It is a play which is technically more nearly perfect than *The Seagull*, chiefly because in it Chekhov made use of the peripetia element in its most simple form. It is a mistake to think that simplicity of technique is a hindrance to the expression of the most complex and evanescent feelings. On the contrary, as Stanislavsky made it so plain during the last years of his life, the easiest and most effective way of representing the most complex emotion on the stage is through the simplest possible physical action. *Uncle Vanya* is so compact and dramatically expressive just because its peripetia element is so simple. This enabled Chekhov to make much more effective use of the other elements through which the functions of action are expressed in an indirect-action play. He had not, for instance, to send one of his characters away on a voyage before filling in the narrative part of the play. Indeed, the messenger element in *Uncle Vanya* is so closely inter-woven with the peripetia element that it accelerates rather than impedes the movement of the play. It also contributes greatly to the tension of the action, particularly in the first act. The sub-plot, too, that is the relationship between Astrov and Helen and, as a consequence, between Astrov and Sonia and Uncle Vanya, respectively, depends for its dramatic development on the peripetia element. At the beginning of the play, Astrov, tired and even disillusioned, can still come to the Voynitsky estate for rest and comfort; at the end the situation is completely reversed: the incursion of Helen has changed everything and never again will the relationship between Astrov, Sonia and Uncle Vanya be the same. None of them are the same, in fact. It is as if a hurricane had swept through their lives and uprooted everything. And it is the young girl's faith and courage alone that will rebuild the ruins.

# 21

# The Three Sisters

ACCORDING TO his own admission, Chekhov found the writing of *The Three Sisters* extraordinarily difficult. "I find it very difficult to write *The Three Sisters*," he wrote to his sister Mary from Yalta on September 9th 1900, "much more difficult than any other of my plays." And after he finished the play, he wrote to Maxim Gorky on October 16th, 1900: "I found the writing of *The Three Sisters* terribly difficult. You must remember that it has three heroines, and each of them has to be made according to her own pattern, and all three of them daughters of a General! The action takes place in a provincial town like Perm, the environment is military—artillery." But the truth is that Chekhov found the writing of the play so difficult not because it had three heroines (as a matter of fact, as Chekhov himself pointed out in a letter to his wife, it has four heroines), but because he had given particular prominence in it to one of the most difficult elements of the indirect-action play, namely, the chorus element. That is what distinguishes it from any of his other plays and what makes it so easy for a producer and an actor to misunderstand its themes and overlook the significance of its symbols. In this play as in no other play of Chekhov's the "inner man" is always to the fore; its characters seem to say the most inconsequential things, sometimes sounding as though they had no apparent connexion either with its plot or with its dialogue and yet bearing the most intimate connexion with both. It is a play which deals with the inmost mysteries of man's soul, the purpose of man's existence, and the ultimate values of life.

Chekhov seems to have first discussed the play with Alexander Vishnevsky, who was to play the schoolmaster Kulygin in *The Three Sisters*, during his visit to Moscow in the late summer of

1899. "The play we discussed," Chekhov wrote to Vishnevsky on October 8th, 1899, "still does not exist and I don't think it will be written soon. I began it twice and every time I gave it up as I got something quite different from what I wanted. . . . So I'm afraid there is no play, but the future is still with us, and all that is left for me to do is to put my trust in the future." Six weeks later he wrote to Nemirovich-Danchenko, who had been bombarding him with letters for a new play, that he had not begun writing the play yet. "I have a subject, *The Three Sisters*, but I shall not start writing the play before I have finished the short stories which have lain on my conscience a long time. The coming season (of the Moscow Art Theatre) will have to do without a play of mine— that's definite." On December 3rd, 1899, he again wrote to Nemirovich-Danchenko, who was urging him to stop reading the newspapers as they interfered with a writer's creative work (we find an echo of this advice in *The Three Sisters*), that he was well aware of his anxiety to have a new play for the coming season, but "what if the play just doesn't write itself? I shall of course do my best," Chekhov went on, "but I don't guarantee or promise anything. However," he added, "we shall talk it over at Easter when, if I am to believe the papers and Vishnevsky, the theatre will be coming to Yalta. We shall discuss it all then." The Moscow Art Theatre, as Stanislavsky explained in *My Life in Art*, was so anxious to get a new play from Chekhov that it was decided to go to the Crimea and show Chekhov, who was prevented from going to Moscow by bad health, that the misgivings about the theatre he had had ever since he saw a private performance of *The Seagull* in Moscow, were unjustified. In his last letter to Nemirovich-Danchenko before the Moscow Art Theatre's visit to the Crimea Chekhov assured him that the play was beginning to take shape in his mind, but that he had not as yet started writing it. "I somehow don't feel like it," he declared, "and, besides, I'd like to wait till it gets a little warmer." After the visit of the Moscow Art Theatre Chekhov evidently began working on the play in earnest, for on August 5th, 1900, he could already tell Vishnevsky that he was writing it. "I have already written a lot," he wrote, "but until I am in Moscow I shall not be able to pass any judgment on it. Quite possibly what I am getting is not a play but some Crimean nonsense. Its title is (as you already know) *The Three Sisters*, and I am preparing the part of second master at a grammar school, the husband of one of the sisters, for you. You will wear a schoolmaster's uniform with a decoration round your neck." (The mention of Kulygin's decoration shows that by that time Chekhov must have already been working on the fourth act of the play, for it is only in that act that Kulygin appears with it on the stage.) On August 14th, Chekhov wrote to his wife, Olga Knipper, that he was writing "not a play but a sort of mishmash. Many characters—it is quite possible that I shall get all muddled up and give up writing it altogether." Three days later, he complained to his wife that people were constantly interfering with his writing, that he was in a bad temper and had to start all over again. At the time he was writing the play from nine o'clock in the morning till the evening. Next day, on August 18th, he wrote to Olga Knipper again, assuring her that the play as a whole was firmly fixed in his head, and that it had already taken final shape and was just asking to be put on paper. The beginning, he told her, was not so bad— "quite smooth, I think." However, two days later, he had changed his mind about it. He had "cooled off" to the beginning and he was wondering what to do. A play, he explained, had to be written without interruption, at one go, and that morning was the first he had been left alone without interference. And he finished with one of Chebutykin's stock phrases in the play, "anyway, it's all one". The difficulties arising out of the entirely new form of the play were accumulating fast, for three days later Chekhov warned his wife that even if he finished the play, he would most probably put it away till the following year or even later till he felt like writing again. And once more he seemed to have changed his mind. Writing to Vera Kommissarzhevskaya, the famous actress who had played Nina in *The Seagull* in the five ill-omened performances at the Alexandrinsky Theatre and who wanted his new play for her benefit night, Chekhov assured her only two days after his last letter to Olga Knipper that his play would probably be finished in September, when he hoped to send it to her. On August 30th he apologised to his wife for not writing to her because he had been busy writing the play. "I am writing slowly—that's the surprising part of it." If it did not work out as he wanted, he would put it off till the coming year. He hoped, however, to finish it soon, one way or another. About a week later he was still unhappy about the progress of the play. He might even have to leave it unfinished before going to Moscow. There were too many characters, there was a sort of crowded feeling about it, and he feared that the final effect might be "indistinct or pale", and therefore he really thought it would be best to put it off till the next year. Three days later he wrote to his wife announcing his intention of leaving for Moscow on September 20th. One of the sisters in the play had "developed a limp", and he could not do anything with her, which made him angry. In the meantime he fell ill, and on September 13th, he wrote again to Kommissarzhevskaya: "My play, begun so long ago, is lying on my desk, waiting in vain for me to sit down again and resume work. I shall in all probability start writing it again soon, but I cannot possibly say now when I shall finish it. In any case, I do not think the play will be suitable for a benefit performance and I doubt whether you will want to put it on for your benefit night. However, we shall see about that later, perhaps in October, when I finish the play and send it to you for your decision." (Even at that late date, it seems, he had not yet made up his mind definitely whether or not to give the play to the Moscow Art Theatre. Stanislavsky had to undertake another hurried journey to the Crimea before Chekhov finally agreed to let the young and still inexperienced company of the Moscow Art Theatre tackle so difficult a play.) On September 14th, he wrote to his wife: "My play looks gloomily at me as it lies on my desk; and I, too, am thinking gloomily about it." A day later he wrote to his wife again, refusing to commit himself about a definite date for finishing the play. It might be ready in September, or October, or November. He did not know. But even if he should finish it, he was not sure whether he would decide to put it on during the current season. He could not make up his mind, first of all, because the play was not finished and he wanted it to lie on his desk a little, and, secondly, because now that he had promised the play to the Moscow Art Theatre he simply had to be present at the rehearsals. "Four highly important women's parts, four well educated women, I can't leave to Alexeyev, however greatly I may respect his gifts and understanding. It is essential that I should see the rehearsals even with one eye." So there it was. His mistrust of Stanislavsky was deep-rooted and, as it turned out, justified. The same day Chekhov wrote a letter to Victor Mirolyubov, a publisher of cheap editions of the Russian classics, in which he referred to *The Three Sisters* in a phrase that is rather significant for a proper understanding of his art as a playwright. "I have also," he wrote, "to mould a play." What he meant was that he was engaged on giving the play on which he had been working just then an artistic form suitable for stage presentation. He was trying, that is, to mould its characters for the three-dimensional medium of the stage by expressing their hidden emotions in terms of action, or, in other words, he was trying to reveal to the audience the "inner man" of his characters without sacrificing the movement of the play within a certain time limit (actually, of three and a half years) and along an ever rising line of dramatic suspense. That is why he was so anxious for the play, as he wrote to his wife on September 28th, "to lie about a little. Let it sweat," he went on, "or as the wives of our merchants say about a hot pasty which is put on the table—let it heave a sigh."

Chekhov fell ill again and had to interrupt his work on the play for ten days. But by the middle of October it was finished. "Can you imagine it," he wrote to Maxim Gorky in the already quoted letter of October 16th, "I have written a play. However, as it will not be put on now but during the next season, I have not made a clean copy of it. Let it lie about."

He arrived in Moscow from Yalta on October 23rd. He took the play with him and was present at the reading by the company of the Moscow Art Theatre. He was so appalled by the interpretation given to it by Stanislavsky and Nemirovich-Danchenko that he left the theatre in a huff and had a real row with Stanislavsky who had hurried after him to his hotel. He then left for Nice where he was busy revising the play. He made only minor changes in the third act, but altered Act IV drastically. By December 23rd the revised play was already in the hands of the directors of the Moscow Art Theatre. Chekhov himself was not present at its first performance on January 31st, 1901, which was far from successful. The play was published in the February number of *Russian Thought* while Chekhov was still abroad, the editor refusing to wait for the corrected proofs, which annoyed Chekhov greatly. He revised the text of the play in 1902 for the new edition of the seventh volume of his collected works, inserting many new stage directions, making small cuts in the dialogue, and adding the long stage direction and Olga's last line at the end of Act IV. Originally, he intended that Tusenbach's body should be carried across the stage before the fall of the final curtain. Stanislavsky, however, asked Chekhov to omit this as the stage of the Moscow Art Theatre was too small for the crowd scene he would have had to introduce and as it would also have interfered with "the trio of the three sisters". Chekhov assented to this change and later incorporated it in the published text of the play.

He took a very active part in the rehearsals of the play before its revival in the autumn season of 1901. According to V. Luzhsky, one of the assistant producers of the Moscow Art Theatre, who took the part of Andrey in *The Three Sisters*, "Chekhov was present at all but the first three rehearsals of the play, gave very detailed instructions about how the parts ought to be played, and even produced the scene of the fire in Act III." But none of these instructions has been preserved. So convinced were the directors of the Moscow Art Theatre that they were right and that Chekhov was wrong in the interpretation of the play that all they have preserved is a short enigmatic remark here and there, usually couched in curiously stilted language. They all seemed to have agreed to look on Chekhov as a genius who did not know himself what he had really written. In the reminiscences of Chekhov which the members of the Moscow Art Theatre company published after the playwright's death, this view of a mild, amusing, childishly mischievous man of genius is given full play. They even made Chekhov use all sorts of verbal idiosyncrasies, such as putting in "Listen," after every other word, which he never did. Stanislavsky himself only refers in his reminiscences to Chekhov's attempt to stage the fire scene in Act III of *The Three Sisters*, but even that he only mentions in order to show up Chekhov's childishly incompetent handling of sound effects. However, Chekhov seemed to have been quite satisfied with the way his play was performed in the autumn of 1901. In a letter to his Yalta friend, Dr. Leonid Sredin, written in Moscow on September 24th, 1901, he declared: "*The Three Sisters* are now having a wonderfully brilliant performance. . . . I rehearsed the play a little, gave a few people to understand what I wanted, and the play, as I am told, is now being much better performed than during last season."

One result of the conflict between Chekhov and the directors of the Moscow Art Theatre[1] was the belief that Chekhov regarded *The Three Sisters* as a comedy. This curious idea is based on some obscure reference by Stanislavsky to Chekhov's dissatisfaction with his interpretation of the play on the ground that he (Stanislavsky) regarded it and *The Cherry Orchard* as tragedies. It is quite true that Chekhov was furious with Stanislavsky for insisting that *The Cherry Orchard* was a tragedy, but so far as *The Three Sisters* is concerned, there is no indication that Chekhov regarded it as anything but a "drama". It is significant that whenever Chekhov wrote a comedy, he always referred to it as such in his letters. *The Three Sisters*, on the other hand, is always referred to by Chekhov in letters as a "play", never as a comedy. And Chekhov's own description of it in the published text is: "A Drama in Four Acts." The only play whose exact nature Chekhov did not specify is *Uncle Vanya*, which bears the description Chekhov gave to *The Wood Demon*, namely,

---

[1] For a fuller discussion of the conflict between Chekhov and Stanislavsky see my biography of Stanislavsky: *Stanislavsky: A Life.*

"Scenes from Country Life in Four Acts", a description he took over from Alexander Ostrovsky.

## 22

# *The Three Sisters*

THE PREDOMINANCE of the chorus element in *The Three Sisters* creates a new kind of relationship between the auditorium and the stage, the spectator's perception of the dramatic action being, as a rule, much more complex than that of the characters. This becomes clear at once from Chekhov's use of the messenger element in this play as an inseparable part of the chorus element. For instance, Olga's part in the opening chorus of the three sisters is mainly narrative in character so far as the audience is concerned. But the sisters themselves as well as Tusenbach and Chebutykin know the facts mentioned by Olga, such as the General's death, his funeral, his arrival with his family from Moscow eleven years earlier, and so on. The only thing about these facts which is of importance to them is Olga's reaction to them; it is the way in which she narrates them and not the narration itself that evokes their comments. But this dual method of treatment of the audience and the characters occasionally provides the spectator with a glimpse into the future which is completely hidden from the characters and in this way helps to intensify the play's suspense. Such an instance occurs at the very opening of the play. The fine spring morning which filled Olga with such a passionate yearning for home and made Irene feel that the whole meaning of life lay in hard work, brought nothing but unhappiness to Mary, the second sister, who is married to a dull-witted schoolmaster and who could hope for no change in her life from the projected return to Moscow. She decides suddenly to go home. Olga sympathises with her. "I understand you, Mary," she says, "with tears." It is at this point that Solyony makes one of his usual rude remarks about the difference between men's and women's intellects. Mary turns on him at once and asks him what he meant by his remark, adding mockingly, "you frightfully terrible man!" Solyony resents this characterisation of him just because it describes too well the affected ferocity of his manner with which he hopes to disguise his natural "shyness" and emptiness of soul. He replies quickly, "Nothing," but, to get his own back on Mary, quotes two very familiar lines from Krylov's fable *The Peasant and the Farm Labourer*: "He had hardly time to catch his breath before the bear was hugging him to death." Now, the relevance of this quotation is obvious: Solyony is referring to the swift way Mary has pounced on him. But this quotation has a much deeper meaning, as appears immediately from the following dialogue.

*Enter Anfissa and Ferapont with a cake.*

ANFISSA. Come in, my good man, come in. Your boots are clean. (*To* Irene.) From the agricultural board, my dear, from Mr. Protopopov, Mikhail Ivanych—a cake.

IRENE. Thank you. Please give my thanks to Mr. Protopopov. (*Accepts the cake.*)

FERAPONT. Beg pardon, Miss?

IRENE (*louder*). Thank Mr. Protopopov!

OLGA. Nanny, please give him some pasty. Ferapont, go to the kitchen, they'll give you some pasty there.

FERAPONT. Beg pardon, Miss?

ANFISSA. Come along, my dear, come along. (*Goes out with Ferapont.*)

MARY. I don't like this Protopopov, this Mikhail Potapych or Ivanych. You shouldn't have invited him.

IRENE. I didn't invite him.

MARY. Excellent.

This is the first mention of Protopopov in the play, the same Protopopov who, though he never appears on the stage, will be responsible for the eviction of the three sisters from their house and the installation of Natasha and himself in it. From the very beginning then, Protopopov makes his presence felt through his unwanted birthday cake. But it is the sensitive Mary, the only true artist in the family, who perceives something ominous about him. She cannot help disliking him. And here Chekhov adds an unexpected touch, connecting Protopopov with the bear in Krylov's fable. Mary seems uncertain about Protopopov's patronymic and, as though still remembering Solyony's quotation, calls him Mikhail Potapych, the humorous name given by Russian peasants to a bear. (The familiar name for a bear in Russian is "Mishka", the diminutive of Mikhail—Michael.) Not one of the characters of course suspects that Protopopov will actually play the part of the bear in the two lines from the fable, but a Russian audience seeing the play for the first time could not help but associate, however vaguely, the very familiar two lines from Krylov's fable with Mary's "Mikhail Potapych". Indeed, Chekhov has here summarised in a symbolic form the whole peripetia element of the play: in the first act the three sisters are the owners of the beautiful house and the considerable fortune their father had left them, but in the last act the situation is completely reversed, for Natasha with the help of Protopopov (she is too stupid and too cowardly a creature to have schemed it all by herself) has evicted the three sisters from their house and grabbed their money. That Chekhov used the Krylov quotation deliberately (another instance, incidentally, of his effective use of literary echoes) because he wanted it to be associated with Protopopov is proved by the fact that he repeats it twice at the end of the play. It is again Solyony who quotes the two lines first. Solyony comes to hurry up Chebutykin, as he wants his duel with Tusenbach to be over as soon as possible. He means to kill Irene's fiancé and he means to do it before Irene leaves the house: his revenge will be more complete that way.

SOLYONY. It's time, doctor. Half past twelve already. (*Exchanges greetings with Andrey.*)
CHEBUTYKIN. One moment, please. I'm sick of the lot of you. (*To Andrey.*) I say, my dear chap, if anyone should ask for

me, tell him that I shall be back presently. (*Sighs.*) Dear Lord!

SOLYONY. He had hardly time to catch his breath before the bear was hugging him to death. (*Going with him.*) What are you groaning about, old man?

CHEBUTYKIN. Well!

SOLYONY. How do you feel?

CHEBUTYKIN (*angrily*). Fit as a fiddle.

SOLYONY. There's nothing to be so upset about, old chap. I shan't go too far, I shall only wing him like a woodcock. (*Takes out his bottle of scent and sprinkles his hands.*) I've emptied a whole bottle on my hands today and still they smell—smell like a corpse. (*Pause.*) Yes, sir. Remember Lermontov's lines—and he, the rebel, the raging tempest seeks, as though in the tempest peace can be found.

CHEBUTYKIN. Yes. He had hardly time to catch his breath before the bear was hugging him to death. (*They go out.*)

There is a double meaning in this repeated quotation of Krylov's lines: they refer not only to Tusenbach's coming death, but also—by a previous association of ideas—to Protopopov's triumph over the three sisters: a double triumph of evil over good synthesised with the help of two lines from a fable.

In a play where the chorus element predominates to such an extent that the whole inner movement of the action is subordinated to it, as is the case with *The Three Sisters*, the contrast between the realistic and symbolic planes of perception assumes quite exceptional importance. That is why almost every character in the play has a number of symbols attached to him or her in order to emphasise the fact that they belong to a world of art rather than to ordinary life. Solyony is one of them, and it is his hands—the hands of a destroyer of life—on which Chekhov concentrates the attention of the audience. The very first words Solyony utters as he comes into the drawing room with Chebutykin are about hands. "With one hand," Solyony says, "I can only lift half a hundredweight, but with two I can lift a hundredweight or more. From that I infer that two men are not only twice as strong as one, but three times or even more." And a

little later Chekhov makes him produce his bottle of scent and
sprinkle his chest and hands. Towards the end of the second act
after Solyony's words, "I even look a bit like Lermontov—so
I'm told," Chekhov makes him again take out his bottle of scent
and, this time, sprinkle only his hands. These two stage directions
Chekhov only added to the text of the play published in 1902,
which shows how much importance he ascribed to this attempt
of Solyony's to deaden the smell of decay which his hands seemed
to exude. In the middle of Act III and at the end of Act IV,
Chekhov gives Solyony the same stage direction, but it is only
in Act IV that he supplies the reason for Solyony's sprinkling his
hands with scent.

Solyony, as has been suggested earlier, is a direct descendant of
Fyodor in *The Wood Demon*, a villain with a literary background,
but while Fyodor is a purely melodramatic villain, Solyony is a
villain with a soul, and it is the utter emptiness of his soul that
provides the key to his character and his actions. He cannot abide
Tusenbach just because the baron has an aim to which he is ready
to devote his whole life. Solyony has no aim except the satisfaction of his own selfish desires. When Irene tells Tusenbach that
she is afraid of Solyony and that he talks nothing but rubbish,
Tusenbach agrees that he is a queer fish, but he finds that it is his
"shyness" that is to blame for his rudeness. "When we're alone
together," he says, "he is very intelligent and friendly, but in
company he is rude and a bully." Solyony himself confirms
Tusenbach's analysis of his character. In Act II he tells Tusenbach
immediately after uttering his veiled threat ("I'm queer, but who
is not queer? Do not be angry, Aleko!"—Aleko being the
character of Pushkin's poem *The Gipsies* who in a fit of jealousy
kills his wife and her lover): "When I am alone with someone,
I'm all right—I'm just like the rest, but in company I feel depressed, I am shy and—I just talk a lot of nonsense. But all the
same," he adds characteristically, "I'm a damned sight better and
more honest than a lot of other people. And I can prove it, too."
He always gets involved in all sorts of absurd arguments, such as
whether there is one or two universities in Moscow. (Chekhov

was referring to the New and the Old University, the names the
Moscow University students of his day gave to two different
buildings of one and the same university.) These arguments
prove both Solyony's utter ignorance and his resentment of the
way people, whom he knows to be better educated than he, react
to it. He does not care a rap whether he is educated or not, or
whether he is right or not; what matters to him is his own opinion.
If he says something, however absurd, it is right and he is "ready
to prove it" by forcing people to accept it whether they agree with
him or not. He is the typical fascist: he exalts his own neurosis to
an article of faith. He is sincere in his love for Irene. "I'm sorry I
behaved so indiscreetly and tactlessly a moment ago," he tells
Irene at the end of Act II, "but you're not like the others—you're
high-minded and pure—you can see the truth." This leads him
quite logically to the conclusion that she alone could understand
him, and having raised her to so high a pinnacle as to be the only
person in the world to be able to understand him, it naturally
follows that he expects her to reciprocate his love. Irene's blunt
refusal to have anything to do with him (IRENE. Goodnight!
Please, go away!) makes no impression on him whatever.

SOLYONY. I can't live without you. (*Going after her.*) Oh, my joy!
    (*Through tears.*) Oh, my happiness! Lovely, exquisite,
    wonderful eyes, the most beautiful eyes in all the world——
IRENE (*coldly*). Don't please!
SOLYONY. It's the first time I've spoken of my love to you and I
    feel as though I am not on earth but on another planet.
    (*Passes his hand feverishly a few times across his forehead.*) Never
    mind. I can't force you to love me, of course. But I shall
    tolerate no successful rivals. I swear to you by all the saints
    that I shall kill my rival. Oh, my wonderful one!

It is in these last few words that the true Solyony is revealed.
The idea that Irene might prefer someone else to him is something
that he is incapable of accepting. If there should be such a man, he
must be destroyed. And he does destroy him. It is the only way
by which he can re-establish himself in his own estimation. No
one seems to take him seriously otherwise. It is only with Natasha

that he succeeds in getting his own back without having to resort
to extreme measures. For in Natasha he meets his match in
stupidity and selfishness. In the second act Natasha is just beginning to feel her way as the future mistress of the house. Her
chief weapon is her little boy. To make the life of the three sisters
as humiliating as possible, she invents an illness of Bobikin, since
that would put an end to the Shrovetide festivities the sisters were
planning for the evening. She overcomes her husband's objections
by simply ignoring them. Then, flushed with her success, she
comes into the drawing-room eager to pounce on anyone who
would be willing to listen to her stories about what a wonderful
child her Bobikin was. But the only person she can get to listen
to her is the always silent and morose Solyony. He listens to her
prattle with feigned attention, waiting patiently for the right
moment to crush her. Then he begins quietly, "If this child had
been mine——" Natasha beams at him in expectation of some
really nice compliment—"I'd fry him in a pan——" Solyony
goes on slowly, enjoying the sudden startled expression in
Natasha's eyes—"and eat him," he finishes with relish, and then
walks quietly off into the drawing-room with his glass of tea and
sits down in a corner, leaving the horrified Natasha to express her
disgust with him as best she can. This is the only time Solyony
can expect the audience to sympathise with him, for Natasha can
make even an innocent child into a horror.

Chekhov was anxious that Solyony should not be acted as a
melodramatic villain. In a letter to Olga Knipper, he insisted that
the actor taking his part should not make him "too coarse".

Chebutykin is the constant butt of Solyony. He is the fourth
and last doctor in Chekhov's plays, but he derives from the improvident Triletsky in *Platonov* rather than from the wise and
humane Dorn or the idealist Astrov. It is characteristic of Chebutykin and Solyony that, though they always argue, they are so
preoccupied with themselves, that they never seem to listen to
each other. For instance, in their furious quarrel in Act II about
the meaning of "cheremsha", a wild onion, and "chekhartma",
mutton roasted in the Caucasian manner, Chekhov has chosen two

unusual words that would sound alike to people who are not so much concerned with convincing each other as with proving that their opponent is wrong. And in contrast to the great issues discussed by Vershinin and Tusenbach, the subject of their disputes is always trifling. All this is brought out immediately on their first appearance in Act I. Solyony is preoccupied with his hands. He is trying to convince Chebutykin that with two hands he can lift a weight three times as heavy as with one hand (an absurdly futile argument considering that he wants only one hand to kill a man). But Chebutykin is not listening to him. He is reading his newspaper, which is treated by Chekhov as the symbol of Chebutykin's crass ignorance. He never reads serious books, or indeed any books. He has forgotten all he has ever known about medicine. His mind has been frittered away. His soul, too, is empty. The popular newspaper (in the earlier versions of the play Chekhov actually mentioned the two popular newspapers Chebutykin is reading) is the only source from which he can fill his vacant mind, since a vacant mind has to be filled with something. (It is very likely that the idea of using the newspaper as one of the visual symbols of Chebutykin's character was indirectly suggested to Chekhov by Nemirovich-Danchenko, who in one of his letters urging Chekhov to get on with the writing of *The Three Sisters* warned him against reading newspapers as they tended to distract the mind from serious work.) But Chebutykin not only reads his newspaper, he also puts down everything that strikes him as important into his note-book, a pathetic reminder of his university days when he used to take down his lectures in the same way:

CHEBUTYKIN (*walks in reading a paper*). For falling hair—130 grains of naphthaline in half a bottle of spirit—dissolve and apply daily. (*Writes it down in his notebook.*) Let me make a note of it.

His very first words, then, give the audience a clear idea of this old doctor whose medical knowledge has been reduced to taking down some absurd prescription from a popular newspaper.

But while in the stage directions the newspaper appears many times, it is only on three occasions that Chekhov actually makes Chebutykin read out an item of news from it. The second time it supplies Chebutykin with one of his most famous lines: "Balzac was married in Berdichev." This line comes after the argument between Vershinin and Tusenbach about happiness. Vershinin argues that happiness does not exist, or, at any rate, that it cannot and must not exist for them. "We must only work and work, but happiness—that's for our remote descendants. (*Pause.*) If not for me, then at least let it be for the descendants of my descendants." Tusenbach does not agree, for he, poor man, is happy! And he goes on to argue that life will always be the same. for it follows certain laws which man will never know. And when Mary asks him whether he really thinks that life has no meaning at all, he replies: "A meaning? Look, it's snowing. What meaning is there in that?" Mary, however, refuses to accept such a complete dissociation of man from his fate, and she insists that man must have faith, or must seek some kind of faith, for otherwise his life is empty. Man, she demands, must know what he is living for, or else (and here she would have been justified in pointing to Chebutykin who was immersed in reading his paper) nothing in life matters any more. Vershinin, looking at Mary, with whom he could have been happy, bursts out: "All the same it is a pity that I'm no longer young." Mary, catching the hidden meaning of his words, quotes the last line from Gogol's famous story of the quarrel between Ivan Ivanovich and Ivan Nikiforovich (another literary echo!): "It's a boring world, my friends!"

TUSENBACH. But I say it's difficult to argue with you, my friends. Oh, let's drop the subject——

CHEBUTYKIN (reading his paper). Balzac was married in Berdichev.

(*Irene hums softly*)

CHEBUTYKIN. I think I'll make a note of that. (*Writes it down in his notebook.*) Balzac was married in Berdichev. (*Reads his paper.*)

IRENE (*laying out patience, reflectively*). Balzac was married in Berdichev.

What is the meaning of this thrice repeated phrase? Berdichev, the Wigan of Russia, is the last place one would expect one of the greatest of French writers to be married in, or, to go back to the rather inconclusive ending of the argument about happiness, to find happiness in. And it is Irene who has been counting the days (there were seemingly only a few of them left) before her return to Moscow, where alone she believed she could find happiness, who repeats the line reflectively: happiness (and this is emphasised again and again by Chekhov whenever the Moscow theme is brought up) is not only to be found in Moscow, where people are also searching in vain for happiness, but even in such a proverbially dull town as Berdichev, and not only ordinary people can find happiness there, but even a great genius like Balzac. It is in this way that Chekhov uses the chorus element both to provide an answer to an inconclusive argument and a comment on one of the main themes of the play. (The association of marriage with happiness is here purely subjective: Irene's dreams of Moscow revolve round her illusion that it is only there that she would meet the man with whom she would fall in love; Tusenbach is happy because, having sent in his resignation from his regiment, he is now more than ever convinced that Irene will accept his proposal of marriage; and Vershinin's as well as Mary's thoughts of happiness also revolve round their own intimate feelings for one another.)

The other two symbols associated with Chebutykin are the silver samovar and the porcelain clock. To present a young girl of twenty with a tea-urn for her birthday could have occurred only to a man who had lost all touch with life. He wanted to get a really expensive present for Irene, the daughter of the only woman he ever loved, and a silver samovar (usually given as a silver-wedding present in middle-class families) was the only thing he could think of! He is therefore quite incapable of understanding the gasp of horror his present has produced.

OLGA (*covers her eyes*). A samovar! That's awful! (*Goes out.*)

IRENE. Oh, you poor darling, what are you doing?

TUSENBACH (*laughs*). I told you.

MARY. Really, doctor, you ought to be ashamed of yourself!

CHEBUTYKIN. My dear, sweet darlings, you are all I have. You're all I hold most dear in the world. I shall soon be sixty. I'm an old man, a lonely, insignificant old man. There's nothing good about me except my love for you, and but for you, I should have been dead long ago. (*To* Irene.) My darling, I've known you ever since you were born—I used to carry you about in my arms—I loved your mother——

IRENE. But why such expensive presents?

CHEBUTYKIN (*through tears, angrily*). Expensive presents! Don't talk such nonsense! (*To his orderly.*) Take the samovar to the other room. (*In a mocking voice.*) Expensive presents! (*The orderly carries off the samovar to the dining room.*)

This complete divorce from life and living people is of course characteristic of the old doctor. His callousness towards his patients is only another side of it. Life, in fact, no longer exists for him. [It is all a delusion.] "Perhaps," he mumbles drunkenly in his soliloquy in Act III, "I am not a human being at all, but merely imagine that I have hands and feet and a head; perhaps I don't exist at all, but just imagine that I walk, eat and sleep. (*Weeps.*) Oh, if only I did not exist!"

Chebutykin is "not a human being at all" and in this phrase Chekhov has stripped him of all the finer attributes of man, but, unlike Natasha, whom her husband also describes as "not a human being", he had been a human being once when he was capable of devoted and selfless love for a woman, and his final degradation, his final dehumanisation, is symbolically represented in his smashing of the porcelain clock which had been one of the treasured possessions of the woman he loved. It happens shortly after his soliloquy in Act III. Vershinin announces that the brigade to which he is attached is to leave the town soon for some distant destination. Irene declares emphatically that they, too, will leave the town.

IRENE. And we are going too.

CHEBUTYKIN (*drops the clock which breaks*). Smashed to bits!
    (*Pause: everyone is upset and embarrassed.*)

KULYGIN (*picking up the pieces*). To smash an expensive thing like
    that! Oh, doctor, doctor, zero minus for conduct!

IRENE. That was mother's clock.

CHEBUTYKIN. Possibly. So it was your mother's clock. Perhaps
    I didn't smash it, but it just seems as though I did. Perhaps
    we only imagine that we exist, but we don't really exist at all.
    I don't know anything. Nobody knows anything.

But somewhere deep inside him the smashing of the clock has
aroused bitter memories of his own wasted life, for as he is about
to leave the room, he suddenly stops and shouts at them furiously:
"What are you looking at? Natasha is having a disgusting affair
with Protopopov and you don't see it. You're just sitting about
here while Natasha is having her disgusting affair with Protopopov and you don't see it. (*Sings.*) Won't you accept this little
present from me? (*Goes out.*)"

Chebutykin's degradation is completed in Act III. In Act IV
he is no longer a human being. Nothing makes any impression on
him any more. The officers forget to take leave of him, but he
just dismisses it with a shrug. Throughout the whole of the act
he is, according to the stage direction, "in a goodhumoured mood
sitting in a chair in the garden and waiting to be called to the duel
between Solyony and Tusenbach. He could have stopped the duel
by telling Irene about it, but as he says to Mary: "One baron more
or less in the world—what difference does it make?" It does not
occur to him that Tusenbach's death will also affect Irene. When
Irene tries to find out from him about the quarrel between Solyony and Tusenbach the day before, he refuses to tell her anything.
"What's happened?" he says. "Nothing. Rubbish. (*Reads his
newspaper.*) It makes no difference." Kulygin has also heard
rumours of the impending duel, but Chebutykin refuses to
enlighten him. "I don't know," he says. "It's all nonsense."
It is then that Kulygin tells his funny story about the divinity
student whose essay his professor marked with the word "non-

sense", which the student, thinking it was written in Roman and not in Russian characters, read as "renyxa". (The Russian word for nonsense—*chepukha*—when written out can be mistaken for a "Latin" word since all its letters are identical with the letters of the Roman alphabet.) The nonsense word "renyxa", which strikes Chebutykin as the very quintessence of nonsense and which he repeats with such relish, epitomises his own attitude towards life. And when he returns from the duel, he just announces the news of Tusenbach's death and sits down, still in his good-humoured mood, reading his paper and humming "Tarara-boomdeay". He has been reduced to the state of an idiot to whom nothing matters and who keeps his good humour irrespective of what calamities may be happening around him.

Protopopov, of course, never appears, but his cake (the personification of middle-class propriety) is there in Act I and his carriage (the emblem of his good social position) can be heard as it draws up before the house in Act II, and it is standing in front of the house in Act IV, while its owner is listening to his mistress's playing "The Maiden's Prayer" on the piano. A cake and a carriage—what better symbols of middle-class respectability does one want?

Kulygin, the classics master and Mary's husband, is only given one symbol—his own magnum opus, his book describing the history of the school, where he is soon to become second master, for the past fifty years. He presents it to Irene as a birthday present in Act I, having forgotten that he already gave her the same book as an Easter present. Still, that does not dismay him: he presents it to Colonel Vershinin instead—to read when he feels bored!

Andrey, poor Andrey, who is the unwitting instrument of the undoing of his sisters, has quite a number of symbols. There is his fiddle, which, escapist that he is, he plays to drown the realisation of his failure in his chosen career of a university teacher. "He is our scholar," Irene tells Vershinin proudly in Act I. "He will probably be a professor. Father was a soldier, but his son has chosen an academic career." And Mary adds, significantly: "At Father's wish." Then there are the picture frames he makes.

IRENE. Look what a lovely picture frame Andrey gave me as a birthday present! (*Shows the picture frame.*) He made it himself.

VERSHININ (*looks at the picture frame and does not know what to say*). Yes—it's something——

IRENE. And that picture frame over the piano he made, too.

(*Andrey waves his hand and walks away.*)

OLGA. He is a scholar, he plays the violin and he is very clever with a fretsaw—in a word, he can turn his hand to anything. Don't go, Andrey. He has a habit of always walking away. Come here!

(*Mary and Irene take him by the arms and bring him laughing back.*)

Then there is his book. He has been reading it till four o'clock in the morning, he tells Vershinin, then he went to bed, still reading it presumably, but "nothing came of it". It must have been the English book he was proposing to translate during the summer, but nothing comes of it, either. Andrey uses an illuminating phrase about his learning. "Father," he tells Vershinin, "inflicted education upon us." And that, no doubt, explains his failure as a budding university professor. "Today," he tells Ferapont at the beginning of Act II (the old fellow is very deaf and Andrey finds it very convenient to have someone to unburden his soul to, someone, that is, who would not ask awkward questions), "today . . . I picked up this book—my old university lectures, and I could not help laughing. Good Lord, I am the secretary of the agricultural board, the same board over which Protopopov presides, I am a secretary, and the most I can hope for is to become a member of the agricultural board! I—a member of the agricultural board, I—who dream every night that I am a professor of Moscow University, a famous scholar of whom the whole of Russia is proud!" His violin playing and his fretwork are merely outward manifestations of his utter loneliness. He is a stranger even in his own house. And what could be more pathetic than the way he walks quietly in towards the end of Act II and sits down near the candle with his book—the symbol of his shattered academic career.

Then there is the key from the cupboard he has lost—at least
so he says when he comes in to ask Olga for it in Act III; but what
he really has lost is the key to his sisters' hearts. And, finally,
there is the bell. It is Mary, the most poetic and sensitive of the
three sisters, who in Act IV applies this symbol to Andrey as she
sees him wheeling the pram with his little son, while Protopopov is
dandling his own daughter in the house. "And there is Andrey,
our darling brother," she says. "All our hopes have perished.
Thousands of people were raising a bell, much money and labour
was spent on it, and then suddenly it fell and smashed to bits.
Suddenly, for no reason at all. That is Andrey."

Andrey's tragedy is that he realises very well how low he has
fallen but cannot do anything about it. A little later in the fourth
act he has again a talk with the deaf Ferapont during which he lays
bare his soul to the audience. According to Luzhsky, Chekhov
demanded that in this last monologue Andrey should be very
excited. "He must almost threaten the audience with his fists,"
Chekhov said.

Andrey's wife, Natasha, has several symbols, too. There is,
above all, her green belt. She is the personification of the *petite
bourgeoise* in mind, manners, morals, and outward appearance.
"Heavens, how she dresses!" Mary exclaims in Act I. "It isn't
that her clothes are not pretty or fashionable—they are just
pitiful! A queer sort of bright yellowish frock with a cheap-
looking fringe and a red blouse." But when Natasha appears
at the end of Act I, she wears a green belt on her pink dress. Olga
gasps with horror at the sight of it. "My dear," she says in a
frightened voice, "you're wearing a green belt! That's not nice!"
But Natasha misunderstands her. Very typically, she thinks that a
green belt must be unlucky. "No," Olga explains, "it simply
doesn't suit you and—and it looks a little strange." Natasha is
dismayed. She has come dressed for the kill, and now it seems
that she has done something awful. Will Andrey notice it, too?
But Andrey does not notice anything. Earlier Mary remarked
that she did not believe Andrey was in love with Natasha, for
"after all, he has taste!" And, besides, she was told that Natasha

was going to marry Protopopov. But if Andrey had taste, his infatuation for Natasha had killed it, and as for Natasha and Protopopov, they have other plans.

It is characteristic of Natasha that she never forgets Olga's remark about her green belt which she took as a personal snub. At the end of the last act, three and a half years later, when she appears for the last time in the garden of the house which now belongs to her, she turns to Irene with the words: "My dear, that belt doesn't suit you at all. It's such bad taste. You ought to get something bright and shiny."

But the most important symbol associated with Natasha is the lighted candle. There is an interval of about a year between the first and second act. Chekhov's stage directions for the second act are most precise: "It is eight o'clock in the evening. From behind the scenes, from the street, come the faint strains of an accordion. There are no lights in the house. Enter Natasha in her dressing-gown with a lighted candle." What is Natasha doing? She is putting out the lights in the house. The drawing room with the columns which was so bright with sunshine in Act I is dark now. Only Natasha's candle throws a trembling light on the changed scene. It is Natasha, now sure of herself, who plunges the house into darkness. It is she who now gives the orders. Her very first words, addressed to Andrey, so solicitous for the welfare of his sisters, are full of venom and hypocrisy. "And Olga and Irene aren't back yet. Still hard at work, poor things. Olga at her staff meeting, Irene at the telegraph office. Only this morning I said to your sister, 'You must take more care of yourself, Irene, darling.' But she won't listen to me." The sisters won't listen to her: that's what makes her so furious. And almost in the same breath she goes on hatching her plot to show the sisters that it is she who is now the real mistress in the house. But—and this is the characteristic touch—while so anxious to put out all the candles for fear of a fire, Natasha leaves her own lighted candle behind her. At the end of Act II after Solyony's threat to kill his rival, Natasha again appears with a lighted candle in her hand. It is in Act III that her lighted candle assumes a sinister significance. At the end of the act (by that time Natasha has already succeeded in throwing Irene out of her room and making her share Olga's bedroom), when the fire in the town has almost been put out, Natasha enters Olga's bedroom with a lighted candle. Chekhov gives her nothing to say. There is only the stage direction: "Natasha with a candle passes across the stage in silence from the door on the right through the door on the left." It is Mary who remarks, as she sits down: "She walks as if she had set the town on fire herself." But Natasha had not set the town on fire: she had set the house of the three sisters on fire. The house might as well have been burnt down to the ground, for it no longer belonged to them. They had given shelter to the people who had been rendered homeless, but they were as homeless as the people whose houses had burnt down. Here again we get the synthesis of two symbols: the fire in the town and Natasha's candle in the house.

Finally, in the last act, Chekhov again uses several objects as symbols to add the last few touches to Natasha's character: the fir-tree avenue, the beautiful maple tree, the flowers and, last but not least, the fork on the garden seat. (There is nothing super-fluous on Chekhov's stage!) Natasha appears at the end of the act accompanied by her maid. In a few lines of dialogue Chekhov lays bare with superb skill the really devilish nature of Natasha, using his symbols only to deepen the stark horror such a character must evoke. Protopopov and Andrey are to take charge of their respective children, the first nursing his little girl in the house and the second wheeling his little boy in the garden. "Children are such a bother!" Still, with two fathers to look after them things are not too bad. Then she turns to Irene to commiserate hypocritically with her for having to leave the house and to tell her that Andrey is to be thrown out of his room as she was before him. Little Sonia, Protopopov's child, is to have her husband's room. "What a lovely child! Such a darling! Today she looked at me with such big eyes and said—mummy!" She ignores Kulygin's compliment to her "lovely child", and sums up the position in one short sentence: "So I shall be alone here tomorrow," following up her triumphant remark with a hypocritical sigh. It is then that she turns to her future plans: "First of all I shall have this avenue of firs cut down, then that maple—it is so unsightly in the evenings." Full mistress of the house and garden at last, she is destroying beauty everywhere (a little earlier Tusenbach was praising the beauty of the trees Natasha is now going to cut down), and even the flowers, which Vershinin admired so much in the drawing-room in Act I, become an abomination in her mouth: "I shall have flowers, flowers, flowers everywhere and there'll be such a lovely scent!" Her wonderful plans, however, are met with icy silence, and that infuriates her. It is then that she notices the fork on the garden seat and asks "severely": "Why is the fork left lying about on the seat?" But her question is completely ignored, and as she walks off into the house, she vents her spite on the maid: "Why is the fork left lying about on the seat, I ask you? (*Screams.*) Don't answer me back!" The only comment comes from Kulygin: "There she goes again!" Deep down she feels her inferiority to the three sisters, and her last scream of rage is her acknowledgement of the fact that, though she had driven them out of their house, they are still her superiors.

# 23

# *The Three Sisters*

CHEKHOV'S use of symbols with the positive characters of the play, that is, with the three sisters, Tusenbach and Vershinin, is much more subtle. There are, for instance, the images of the grand-piano, the lost key and the dead tree which deepen the poignancy of the farewell scene between Irene and Tusenbach in Act IV. The scene is so poignant because neither of them realises that it is the last time they will see one another, but the symbols help to cast a shadow over a relationship that is none too happy as it is. One cannot help feeling that it is just because Irene does not love Tusenbach that a deeper note of tragedy is added to their last meeting.

TUSENBACH. . . . I'm going to take you away tomorrow. We shall work. We shall be rich. And my dreams will come true. You will be happy, darling. Only one thing—one thing only worries me: you don't love me!

IRENE. I can't help that! I shall be your wife, your true and faithful wife, but I don't love you. We can't do anything about it! (*Cries.*) I've never been in love. Oh, how I dreamed of love, dreamed of it for years and years, night and day, but my heart is like an expensive grand-piano that is locked and the key is lost. (*Pause.*) You look troubled.

TUSENBACH. I didn't sleep last night. There's nothing in my own life I'm afraid of, and it is only the lost key I'm worried about. That's what destroys my sleep. Say something to me. (*Pause.*) Say something to me.

IRENE. What? What do you want me to say? What?

TUSENBACH. Just something.

IRENE. Don't fret, dear. Don't, please!

TUSENBACH. It is strange how little things, mere stupid trifles, sometimes become important in our lives without rhyme or reason, and so suddenly, too. You laugh at them, as you always do, but you go on all the same and you haven't got the strength to stop. Oh, don't let's talk about it! I feel fine. I feel as though I'm seeing these firs, maples and birches for the first time in my life, and that all of them are looking curiously at me and—waiting. How beautiful these trees are and how beautiful life ought really to be near them! (*There is a shout from his seconds who are waiting to take him to his duel with Solyony.*) I must go. It's time. This tree here is dead but it goes on swaying in the wind with the others. So I too, I can't help feeling, if I should die, will go on taking part in life one way or another.

The grand-piano in a more material sense is used by Chekhov at the beginning of Act III to describe in a few sentences the tragedy of Mary's life. Mary is an accomplished pianist, but for the last three or four years she has not gone near her piano, and her art withers because there is no one to appreciate it. Far from encouraging her, all that Kulygin, her husband, thinks about is that the head of his school might disapprove of her taking part in a public concert.

TUSENBACH. I'm being asked to organise a concert in aid of the homeless.

IRENE. But who——

TUSENBACH. It could be arranged if we tried. Mary plays the piano beautifully, in my opinion.

KULYGIN. She plays wonderfully.

IRENE. She's forgotten how. She hasn't played for three or four years.

TUSENBACH. There's absolutely no one in this town who appreciates music, not a soul, but I do and I assure you that Mary plays wonderfully, almost like a concert pianist.

KULYGIN. You're quite right, baron. I love Mary very much. She's a dear.

TUSENBACH. To be able to play so well and to know all the time that there is no one to appreciate it—no one!

KULYGIN (sighs). Yes—but do you think it's the done thing for her to take part in a concert? (Pause.) I know nothing about such matters, of course. It may be all right. I must say our head is a decent fellow, a very decent fellow, indeed, and very intelligent, too, but he has such views——Of course, it isn't his business, but all the same if you like I might perhaps have a talk to him.

Kulygin loves his wife very much, but it never occurs to him that it is he who is destroying her soul. How full of action Chekhov's pauses are can be plainly seen from the one pause in this little scene. Chekhov does not describe the reaction of the other characters to Kulygin's extraordinary statement that Mary's appearance at a public concert may not be "the done thing", but the way Kulygin squirms under their disapproval, which each of them expresses in his or her own way (what latitude Chekhov gives to his producers!) shows clearly how truly dramatic the action of this scene is.

The idea that the yearning of the sisters for Moscow is the

main theme of the play and expresses, as a modern Russian critic put it,[1] "a kind of poetic symbol which introduces a certain unreality in the delineation of everyday facts," is far from true. The producers of *The Three Sisters* make too much of this all too obvious theme in conformity with the popular notion that the chief characters of the play are "Chekhovian" ineffectual characters, whereas the truth is that they are far from ineffectual. The important fact that the play does not end on a note of resignation but on a note of triumph is somehow completely ignored by them. It must be remembered that the Moscow theme is to a large extent autobiographical, expressing, as it does, Chekhov's own yearning to return to Moscow from the Crimea where his illness kept him confined for the last five years of his life. In his play Chekhov uses it to point a moral rather than to wallow in one of those moods which critics are so fond of ascribing to him, but which in fact he detested. It is significant that every time Moscow is mentioned in the play, Chekhov immediately underlines the absurdity of such a purely romantic craving for the unattainable. He does so at the very opening of the play in the chorus scene of the three sisters. Then, in the middle of Act I, Vershinin, in reply to the ecstatic cries of Olga and Irene when they find out that he, too, had been in Moscow, tells them of the "gloomy bridge" which made him feel so depressed every time he had to cross it, and—immediately after Irene's remark that her mother was buried in the cemetery attached to the Novo-Devichy Monastery, one of the oldest monasteries in Moscow (Chekhov was buried there), Vershinin says that with time "what seems so very important to us now, will be forgotten and will seem trivial". In Act II, in the scene between Andrey and Ferapont, Andrey's wish to sit in a large restaurant in Moscow where he would not feel as lonely as he does at home, is countered with Ferapont's story of the merchant who choked himself to death with a pancake in a Moscow restaurant, the whole point of the story being that Moscow can be as coarse and as uncivilised as the least cultured provincial town. A little later in the same act

[1] A. Roskin. *The Three Sisters* on the Moscow Art Theatre Stage. Leningrad, 1946.

the whole unreality of Irene's dream about Moscow is emphasised twice. First, in her unconscious failure to realise that Andrey's losses at cards would prevent her from going to Moscow.

IRENE. A fortnight ago he lost, and in December he lost. I wish he'd hurry up and lose everything he's got—perhaps we'd leave for Moscow then. Oh dear, I dream of Moscow every night. I'm going quite off my head. (*Laughs.*) We move there in June, and before June there is still—February, March, April, May—nearly half a year!

And later in the same act when Irene is laying out the cards in a game of patience——

IRENE. It's coming out—I can see. We shall go to Moscow.
FEDOTIK. No, it won't come out. See? The eight of spades is on top of the two. (*Laughs.*) That means that you won't go to Moscow.
CHEBUTYKIN (*reads the paper*). Tsitsihar. A smallpox epidemic is raging here.

Here again, as in the case of Berdichev, Chekhov introduces an apparently irrelevant statement, but what he really does is to use the chorus element as a detached comment on the dialogue, in this instance Irene's remark about Moscow. Tsitsihar—what an exotic place, even more desirable and unattainable than Moscow, and yet in reality it is nothing but a pest hole. (An English spectator would see the point of Chebutykin's line more clearly if Chekhov had used Samarkand instead of Tsitsihar.) And a little later after Mary's remark that if she had been in Moscow she would not notice the bad weather, Vershinin tells them the parable of the imprisoned French Cabinet Minister who for the first time in his life found real delight in watching the birds from his prison window, but who did not notice them any more after his release from prison. "So," Vershinin goes on, "you won't notice Moscow when you live there."

Chekhov ends Act II and Act III with the Moscow theme, but in both these curtains it is used merely to emphasise the delusive nature of Irene's dream. In Act II it follows close upon Natasha's departure for her sleigh ride with Protopopov, the two persons who will rob the sisters of their fortune and will make it impossible for them to go to Moscow; and in Act III it follows Irene's decision to marry Tusenbach, who has got himself a job far away from Moscow. Indeed, a little earlier in the same act Irene herself realises at last that she would never go to Moscow.

In Act IV comes Irene's final reconciliation with the idea that she would never see Moscow again. She says: "What I have decided is that if I am not going to live in Moscow, then it just can't be helped. I suppose it's fate, and there's nothing to be done about it." And the same note of reconciliation rather than resignation is sounded by Olga at the end of Act IV: "There won't be a single soldier left in town tomorrow, everything will become just a memory, and for us of course a new life will begin. Nothing has turned out as we expected. I did not want to be a headmistress, but I've become one. Which means that I shall never go to Moscow. . . ."

The whole thing, in fact, is nothing but a delusion, and the time has now come for the sisters to face reality, and they do it with courage and hope, as the final chorus of the three sisters shows— and it is this and not Moscow that is the leitmotif of the play.

The love theme forms almost as complex a profusion of triangles in *The Three Sisters* as in *The Seagull* and in *Uncle Vanya*. There is the Irene-Tusenbach-Solyony triangle, the Mary-Kulygin-Vershinin triangle, and the Natasha-Andrey-Protopopov triangle. And again as in the two previous plays the love affairs end unhappily: Tusenbach is killed, Vershinin has to leave with his regiment, and Andrey becomes a stranger in his own house in more senses than one. But of all these love affairs the only real one is between Mary and Vershinin. Irene does not love Tusenbach and their proposed marriage is just an arrangement which she accepts because there seems nothing better she can hope for. And even then she is practically pushed into it by her elder sister.

IRENE. . . . I'm twenty-three now, I've worked for a long time, and my brain has dried up, I'm growing thin, I'm losing my looks, I'm getting old, and there's nothing, nothing I can look forward to, no satisfaction out of life I can hope for. Time is flying past, and I seem to be getting further and further away from real life, from a life that is beautiful, and heading for some horrible disaster. I'm in despair and I simply can't understand how I go on living, how I haven't killed myself before now.

OLGA. Don't cry, darling. I can't bear to see you cry.

IRENE. I'm not crying—I'm not crying. I've stopped now. See? I'm not crying any more. I've stopped—I've stopped!

OLGA. Darling, I'm telling you this as your sister, as your friend— if you take my advice, you'll marry the baron.

IRENE. (*Cries softly.*)

OLGA. You do respect him, don't you? You think highly of him. It's true he's not handsome, but he's such an honest and decent man. People don't marry for love but to fulfil their duty. At least, I think so, and I wouldn't hesitate to marry a man I didn't love. I would marry anyone who asked me, if he was a decent man. I would even marry an old man.

Olga with her deep sense of duty and Irene with her deep sense of the sanctity of labour—how carefully drawn their characters are and how absurd it is to regard either of them as ineffectual! But it was on Mary that Chekhov lavished all the rare gifts of his genius. Mary with her sensitive soul of an artist, with her superstitions and her bluntness of speech and manner. "Remember, no drinking today," she tells Chebutykin in Act I shortly after being told by her husband that he expected her to spend the evening with him at the headmaster's. "Do you hear? It's bad for you!" And in reply to Chebutykin's assurance that he had not been really drunk for the past two years, and what did it matter, anyway, Mary says: "All the same, don't you dare to drink! Don't you dare! (*Gruffly, but not so loud as to be overheard by her husband.*) Damn, I shall have to spend another boring evening at the headmaster's, it seems!" And later at the dining-room table it is she who offends against all middle-class proprieties by banging her fork against her plate and exclaiming: "Let's have a glass of vodka! Oh, life is sweet—what the hell——" Which at once brings down the rebuke of her husband on her:

KULYGIN. Black mark for conduct.

But it is Natasha, that typical *petite bourgeoise*, who is really shocked by Mary's language. When in Act II Mary, worried by Vershinin's wife's latest attempt to poison herself, shouts at the old nurse, mixes up Irene's cards, and tells Chebutykin that at his age he should not be talking such damned nonsense, Natasha gives her a lecture on how a lady ought to behave in society.

NATASHA (*sighs*). My dear Mary, why must you use such expressions? I assure you that with your attractive appearance you'd be simply bewitching in any refined society if it were not for your language. *Je vous prie, pardonnez moi, Marie, mais vous avez des manières un peu grossières.*

How revealing Natasha's hypocritical sigh is and the French sentence with which she shows off her own refined education and which make Mary's *manières un peu grossières* more attractive. No wonder Tusenbach can hardly restrain himself from laughing at Natasha's lady-like pretensions. Natasha, indeed, uses the most vulgar expressions when in a temper, while Mary is never vulgar. "Coarseness," she tells Vershinin in Act II, "hurts and upsets me. I can't bear it when a man is not sufficiently sensitive or sufficiently gentle and courteous."

But it is in the unfolding of Mary's love for Vershinin that Chekhov reveals her truly poetic nature. He achieves it by the use of a literary echo, the two first lines from Pushkin's fairy-tale poem of *Ruslan and Lyudmila*, twice in Act I and twice in Act IV, and by the exchange of a snatch of a tune between Mary and Vershinin in Act III. Ever since she had got up on the morning of Irene's birthday, Mary had felt a strange uneasiness, a vague premonition that something important was going to happen that day, and at the beginning of Act I she just sits quietly over her book, lost in thought and whistling some tune. The very first words she utters are the two lines from *Ruslan and ˌudmila*, lines that are full of magic and mystery and that evoke a mood full of wonder and expectation. She then gets up, humming a tune quietly, and is about to leave.

OLGA. You're not very cheerful today.
MARY. (*Puts on her hat, still humming the tune softly.*)
OLGA. Where are you off to?
MARY. Home.
IRENE. Strange—
TUSENBACH. Leaving a birthday party!

But Mary will not be persuaded to stay. She tries to rationalise her feeling of uneasiness by putting it down to the few people who turned up at the birthday party as compared with the thirty or forty officers who used to come to it when her father was still alive. Olga sympathises with her: it is only a year since their father died and the contrast between the past and the present can still be felt acutely, but that is not what makes Mary feel so sad. "Don't howl!" she tells Olga gruffly. Then, after the short episode with Chebutykin's silver samovar, Vershinin comes in. What were Mary's feelings during their first meeting? She tells her sisters about it in Act III: "At first I thought him queer, then I felt sorry for him and—and then I fell in love with him." Her first words to Vershinin, after he told her that her face was familiar, are: "I don't remember you!" But in another minute she does remember him:

MARY. . . . Now I've remembered! (*To Olga.*) Don't you remember we used to talk of the love-sick Major? You
were only a Lieutenant then and you were in love with
someone, and for some reason everyone used to tease you by
calling you a Major.
VERSHININ (*laughs*). Yes, yes—the love-sick Major—that's right.

Then quite unaccountably Mary bursts into tears. "You had only a moustache then," she says to Vershinin. "Oh, how old you've grown! How old you've grown!" A wave of pity for the prematurely old colonel, who can still talk with such boyish enthusiasm, passes over her, and after his first long speech of the wonderful world there will be in two or three hundred years time she forgets all about her depression and her wish to leave the party.

MARY (*takes off her hat*). I'm staying for lunch.

At the end of Act I, those two magic lines of poetry came spontaneously to her lips again, but this time she already perceives the stirrings of a great passion in her and she is annoyed with herself for mumbling words the full significance of which she is as yet unable to grasp:

MARY. . . . (*Tearfully.*) Now why do I keep on saying that? I just haven't been able to get it out of my head all day.

It was indeed a fateful day for Mary, and an ominous one, too, for no sooner did she become aware of her feelings for Vershinin than her husband announced: "There are thirteen at the table." And she was so superstitious!

Act II begins about nine months after the end of Act I. The time element in the play is curiously relative. The whole action lasts about three and a half years, for Chekhov gives us the most precise information about the beginning and the end of the play. It opens on May 5th, Irene's twentieth birthday, and Act IV takes place in the autumn when Irene is in her twenty-fourth year. Between Act I and Act II Andrey and Natasha get married and have a child. Act II takes place in February—Shrovetide. (Irene, counting the months before their proposed moving to Moscow, starts with February.) Act III quite likely follows almost immediately after Act II, that is to say, the fire in the town must have occurred only a few months after the end of the second act. That seems to agree with the small lapse of time that is implicit in the lighted candle symbol and Irene's expulsion from her room. But if that is so, then two and a half years must have passed between Act III and Act IV, which is most improbable since in Act III Vershinin announces that his regiment is leaving town, while in Act IV we are actually present at its departure. And yet Natasha bears Protopopov a child between Act III and Act IV! There is therefore an artistic compression of time in the whole play, and this relativity of time is particularly noticeable in the case of Mary and Vershinin. For while the other characters in the play clearly reveal the lapse of time at the beginning of Act II, the first scene between Mary and Vershinin in that act seems to follow immediately after the end of Act I. It is almost as if it is their second meeting. Indeed, if, as it seems likely, they had met several times before, there is no indication of any such meeting. And yet it is in this scene that Vershinin declares his love for Mary and that we hear for the first time Mary's soft, happy laughter. Their love, then, has something of a fairy-tale in it: time means nothing to two truly loving hearts. But their real understanding comes only in Act III. By that time, however, their spiritual intimacy has become so close that all they need is to exchange a few snatches of a tune—the most original love declaration in the whole literature of the stage!

MARY. Trum-tum-tum—
VERSHININ. Tum-tum—
MARY. Tra-ra-ra—
VERSHININ. Tra-ta-ta—(*Laughs.*)

A few minutes later a shorter exchange of the same snatch of a tune takes place, but this time, according to Chekhov, "Vershinin says 'trum-tum-tum' in the form of a question and Mary in the form of an answer. Mary thinks it such an original joke that she pronounces her 'trum-tum' with a grin and, having uttered it, bursts out laughing, but not loudly, just a little laugh, barely audible." What happens, then, is that at first this exchange is just a declaration of love, a confirmation that they belong to each other; the second time, Vershinin asks Mary whether she will be his and she replies in the affirmative; the third time, Vershinin sings the tune behind the stage, that is to say, he uses it as a signal to tell Mary that he is waiting for her. Mary gets up and replies in a loud voice: "Tra-ta-ta!" to tell him that she is coming. She then takes leave of her sisters and her brother: "Goodbye, Olga. Bless you, my dear. (*Goes behind the screen and kisses Irene.*) Sleep well. Goodbye, Andrey. Go away now, they're tired. You'll talk to them tomorrow. (*Goes out.*)"

But immediately before this last exchange with Vershinin,

Mary tells her sisters of her love, beginning with the words: "I should like to confess to you, my dears." Chekhov was very anxious to make it absolutely clear that "Mary's confession in Act III is not a confession at all but merely a frank conversation. Mary," Chekhov went on, "must act this scene nervously, but not hysterically. She must not raise her voice; she must smile occasionally; above all, her acting must convey the fact that it is very late and that she is very tired. She should also make the audience feel that she considers herself much more intelligent than her sisters."

The whole action of Act III, Chekhov insisted in his instructions to the actors, must be conducted quietly "so that the audience should feel that the people on the stage are tired and want to go to to sleep. . . . The noise of the fire should come from a distance, from behind the scenes, and it should be subdued and indistinct."

In Act IV the parting scene between Mary and Vershinin is very brief. Before that Mary appears for only a short time to exchange a few words with Chebutykin. "When you have to snatch your happiness piecemeal, in little bits," she tells him, "and then lose it, you gradually become coarse and bitter. (*Pointing to her breast.*) I feel it seething here." That is all we know of her feelings, except for her last words, expressing her longing to go away with Vershinin, as she walks away along the avenue of trees: "And the birds are already flying away. (*Looks upwards.*) Geese or swans. Oh, my dear ones, my happy ones! (*Goes out.*)" Brief though it is, the parting scene is charged with emotion.

VERSHININ. I've come to say goodbye. (*Olga walks away a little so as not to interfere with them.*)
MARY (*gazes at his face*). Goodbye! (*A long kiss.*)
OLGA. There, there, Mary, be brave.
MARY. (*Sobs bitterly.*)
VERSHININ. Write to me. Don't forget me. Let me go now—it's time. Olga, please take her. I have to go. I'm late as it is. (*Deeply moved he kisses Olga's hands, then embraces Mary again and goes out quickly.*)

Kulygin comes in and, as usual, says the wrong things. It is then that Mary again repeats the two lines from Pushkin's poem, but this time they have lost their magic and the words convey nothing to her. "I'm going mad," she murmurs desperately. Olga tries to calm her, but she has already stopped crying. A distant shot is heard: Tusenbach is killed. Then again the words of Pushkin's poem burst confusedly from her lips. One word sticks in her mind, but she doesn't know even what it means any more. Irene comes in. Mary refuses to go inside the house. "I'm not going into that house again," she declares firmly, "and I shan't go in there ever!" Irene reminds her that she is going away next day and proposes that they should spend a few minutes quietly together. Kulygin, the pathetic idiot, tries to amuse his wife by putting on a false beard he has confiscated from one of his schoolboys. (Chekhov made him shave off his beard specially for this scene.)

KULYGIN. I look like our German master, don't I? (*Laughs.*) Those boys are funny beggars.
MARY. You do look like your German.
OLGA. (*Laughs.*) Yes.
MARY. (*Cries.*)
IRENE. Stop it, Mary.
KULYGIN. Yes, I certainly look very like him.

Nothing in this scene is irrelevant; everything in it has been nicely calculated to evoke the right kind of response from the audience; everything shows the touch of a master of stage technique. And it would be the greatest mistake to interpret this scene as an instance of what is so generally assumed to be the expression of "Chekhovian" frustration and gloom. Mary, indeed, says in the bitterness of her heart that her life is a failure and that there is nothing more she wants, but as her little speech in the chorus of the three sisters shows, she soon recovers from her feeling of desolation. Parting is such sweet sorrow—and Chekhov makes it quite clear that it is not by any means the end.

The other great themes of the play—the theme of the illusion of happiness, the theme of mankind's future, and, above all, the theme of the regenerative powers of work—are all carefully interwoven with the action and find a *gay* affirmation of life in the final chorus of the three sisters to the accompaniment of an invigorating march by the band of the departing regiment.

MARY. Oh, how gay the music sounds! They are going away from us—one has already gone, gone for ever—and we shall be left alone to start our life anew. We must live. We must live. . . .

IRENE (*lays her head on Olga's breast*). The time will come when there will be no more secrets, when all that is now hidden will be made plain, and when all will know what these sufferings are for. Till then we must live—we must work, just work! Tomorrow I shall go away alone, I shall teach in a school, and I shall give my life to those who may need it. It is autumn now; it will be winter soon and everything will be covered with snow. But I shall be working—I shall be working.

OLGA (*embraces the two sisters*). The music is so cheerful and gay and I want to live! Dear God! Time will pass and we shall be gone for ever. We shall be forgotten, and people will no longer remember our voices, or our faces, or how many of us there were. But our sufferings will pass into joy for those who live after us—peace and happiness will reign on earth, and we who live now will be remembered with gratitude and will be blessed. Oh, my dear, dear sisters, our lives are not finished yet. Let us live! The music is so gay, so joyful, and it almost seems that in a little while we shall know why we live and why we suffer. Oh, if only we knew—if only we knew!

# 24

# The Cherry Orchard

*T*he Cherry Orchard has been so consistently misunderstood and misrepresented by producer and critic alike that it is only by a complete dissociation from the current misconceptions about the play that it is possible to appreciate Chekhov's repeated assertions that he had written not a tragedy but "a comedy, and in places even a farce."[1] Structurally, this last play of Chekhov's is the most perfect example of an indirect-action play, for in it all the elements are given equal scope for the development of the action. And in no other play is the peripetia element so important for a proper understanding of situation and character without which any appreciation of the comic nature of the play is impossible. Long before Chekhov sat down to write his last play, he had made it clear that it was going to be a comedy. He told his wife, Olga Knipper, on March 7th 1901, that is to say, barely six months after the completion of The Three Sisters, that his next play would be "an amusing one, at least in conception." In April of the same year he again wrote to her that he was overcome by a strong desire "to write a four-act vaudeville or comedy for the Moscow Art Theatre," and that if nothing interfered with him he would write it, though he would not let the theatre have it before the end of 1903. And in January, 1902, he assured his wife, who complained that he did not write to her about his new play because he had no faith in her, that the real reason why he never mentioned his play was that he still had no faith in it. "I am only just able to catch a faint glimmer of it, like the faint glimmer of an early dawn," he wrote, "and I myself don't understand what it is really like or what form it is likely to assume, for it

---

[1] "I'm afraid my play has turned out to be not a drama but a comedy, and in places even a farce, and I fear Nemirovich-Danchenko will never forgive me for that." (Letter to Maria Lilina, Stanislavsky's wife and one of the leading actresses of the Moscow Art Theatre, September 15th, 1903.)

changes every day." In the same year his wife fell seriously ill and it is only in October that we find a reference to the play in a letter to Stanislavsky. "I shall be in Moscow on October 15th," Chekhov wrote, "and I shall then explain to you why my play is not yet ready. I have a subject for it, but I haven't the strength to sit down to it." This is the first indication we have of Chekhov's rapidly deteriorating health. In his letter to his wife he was more careful. "I should like to write a vaudeville," he told her in his letter of December 12th, 1902, "but I can't set about it. Besides, it is too cold for writing; it is so cold in my room that I have to walk about to keep warm." Two days later he already gave her the title of his new play: "When I sit down to work on The Cherry Orchard," he wrote, "I shall let you know about it." On December 22nd he again made it clear to his wife that what he had in mind was a "vaudeville." He had a kind of presentiment, he told her, "that vaudevilles will soon come into fashion again". Two days later he wrote to her that he thought his play would have three acts, though he was not sure. "I shall soon get well," he at last thought it expedient to mention his illness, "and I shall start considering it again. Now I have put everything aside." In January of the following year he was still uncertain about the final form of the play. "I meant to make The Cherry Orchard into three long acts," he wrote to his wife, "but I can also turn it into four. I don't mind, for whether it is in three or four acts, it will be the same thing." He had not yet begun to write the play, being too ill to do anything. "I shall start writing the play in February," he informed Stanislavsky on January 1st, 1903. At the end of January he wrote to Kommissarzhevskaya: "It is quite true that I have already planned out my play and that I have even got a title for it (The Cherry Orchard—this is still a secret), but I shall probably begin to write it not later than the end of February, provided, of course, my health is good." It is in the same letter that Chekhov for the first time mentioned the important fact that the chief character in the play would be "an old woman."[1]

[1] It must have been at the same time that Chekhov wrote down in his note-book: "A liberal-minded old woman, dresses like a young one, smokes, can't do without society, sympathetic."

On February 11th, in a letter to Maria Lilina, in which he asked
her to act in his play without, however, mentioning what part
he had in mind for her, he wrote: "I don't know what my play
will be like and I am not sure whether it will turn out as I want.
It will be finished in the spring when I hope to take it to Moscow
myself." On the same day he wrote to his wife that he would begin his play on February 21st. On February 22nd, however, he
could still tell her nothing about the play. He did tell her, though,
that her part would be that of a "perfect fool" (Varya). In the
final casting of the play Olga Knipper was given the part of Mrs.
Ranevsky, but it is obvious that Chekhov thought his wife too
young to play the part of "an old woman." On March 1st he had
"only laid out the paper for the play and written the title," he wrote
to his wife, who did not seem to realise how serious his illness was
and scolded him for being "lazy" and threatened to "take him in
hand." But Chekhov reminded her on March 4th that "since the
days of Noah" he had been telling them that he would set to work
on the play at the end of February or at the beginning of March.
"My laziness does not come into it at all," he wrote. "I am not
my own enemy and if I had the strength I would write twenty-
five plays." On March 5th he told her for the first time that the
part he had in mind for her was that of Varya, "an adopted
daughter, aged 22". And on March 6th he was already so confident about the play that he wrote to her: "If my play does not
turn out as I have conceived it, you may hit me on the head with
your fist. Stanislavsky has a comic part (Lopakhin) and so have
you." On March 18th he seemed to have had some trouble with
one of the characters which "was not sufficiently thought out,"
but by Easter he hoped that it would be quite clear to him and he
would have got rid of his difficulties. On March 21st he assured
his wife that *The Cherry Orchard* would be finished soon. "I am
trying," he wrote, "to have as few characters as possible; it will
be more intimate so." On April 11th he was beginning to feel
worried because the Moscow Art Theatre had no actress for "the
old woman in *The Cherry Orchard*. If not," he added, "there will
be no play. I am not going to write it." On April 15th he referred

to it again. "I have no desire to write for your theatre," he wrote
to Olga Knipper, "chiefly because you have no old woman. They
will be making you play the part of the old woman, though
there is another part for you, and, besides, you have already been
acting an old woman in *The Seagull*." Chekhov's work on the
play was interrupted in April by his journey to Moscow and
Petersburg and was probably resumed only after his return to
Yalta in July. In reply to a letter from Stanislavsky, Chekhov
wrote on July 28th: "My play is not ready yet. It is moving along
slowly, which may be due to my laziness, the beautiful weather
and the difficulty of the subject." In August he must have been
working on Act II, for in a letter to Nemirovich-Danchenko he
discussed the scenery of this act which, he wrote, he had reduced
to a minimum, having substituted an old chapel and a well for
a river. The scenery for this act, he told Nemirovich-Danchenko,
would be "a green field, a road, and a distant view unusual for
the stage". On September 2nd he wrote to Nemirovich-Danchenko: "My play (if I go on working as I have been doing till
today) will be finished soon. Don't worry. It was difficult, very
difficult to write the second act, but I think it came off all right.
I shall call the play a comedy." By the middle of the month he
wrote to his younger brother Michael: "I have nearly finished
my play. I ought really to have begun copying it out, but my
illness is interfering with my work and I can't dictate."

On September 18th a notice appeared in the Moscow papers
announcing that the première of *The Cherry Orchard* would take
place in December. Chekhov agreed, stipulating, however, that
it should be the beginning and not the end of December. On
September 21st he wrote to his wife: "The last act will be merry
and frivolous. In fact, the whole play will be merry and frivolous:
Sanin[1] won't like it. He will say I have become shallow." Four
days later he assured his wife that the fourth act was shaping quite
well and apologised for not having finished it because of his illness.
He thought he could claim that there was something new in the

[1] Stage name of Alexander Schoenberg, actor and assistant producer of the Moscow
Art Theatre.

play and he emphasised the fact that there was "not a single pistol shot in it". On September 26th he wired Olga Knipper that the play was finished and that it was being copied. But the copying went on very slowly as Chekhov was altering the play all the time. "Some passages," he wrote to his wife, "I don't like at all, and I am re-writing them and copying them out again." On October 8th he finished copying Act III and began the revision of Act IV. "The third act," he wrote to Olga Knipper, "is the least dull, but the second act is as dull and monotonous as a spider's web." Next day he wrote to his wife again, assuring her that the play would be finished soon and that every extra day he spent on it was only to the good, for the play was "growing better and better and the characters are clear now." On October 10th he wrote to Stanislavsky: "I am re-writing the play a second time and that is why I am so late. I shall send it in three days." On October 12th the revision was finished. He still thought that some slight alterations might be needed. "The worst thing about the play," he wrote to his wife, "is that I have not written it at one sitting but over a long, long period, so that it is bound to seem spun out. Oh, how hard it was for me to write this play!" He returned to the subject of "alterations and finishing touches" in his letter to his wife five days later. Act IV, he warned her, was not quite finished, and he thought that there ought to be a little more movement in Act II, and two or three words perhaps should be changed in Anya's concluding speech in Act III as otherwise it might sound too much like Sonia's last speech at the end of *Uncle Vanya*. But all that he proposed to do on his arrival in Moscow.

In November the play was examined by the dramatic censor. Already on October 9th Chekhov wrote to Olga Knipper that he was afraid the censor might object to certain passages in the play. "That," he wrote, "would be awful!" His fears proved justified. The censor cut out two passages in Trofimov's speech in Act II. In the first passage Trofimov's words about the Russian intelligentsia read originally: " . . . They are all so serious, they have such solemn faces, they all talk of nothing but important matters, and yet before our very eyes the workers live in terrible squalor, sleep on the floor, thirty and forty in a room—bugs, stench, damp and moral depravity everywhere." The censor cut out the reference to the workers and the conditions under which they lived.

The second passage, which occurs at the end of Act II in Trofimov's speech beginning with the words, "All Russia is our garden," read originally: " . . . do you not hear their voices? To be the owners of living souls—that has made you all into different human beings so that your mother, your uncle and you yourself don't even notice that you live on credit, at the expense of other people, at the expense of those whom you do not admit farther than your entrance hall. . . ."

Though Chekhov substituted different versions for those the censor (for obvious reasons) insisted on cutting out, he did not cross them out himself but merely put them in brackets in his manuscript, a clear indication that he wanted them restored.

The alterations Chekhov made in the text of the play during its production were of minor importance. The only major change was in the second act. At the insistence of Stanislavsky, who found this act particularly difficult, Chekhov permitted a few cuts, and after the first few performances also decided to cut out the final scene. In preparing the play for publication, however, Chekhov altered Act II radically. In the original text Charlotte did not open the act with her soliloquy. Instead it was opened by Trofimov and Anya:

ANYA. Granny is very rich and lonely. She doesn't like mother. At first I felt very unhappy in her house. She spoke very little to me. But afterwards she was all right. She laughed. She promised to send the money and she gave Charlotte and me enough money to take us back home. But how horrible it is to feel that you are a poor relation.

TROFIMOV. There's someone here already, I think. Sitting there. Let's walk on a little.

ANYA. I was away for three weeks. I was so homesick! (*They go out.*)

The scene between Dunya, Yasha and Yepikhodov followed with few alterations. But the next scene between Mrs. Ranevsky, Gayev and Lopakhin was interrupted after Mrs. Ranevsky's words, "Perhaps we shall think of something," by a little scene between Varya and Charlotte, who walk across the stage.

VARYA. I know she's an intelligent and well brought up girl and that nothing will happen, but at the same time it is not proper to leave her alone with a young man. We're having supper at nine, Charlotte. Please, don't be late.

CHARLOTTE. I'm not hungry. (*Hums a tune softly.*)

VARYA. That makes no difference. Everyone must be in his place at supper. Look, there they are! Sitting on the bank.

*Varya and Charlotte go out.*

The end of Act II of the original version was quite different from the published version. After Anya's words, "How beautifully you said that!" the dialogue went on as follows:

TROFIMOV. Hush! Someone's coming. It's that Varya again! (*Angrily.*) It's sickening!

ANYA. Well, let's go down to the river. It's lovely there.

TROFIMOV. All right, let's.

ANYA. The moon will rise soon. (*They go out.*)

*Enter Firs, followed by Charlotte. Firs is muttering and looking for something on the ground near the seat; lights a match.*

FIRS (*mutters*). Oh, you duffer!

CHARLOTTE (*sits down on seat and takes off her cap*). Is that you, Firs? What are you looking for?

FIRS. Mistress lost her purse.

CHARLOTTE (*looks for it*). Here's her fan. And her handkerchief— scented. (*Pause.*) She's always losing something. She's lost her life, too. (*Hums a tune softly.*) I haven't a real passport, grandpa, and I don't know how old I am, and I sort of can't help feeling that I am a very young girl. (*Puts her cap on Firs who remains sitting motionless.*) Oh, I love you, sweet sir! (*Laughs.*) Ein, zwei, drei! (*Takes the cap off Firs and puts it on herself.*) When I was a little girl my father and mother used to travel about to fairs and give performances—very good ones. I used to perform the death leap and all sorts of other things. And when father and mother died, a German lady took me and had me educated. All right. I grew up and then became a governess. But where I came from and who I am, I don't know. Who were my parents? Perhaps they were never married—I don't know. (*Takes a cucumber out of her pocket and eats.*) I know nothing.

FIRS. I must have been twenty or twenty-five when our deacon's son, our cook Vassily and myself went for a walk past this place and saw a man sitting on that stone there. He didn't belong to us—a stranger he was. I got frightened—don't know why—and went away, but as soon as I was gone they killed him. He had money on him.

CHARLOTTE. Well? *Weiter!*

FIRS. Well, then of course the police came and started questioning everybody. They took me, too. Was imprisoned for two years, but they let me go after that. Years ago it was. (*Pause.*) Can't remember everything.

CHARLOTTE. Time you were dead, grandpa. (*Eats her cucumber.*)

FIRS. Eh? (*Mutters.*) And so, you see, Miss, they all drove off together. Then they had to stop. My uncle—he jumps off the cart and picks up a bag. And there was another bag inside it, and inside that one something was moving—jerk, jerk!

CHARLOTTE (*laughs, softly*). Jerks, jerk! (*Eats her cucumber.*)

(*Someone can be heard walking quietly on the road and quietly strumming a balalaika. The moon rises. Somewhere near the poplars Varya is looking for Anya and calling:* "Anya, where are you?")

### Curtain

Except for Charlotte's life story, the scene between Charlotte and Firs does not appear in the published version of the play. The other acts of the play underwent only minor alterations.

# 25

# The Cherry Orchard

IN DECLARING that there was not a single pistol shot in *The Cherry Orchard*, Chekhov overlooked another remarkable feature which distinguishes his last play from all his other plays, namely that there is not a single love triangle in it, either. Indeed, Chekhov seems to have been so anxious that nothing should obscure the essentially comic character of the play that he eliminated everything from it that might introduce any deeper emotional undercurrents. The play, it is true, has plenty of emotional undercurrents, but they are all of a "comic" nature, that is to say, the ludicrous element is never missing from them. *The Cherry Orchard*, in fact, conforms entirely to Aristotle's definition of comedy as "an imitation of characters of a lower type who are not bad in themselves but whose faults possess something ludicrous in them". What—to take one instance—can be more ludicrous, nay, grotesque, than a typical patrician like Gayev, whose main characteristics, according to Chekhov, were "suavity and elegance," turning to his sister and demanding that she should choose between him and some absurd fool of a footman like Yasha? And is not the fact that Gayev became "a bank official" ludicrous, particularly as it is quite clear that he would not be able to hold down his job even for a month? And is not his sister's love affair ludicrous from beginning to end? (Chekhov was very anxious to make it absolutely clear that he regarded it as an unwarranted distortion of Lyubov Ranevsky's character to represent her on the stage as "subdued by suffering". In a letter to his wife he pointed out that "nothing but death could subdue a woman like that." He saw her as "tastefully but not gorgeously dressed; intelligent, very good-natured, absent-minded; friendly and gracious to everyone, always a smile on her face." These are all the outward expressions of a woman who, as Charlotte says at the end of the first version of Act II, "has lost her life," or in other words has thrown it away on trifles, and it is this that forms the ludicrous or comic essence of her character.) Or—to take another instance—are not the circumstances leading up to the sale of the cherry orchard and the Gayev estate ludicrous in the extreme? And is not the attitude of Gayev and his sister to this incident of the play ludicrous? At first the sale of the country seat, which has belonged to their family for generations, is regarded by them as a great tragedy, but does their attitude after the sale justify all the heartbreak which it has aroused? According to Chekhov's stage directions, Gayev in the last act says *gaily*: "Really, everything is all right now. Before the cherry orchard was sold we were all worried and upset, but afterwards when the question was finally and irrevocably settled we all calmed down and even felt cheerful. I am a bank official now—a financier—cannon off the red—and say what you like, Lyuba, you certainly look much better than you used to." To which his sister replies: "Yes, my nerves are much better, that's true. I'm sleeping well." That is hardly the way people in a tragedy would react to an event which forms the dramatic core of the play.

The misinterpretation of *The Cherry Orchard* as a tragedy (Stanislavsky, in the first flush of excitement after reading Chekhov's last play, rushed off a letter to Chekhov in which he vowed that it was a tragedy and not, as Chekhov insisted, a comedy) is mainly due to a misunderstanding of the nature of a comic character. A "comic" character is generally supposed to keep an audience in fits of laughter, but that is not always so. No one would deny that Falstaff is essentially a comic character, but his fall from favour is one of the most moving incidents in *Henry IV*. Don Quixote, too, is essentially a comic character, but what has made him immortal is his creator's ability to arouse the compassion and the sympathy of the reader for him. The same is true of the chief characters of *The Cherry Orchard*: the sympathy and compassion they arouse in the spectator should not be allowed to blind him to the fact that they are essentially comic characters.

It should be the producer's aim to bring out their comic traits and not, as is all too often done, to sentimentalise them. All the characters in the play, in fact, with perhaps the single exception of the seventeen-year-old Anya, possess this unmistakably ludicrous streak in their natures which makes them into comic characters.

The main theme of the play is generally taken to be the passing of the old order, symbolised by the sale of the cherry orchard. But that theme was stale by the time Chekhov wrote his play. Alexander Ostrovsky had practically exhausted it, and so had many other Russian novelists and playwrights before Chekhov, who himself had already used it in *Platonov*. What is new about this theme is the comic twist Chekhov gave it. Stanislavsky, who was himself a member of the old order, could not help regarding the passing of the Gayev estate into the hands of a successful business man who had once been a peasant on it as a tragedy. But Chekhov belonged to "the lower orders" himself and he could therefore take a completely detached view of it. Not being personally involved, he saw the comedy of it all and gave it an artistic form of a play full of comic characters. Nothing indeed was further from Chekhov's thoughts than that his characters should spread a feeling of gloom among his audience. In reply to a telegram from Nemirovich-Danchenko who complained that there were too many "weeping characters" in the play, Chekhov wrote: "Where are they? There is only one such character—Varya, but that is because she is a crybaby by nature and her tears ought not to arouse any feelings of gloom in the audience. I often put down 'through tears' in my stage directions, but that shows only the mood of the characters and not tears."

The symbolism of the cherry orchard, then, has nothing to do with its sale. All it expresses is one of the recurrent themes in Chekhov's plays: the destruction of beauty by those who are utterly blind to it. "All Russia is our garden," Trofimov says to Anya at the end of Act II, and he adds: "The earth is great and beautiful and there are many wonderful places in it." And his words are meant not only as a consolation to Anya, but as a warning against the Lopakhins of this world, a warning that can be understood everywhere, since the menace of the speculative builder has been felt not only in Russia. The cherry orchard indeed is a purely aesthetic symbol which its owners with the traditions of an old culture behind them fully understand; to Firs it merely means the cartloads of dried cherries sent off to town in the good old days, and to Lopakhin it is only an excellent site for "development."

That the sale of the cherry orchard does not form the main theme of the play can also be deduced from the fact that the peripetia element has very little, if anything, to do with it. Indeed, the moment its owners appear on the stage, it ought to become clear to the discerning playgoer that they are certainly not going to save it. The whole dramatic interest of the play is therefore centred on Lopakhin, the future owner of the cherry orchard. "When I was writing Lopakhin's part," Chekhov wrote to Stanislavsky, "I could not help thinking of it as yours. It is true, Lopakhin is a merchant, but he is a decent fellow in every respect; he must behave with the utmost courtesy and decorum, without any vulgarity or silly jokes, and that is why it seemed to me that you would have handled this part, *the central one in the play*,[1] brilliantly. . . . In choosing an actor for this part," Chekhov added, "it must be borne in mind that such a serious and religious girl as Varya was in love with Lopakhin; she would never have fallen in love with some cheap moneymaker." And in a letter to Nemirovich-Danchenko Chekhov gave this further characterisation of Lopakhin: "Lopakhin—a white waistcoat and brown shoes, walks about waving his hands and taking large steps; he is always deep in thought—he walks along one straight line."

In this description Chekhov put his finger on the most essential point of Lopakhin's character. Lopakhin, Chekhov pointed out, "is not a merchant in the vulgar sense of the word—that must be clearly understood. He must not be played as a loud and noisy man. There is no need for him to be the typical merchant. He is a tender-hearted man." Lopakhin, however, waves his hands about, that is, he is full of himself as a successful business man and a

[1] My italics.

self-made man, too, but he does not realise that his success has killed the finest traits of his character: it has killed the artist in him. He has, Trofimov remarks, the delicate fingers and the sensitive soul of an artist. He makes a profit of forty thousand roubles from his poppy seeds, but what really moves him is the fine sight of his fields of poppies in flower. He walks through life like a blind man, keeping to the one straight line which he believes has already led him to success and which he hopes will lead him to even greater success. Nothing in the world will convince him that it really leads him to failure, the failure of a man who is deeply sensitive to beauty, but whose obsession with worldly success makes him into a destroyer of beauty. It is the absence of a conflict between the artist and the money-maker in Lopakhin that makes him into a typically comic figure.

Lopakhin can well afford to buy the estate on which his father has been a serf, but it never occurs to him to do so. At first he is absolutely genuine in trying to save the estate for its owners, but in the end it is he who becomes the owner of the estate—a complete reversal of the situation. It is the inner conflict between the son of the former serf and the rich business man round which the peripetia element in the play revolves. At the very beginning of the play Chekhov makes use of a device he used with equal effect in *The Three Sisters*, the device of the chorus element which gives the audience a vague hint of what the development of the plot is going to be while leaving the characters themselves completely in the dark. In *The Three Sisters* this device is associated with Protopopov and the two lines about the bear from Krylov's fable. In *The Cherry Orchard* it is more openly comic in character. It occurs at the very beginning of Act I in the scene between Varya and Anya:

ANYA. Well, what's happening? Have you paid the interest on the mortgage?
VARYA. Good heavens no.
ANYA. Oh dear, oh dear. . . .
VARYA. In August the estate will be sold.
ANYA. Oh dear——
LOPAKHIN (*peeps through the door and bleats*). Bah-h-h! (*Goes out.*)

This is the first time the impending sale of the cherry orchard is mentioned in the play and at once we get this comic intrusion of its future owner: the peripetia element compressed in a few lines. Lopakhin's mocking bleat epitomises both the hopelessness of the position of the hereditary owners of the estate and his own powerful position as the heir of all the thousands of serfs whose sweat and toil went to the upkeep of the old country mansion. ("The house," Chekhov was careful to explain in a letter to his wife on October 14th, 1903, "is an old country mansion: at one time people lived in great style there and this ought to be felt in the staging. Wealthy and comfortable.") The symbolic meaning of this brief scene is much cruder than of the scene at the beginning of Act I of *The Three Sisters*, but this is so because *The Cherry Orchard* is a comedy while *The Three Sisters* is a "drama." On the realistic plane, it is true, Lopakhin's intrusion can be interpreted as merely showing his goodnatured contempt for Varya, whom Chekhov characterised in his correspondence as "a perfect fool," "a goodnatured fool," "a nun, a foolish creature," and, finally, as "crude and rather stupid, but very goodnatured." She is the only "crybaby" in the play, a deeply religious girl who is in love with Lopakhin. It is both in his relations to Varya and in his attitude towards the owners of the Gayev estate that another side of the "comic" element in Lopakhin's character is revealed. It is the serf in him he cannot get rid of. The long years of serfdom and humiliation have left an indelible mark on his soul. He does not cringe, it is true. He speaks to his former masters not as his superiors but as their equal. But deep down inside him the serf is still lurking. In the fine drawing room of the Gayev country house he can't help feeling that he is just a country yokel. He has plenty of money, but at heart he is still a common peasant.

This dualism in Lopakhin's nature is brought out at once in the opening scene of the play. That is why in spite of his "white waistcoat and brown shoes" the idea that he might become the owner of the Gayev estate never occurs to him. And that is why his marriage to a gentlewoman like Varya seems unreal to him, though when pressed by Mrs. Ranevsky in Act II, he declares that he is quite ready to marry her, and in Act IV when Mrs. Ranevsky again expresses her surprise at the way he and Varya are avoiding each other, he replies: "I must say I don't understand it myself. The whole thing is sort of queer. If there's still time, I'm quite ready even now to—— Let's settle it once and for all, and let's get it done with. But," he adds significantly, "without you I feel I shall never propose to her." And that of course is quite true. Face to face with Varya he is so conscious of her social superiority that he cannot bring himself to propose to her, while Varya ("the perfect fool") is quite incapable of disregarding the conventions which demand that the lady has to wait for the gentleman to propose to her. It is to conceal this typically peasant feeling of awe for the gentry that is so deeply embedded in his character which makes Lopakhin treat Varya with such good-humoured contempt. When in Act II Varya, in reply to Mrs. Ranevsky's congratulations on the satisfactory result of her attempt to arrange a match between her and Lopakhin, exclaims *through tears*, "You mustn't joke about that, mother!" Lopakhin cannot but interpret this exclamation as an expression of Varya's reluctance to marry beneath her, and that is why he immediately hurls the two quotations from *Hamlet* at her. Lopakhin's contempt is expressed in his deliberate distortion of Ophelia's name into its vulgarised Russian equivalent of "Okhmelia." And while it is quite possible that Lopakhin would use the first quotation without distorting it, namely "Okhmelia, get thee to a nunnery," he would never use the second quotation in its original form of "O nymph, in thy orisons be all my sins remember'd." Lopakhin, as he himself confesses, is an uneducated man. "My father," he tells Mrs. Ranevsky in Act II, "was a peasant, an idiot. He knew nothing and taught me nothing. Only beat me when he was drunk, and always with a stick. And I too am really the same stupid idiot. I haven't learnt anything and my hand-writing is just awful—makes me feel ashamed before people." And a little earlier in the same act Chekhov gives us a hint of the sort of plays Lopakhin went to see in the snatch of a song from a popular musical play he hums. "What a wonderful play I saw last night," he says. "It was very funny." It is quite clear that Lopakhin would never have seen *Hamlet* performed, and he most certainly never read it. He must have just heard people quoting from it and he could not possibly be expected to quote the second line from *Hamlet* correctly. Indeed, Chekhov himself makes him misquote the line. What Lopakhin says is: "Okhmelia, O nymph, remember me in your prayers!" To make Lopakhin use the exact quotation of this line on the English stage is to distort his character and give the audience quite a wrong impression of his background. (In *Platonov* Voynitsev quotes the same line correctly at the end of Act II.)

It is in Act III that the peasant in Lopakhin breaks through his "white waistcoat and brown shoes" and for once asserts himself. Why did Lopakhin buy the estate after all? He bought it because his chief opponent at the auction was not Gayev (he would never have bid against him) but another rich merchant like himself. Already in Act II Lopakhin sounds the alarm:

LOPAKHIN. The rich merchant Deriganov is thinking of buying your estate. I'm told he's coming to the auction himself.

MRS. RANEVSKY. Where did you hear that?

LOPAKHIN. That's what they say in town.

GAYEV. Our Yaroslavl aunt has promised to send us money, but when and how much we don't know.

LOPAKHIN. How much will she send? A hundred thousand? Two hundred?

MRS. RANEVSKY. Well, I hardly think so. Ten or fifteen thousand at most, and we must be thankful for that.

LOPAKHIN. I'm sorry, but such improvident people as you—such queer, unbusiness-like people—I've never met in my life. You're told in plain language that your estate is going to be sold and you don't seem to understand.

MRS. RANEVSKY. But what are we to do? Please, tell us.

LOPAKHIN. I tell you every day. Every day I say the same thing over and over again. You must let the cherry orchard and the land under building leases for summer cottages, and you must do it now, as quickly as possible, or the auction will be on top of you! Try to understand! The moment you decide to let your land for summer cottages, you will be able to raise as much money as you like and you'll be saved.

MRS. RANEVSKY. Summer cottages and holiday-makers—excuse me, but it is so vulgar.

GAYEV. I'm entirely of your opinion.

LOPAKHIN. I'll burst into tears or scream or have a fit. I can't stand it. You're driving me mad. (*To* Gayev.) You're an old woman!

GAYEV. I beg your pardon?

LOPAKHIN. An old woman! (*Gets up to go.*)

MRS. RANEVSKY (*in dismay*). No, don't go. Please, stay. I beg you. Perhaps we'll think of something.

LOPAKHIN. What's there to think of?

MRS. RANEVSKY. Please, don't go. I feel so much more cheerful with you here. (*Pause.*) I keep expecting something to happen, as though the house were going to collapse on top of us.

As for Gayev, he does not seem to care whether the house collapses on top of him or not. He is *deep in thought*, wondering how to retrieve an imaginary billiard shot.

Even the intervention of another rich merchant, then, does not change the situation as far as Lopakhin is concerned. He still tries to save the estate for the two comic characters who even in the hour of their greatest peril are entirely ignorant of what is happening around them. It is only at the auction itself after Deriganov's first bid of "thirty thousand over and above the arrears," as Lopakhin, still apologetic in the hour of his greatest triumph, tells them at the ball, that he enters the fray himself. Nothing now stands in the way of his becoming the owner of the estate where "his father and grandfather were slaves and where they were not even admitted to the kitchen." But back at the country house he is once more overwhelmed by his old qualms of conscience: the serf re-awakens in him. When Mrs. Ranevsky presses him to tell her what happened at the auction, he is embarrassed, *afraid of betraying his joy*, as Chekhov puts it in his stage direction. His return as the owner of the Gayev estate, by the way, is accompanied by another comic interlude. As he enters, Varya hits him over the head with a stick. It is as if Varya, who had intended the blow for Yepikhodov, wanted to remind the new "squire" of his childhood beatings. (The stick is the symbol of the serf in Lopakhin.)

LOPAKHIN. Thank you very much.

VARYA (*angrily and ironically*). I'm so sorry!

LOPAKHIN. It's all right, ma'am. I'm greatly obliged to you for the kind reception, I'm sure.

VARYA. Don't mention it. (*Walks away, then looks round and inquires gently.*) I haven't hurt you, have I?

LOPAKHIN. Oh no, not at all. But there's going to be an enormous bump on my head for all that.

Even his triumphant entry into his new possessions (Lopakhin is so intoxicated with his transformation into a landed gentleman that he behaves like a man drunk), Chekhov marks by a comic incident:

LOPAKHIN. . . . (*Ironically.*) Here comes the new squire, the owner of the cherry orchard. (*He tips over a little table accidentally, nearly upsetting the candelabra.*)

But at first Lopakhin refuses to speak, and it is only after Gayev has rushed out of the room in tears, having handed to Firs the anchovies and the Kerch herrings he had not forgotten to bring from town in spite of the disaster of the auction, that he cannot hold out any longer.

PISHCHIK. Well, what happened at the auction? Come on, tell!

MRS. RANEVSKY. Has the cherry orchard been sold?

LOPAKHIN. It has.

MRS. RANEVSKY. Who bought it?

LOPAKHIN. I bought it. (*Pause.*)

It is a perfect climax brought about by only three short words, perhaps the most perfect climax in any of Chekhov's plays. The reversal of the situation is not only complete, it is not only underlined by the absurd ball arranged at that "inopportune moment," as Mrs. Ranevsky remarks earlier, humming a tune (did she really hope in spite of everything that the estate would somehow or other remain her property?), but it also contains a double surprise: "the most beautiful estate in the world" has passed out of the hands of its aristocratic owners and into the hands of the son of one of their former serfs. It is the last circumstance that in one blinding flash opens up the great social gulf that divides Lopakhin from the Gayevs. That is why Lopakhin is so terrifically excited. That is why Mrs. Ranevsky is so crushed by the news that *she would collapse if she were not standing near a table and a chair*, as the stage direction states. And would Varya have flung her keys with such contempt at Lopakhin's feet and stormed out of the room if she, too, had not become aware of the social implications of the sale of the cherry orchard? Lopakhin's remark as he picks up the bunch of keys that Varya "wanted to show that she was no longer mistress here" has a much wider implication than would appear at first sight. This indeed emerges from Lopakhin's words to Mrs. Ranevsky:

LOPAKHIN (*reproachfully*). Why, why did you not listen to me? You poor darling, you will never get it back now. (*With tears.*) Oh, if only all this could be over soon, if only our unhappy and disjointed life could somehow be changed soon!

The social implications of the play emerge more clearly in the character of Peter Trofimov. Here again Chekhov was faced with the dilemma of either having his play banned or getting it past the censorship by avoiding all purely controversial issues of a political nature. Writing to his wife on October 19th, 1903, he expressed his fear of "a certain incompleteness" in the characterisation of Trofimov. "You see," he wrote, "Trofimov has been exiled many times for his political views, he is being continually sent down from the university, and how is one to show all these things?" But even Trofimov, the only idealist in the play, is essentially a comic character. His exterior itself is comic. "A motheaten gentleman," a shrewd country woman called him, and Mrs. Ranevsky half cries and half laughs when she looks at his beard. But his outward appearance is merely a pointer to the deep-seated comic streak in his nature. He is "an eternal student" in more senses than one. He is the eternal adolescent because reason means everything to him and experience nothing. He belongs to those men who never really grow up because they can never see the distinction between what is reasonable and what is wise. Trofimov sees through everybody except himself. "For once in your life," he tells Mrs. Ranevsky in Act III, "you must look truth straight in the face." But when it comes to himself, all he does is to utter clichés. "We are higher than love," he tells Mrs. Ranevsky apropos of himself and Anya. And when Mrs. Ranevsky exposes the silliness of such a remark by telling him that it is absurd for a man of his age not to have a mistress, all he can do is to deliver himself of another cliché: "All is finished between us!" and rush out of the room.

Chekhov underlines this comic streak in Trofimov's nature by involving him immediately in a comic incident.

MRS. RANEVSKY (*shouts after him*). Peter, wait! You funny man, I was only joking.
(*Someone can be heard running quickly downstairs and suddenly falling down with a crash. Anya and Varya utter a scream, which is at once followed by laughter.*)
MRS. RANEVSKY. What's happened?
(*Anya runs in.*)
ANYA (*laughing*). Peter fell down the stairs.
MRS. RANEVSKY. What a queer fellow that Peter is!

And that is true: Peter is a queer fellow, but being queer does not prevent a man from having a great aim in life. Trofimov, besides, is the kind of idealist who not only dreams, but also works for the fulfilment of his dream. It is in that that he differs from Vershinin, whom he resembles in many other respects. It is through Trofimov's mouth that the theme of hard work as the key to future happiness is expressed in *The Cherry Orchard*. And it is to the seventeen-year-old Anya, who personifies this brighter future, that Trofimov turns for the realisation of his ideal of a better life. He sees it coming. "Already," he tells Anya at the end of Act II, "I can hear its footsteps. And," he adds, "if we never see it, if we never know it, what does it matter? Others will see it!"

Anya, who, according to Chekhov, "is first and foremost a child, lighthearted all through, and not crying once, except in Act II, and then she only has tears in her eyes," does not join in her mother's and uncle's lamentations over the sale of the cherry orchard. She is glad to bid farewell to the past. "Goodbye, my home!" she exclaims gaily at the end of Act IV. "Goodbye, my old life!" And Trofimov echoes her confidently and ecstatically: "Welcome, new life!"

Chekhov endowed the minor characters of his last play with many purely farcical features without, however, sacrificing their essential humanity. Simeonov-Pishchik is such a broad comic figure, as his double-barrelled name implies. The first half of it is impressively aristocratic and the second farcical (its English equivalent would be Squeaker). Yepikhodov, too, is a broadly comic characterisation of a conceited half-wit who imagines himself a highly educated person because he possesses the bovine patience to wade through "learned" books he has not the brains to understand. The only love triangle in the play is that in which he figures—Yepikhodov-Dunya-Yasha—and it is entirely farcical. Chekhov drew him partly from a well-known circus clown. Charlotte, another broadly comic character, was also partly drawn from life. While staying at Stanislavsky's country house during his wife's convalescence in 1902, he became friendly with the family of Stanislavsky's cousin Smirnov and it was at his house that he met an English governess ("A very plain girl, neither man nor woman," Stanislavsky's daughter described her), who seems to have been a very jolly person to whom Chekhov took a great liking. It was she he used for his model of Charlotte.

The two servants, Dunya and Yasha, are also broad comic figures. In *Platonov* Dr. Triletsky (Act II, Sc. 1) tells the two drunken footmen that they are "awfully like their masters," and that is also true of Dunya and Yasha. They are caricatures of their masters. The relations between them and their masters are not what one would expect the relations between servants and masters to be. Yasha openly makes fun of Gayev and treats his mistress almost like an equal. "If you go back to Paris," he says to her in Act III, "will you please take me with you. Do me a favour. It is absolutely impossible for me to stay here. You can see for ourself how uncivilised this country is. The people have no morals, it's so dull here, the food in the kitchen is horrible, and there's that Firs walking about the place and muttering all sorts of objectionable words. Take me with you please!"

The "objectionable word" which Firs uses all through the play and which Yasha dislikes so much because it describes him so neatly, has been variously translated as "ne'er-do-well," "good for nothing," and even by one translator, who was obviously expressing his own views of Cnekhov's characters, as "a job lot." Actually, the word Firs is so fond of happens to have been a word Chekhov himself often used during the last years of his life—*nedotyopa*, a very colloquial word which could perhaps be best translated by "duffer," which the Oxford English Dictionary defines as "a person without practical ability or capacity, or, generally, a stupid or foolish person." In his note-book Chekhov gave Varya, "the perfect fool," the family name of Nedotyopina. Another reference to the same word which occurs in Chekhov's note-book is: "*nedotyopa*—on the cross (in a graveyard) someone has written: Here lies a *nedotyopa*." Gayev, Trofimov, Mrs. Ranevsky and Yasha are all people "without practical ability or capacity," they are all "duffers" by nature. And, of course, so is Firs himself, whose loyalty to his masters is perhaps the most farcical, though also the most touching, thing in the whole play. "My life has slipped by as though I hadn't lived," he mutters at the end of the play, and those words could be used as his own epitaph. "Oh, you—duffer!" are his last words, addressed to himself.

In their attempts to wring the last drop of pathos out of the final scene of *The Cherry Orchard*, many producers tend to sentimentalise even Firs by leading their audiences to believe that he has been left to die by his lackadaisical masters. But there is nothing in the play to indicate that Chekhov's stage direction: "lies motionless" means "dies." If Chekhov had meant Firs to die, he would have said so. But in fact nothing could have been further from Chekhov's thoughts than to end his play with the death of an abandoned old servant. That would have introduced a completely alien note in a play which Chekhov never meant to be anything but a comedy.

The dying, melancholy sound of a broken string of a musical instrument (the Russian word does not specify the particular nature of the instrument, it might have been a balalaika), which first occurs in Act II and with which the play ends, is all Chekhov needed to convey his own attitude to the "dreary" lives of his characters. It was a sound Chekhov remembered from his own boyhood days when he used to spend his summer months at a little hamlet in the Don basin. It was there that he first heard the mysterious sound, which seemed to be coming from the sky, but which was caused by the fall of a bucket in some distant coal-mine. With the years this sound acquired a nostalgic ring, and it is this sad, nostalgic feeling Chekhov wanted to convey by it. It is a sort of requiem for the "unhappy and disjointed" lives of his characters.

So many unnecessary tears have been shed in this play both on the stage and in the auditorium that it would seem almost hopeless to re-establish it as a comedy. It is much easier to misrepresent it as a tragedy than to present it for what it really is, namely "a comedy, and in places almost a farce." But unless it is treated as such, it will never be Chekhov's play.

It has been the purpose of this Essay to provide an analysis of the development of Chekhov's art as a dramatist and, particularly, of the "architecture" of his great plays. For without a thorough understanding of the problems which faced Chekhov when he embarked on the writing of indirect-action plays and the way he solved them, no proper answer can be given either to the perennial question of what it is all about or to the more fundamental question of whether or not these highly original plays contain "a suggestion of a desirable life," or, in other words, whether or not they show us not only life as it is, but also life as it should be. The contention, so frequently repeated and so firmly held, that Chekhov's favourite theme was disillusionment and that, moreover, he was, as Mr. MacCarthy expressed it, "the poet and apologist of ineffectualness," appears in the light of the foregoing argument to be wholly untenable. Nothing, indeed, could be further from the truth than the opinion expressed by Bernard Shaw in his Preface to *Heartbreak House* in a reference to *The Cherry Orchard*, an opinion, incidentally, that has probably shaped the attitude to Chekhov in England more than any other critical appraisal of his plays. "Chekhov," Shaw wrote, "more of a fatalist than Tolstoy, had no faith in these charming people extricating themselves. They would, he thought, be sold up and sent adrift by the bailiffs; therefore, he had no scruple in exploiting and flattering their charm." Now, Chekhov was certainly not a fatalist, nor did he dream of exploiting and flattering the charm of his characters; that is done by the producers and actors who find themselves entirely at sea in face of a drama that seems to defy every canon of stagecraft and yet contains such wonderful stage material; therefore, they fall back on the more obvious and dramatically insignificant details, the mere bricks and mortar of a Chekhov play which, without its steel frame, is more of a picturesque ruin than an enduring monument to a great creative artist.

# Index